IVP PRAXIS

EQUIPPING LEADERS FOR MINISTRY

"...TO EQUIP HIS PEOPLE FOR WORKS OF SERVICE,

SO THAT THE BODY OF CHRIST MAY BE BUILT UP."

EPHESIANS 4:12

God has called us to ministry. But it's not enough to have a vision for ministry if you don't have the practical skills for it. Nor is it enough to do the work of ministry if what you do is headed in the wrong direction. We need both vision *and* expertise for effective ministry. We need *praxis*.

Praxis puts theory into practice. It brings cutting-edge ministry expertise from visionary practitioners. You'll find sound biblical and theological foundations for ministry in the real world, with concrete examples for effective action and pastoral ministry. Praxis books are more than the "how to" – they're also the "why to." And because *being* is every bit as important as *doing*, Praxis attends to the inner life of the leader as well as the outer work of ministry. Feed your soul, and feed your ministry.

If you are called to ministry, you know you can't do it on your own. Let Praxis provide the companions you need to equip God's people for life in the kingdom.

www.ivpress.com/praxis

RESILIENT MINISTRY

WHAT PASTORS TOLD US ABOUT
SURVIVING AND THRIVING

BOB BURNS, TASHA D. CHAPMAN
AND DONALD C. GUTHRIE

IVP Books

An imprint of InterVarsity Press
Downers Grove, Illinois

InterVarsity Press
P.O. Box 1400, Downers Grove, IL 60515-1426
World Wide Web: www.ivpress.com
E-mail: email@ivpress.com

InterVarsity Press® is the book-publishing division of InterVarsity Christian Fellowship/USA®, a movement of students and faculty active on campus at hundreds of universities, colleges and schools of nursing in the United States of America, and a member movement of the International Fellowship of Evangelical Students. For information about local and regional activities, write Public Relations Dept., InterVarsity Christian Fellowship/USA, 6400 Schroeder Rd., P.O. Box 7895, Madison, WI 537077895, or visit the IVCF website at <www.intervarsity.org>.

Scripture quotations, unless otherwise noted, are from The Holy Bible, English Standard Version, copyright © 2001 by Crossway Bibles, a division of Good News Publishers. Used by permission. All rights reserved.

While all stories in this book are true, some names and identifying information in this book have been changed to protect the privacy of the individuals involved.

Design: Cindy Kiple
Interior design: Beth Hagenberg

ISBN 978-0-8308-4103-5

Printed in the United States of America

 InterVarsity Press is committed to protecting the environment and to the responsible use of natural resources. As a member of Green Press Initiative we use recycled paper whenever possible. To learn more about the Green Press Initiative, visit <www.greenpressinitiative.org>.

Library of Congress Cataloging-in-Publication Data
A catalog record for this book is available from the Library of Congress.

P	20	19	18	17	16	15	14	13	12	11	10	9	8	7	6	5	4	3	2	1
Y	30	29	28	27	26	25	24	23	22	21	20	19	18	17	16	15	14	13

CONTENTS

INTRODUCTION

WHAT DOES IT TAKE FOR PASTORS NOT ONLY to survive but to thrive in fruitful ministry over the long haul? With the alarmingly high rate of people leaving the pastorate, the church has a great stake in the answer. Unlike other vocations, ministry work has no formal arrangement for ongoing learning and development and no requirements for continuing education. So how do pastors pursue learning and growth? Where do pastoral couples receive mentoring and pastoral care? How do pastors stay current in our rapidly changing world?

This book, based on seven years of research, seeks to answer these questions. Our research focused on gathering pastors and their spouses into peer cohorts, which met repeatedly in multiday retreats called Pastors Summits where we facilitated heartfelt discussions about the challenges of vocational ministry. This book presents the summary and analysis of those discussions in light of our literature research and experiences. Although the cohort research was limited to the majority demographic in the pastorate of married male pastors and their wives, we believe the findings are relevant enough to help foster resilience for all those in vocational ministry. (See appendix A for research method details.)

RECOMMENDATIONS FOR READERS

When you read nonfiction, do you tend to skip over block quotations and illustrative stories to be efficient? We often do. With this book, however, try flipping that strategy. Instead, focus on the quotations and stories. Listen to what it sounds like when pastors unplug from the stressors of ministry in a safe place. We wrote this book to focus on the actual words of real pastors, serving in real congregations and facing real-life issues. While we don't mention the speakers by name, most direct quotations were said by male pastors during conversations in the peer cohorts. Benefits from this book begin with "hearing" the participants.

Another tip for utilizing this book: consider reading the final chapter first. There we summarize lessons learned in the summit and give helpful advice on how you might put the ideas you will find into practice. This is not material easily skimmed over, so consider some strategies for putting the book to work in your life.

An ounce of reflection can lead to a pound of learning. Therefore, throughout each chapter we include sets of questions worth pondering. These questions can be used in many ways. One idea is personal reflection. Consider writing in a personal journal to ponder these questions, as well as other thoughts and feelings that this book raises. Another strategy is to work through the book with others. The questions can serve as discussion guides. If you study this with a group, you may want to cover only half of a chapter per session. Take time to make it your own by adding stories and insights from your experience to the stories in the book. And at the end of each chapter, we suggest other books and media that will heighten your understanding of the issues. You may find it helpful to pause and utilize some of this material for further reflection or group work.

We wrote this book with five types of readers in mind. First, we hope pastors will read it and share it with their spouses. We also believe other vocational ministry staff will benefit from the book and find the issues to be relevant to their lives. Although we write about vocational ministry in the *church*, the material is applicable to Christian leaders in parachurch ministries and other vocational contexts. Ministry board members will find great value in it for understanding and caring for the pastors and staff who serve their churches. Finally, church members will gain an appreciation for the complexity of ministry leadership, as well as a way to evaluate their own lifestyles and vocations in God's world.

A WORD ABOUT THE AUTHORS

Bob Burns serves as senior associate pastor and head of staff at Central Presbyterian Church in St. Louis, Missouri. During the seven years of leading the Pastors Summit research, Bob was dean of lifelong learning, professor of educational ministries and director of the Center for Ministry Leadership at Covenant Theological Seminary in St. Louis. Bob has been a pastor and teacher for more than forty years, with experiences ranging from church planting to family ministry and from worship and the arts to youth and singles ministries. Bob and Janet, his wife of thirty-five years, have two married children and five grandchildren.

Tasha Chapman serves Covenant Theological Seminary as dean of academic services and adjunct professor of educational ministries. Tasha has over twenty years of experience working with diverse ministries in the United States and overseas. These include university campus ministry, church women's ministry and international women's ministry, as well as consulting for youth ministry, children's ministry, disability ministry and elementary schools. After spending the week with adult learners at the seminary, she enjoys ministering with young children and cognitively handicapped saints on Sunday mornings. She and her husband, David, have two teenaged children.

Donald Guthrie is professor of educational ministries at Trinity Evangelical Divinity School. Following twelve years of campus ministry, Donald joined the faculty of Covenant Theological Seminary, where he served for fifteen years. He directed field education, the doctor of ministry and distance learning programs, and served as vice president for academics. He has enjoyed serving as a ruling elder in several local churches over the past twenty-five years. He is a frequent teacher at conferences and retreats, often addressing cultural trends, intergenerational ministry, calling and vocation, and adult learning. He and his wife, Mary, have two young adult children.

We invite you to join us in a conversation that is stimulating, sobering and ultimately hopeful. Whether read primarily for yourself or on behalf of a loved one or colleague, we hope this book leaves you embracing the gospel of Jesus Christ more deeply, loving others more richly and serving our Lord more joyfully.

ACKNOWLEDGMENTS

The Pastors Summit involved many more people than we could mention here. Besides the pastors and spouses who were involved, we would be remiss without thanking our omnicompetent administrator Denise Wichlan, research coordinators Rebecca Rine and Caroline Wilson, researcher and writer Kim Andrews, writer Kristen Sagar, and transcriber Sarah Bobell. We are also grateful for research assistants Chris and Maggie Genshear, Kelsey Reed, Michael Wichlan and John Early. Stafford Carson, Frank

James and Tim Witmer did an amazing job as coordinators for the summit in their respective seminaries.

Finally, we want to thank the Lilly Endowment, particularly Craig Dykstra and John Wimmer. With the leadership of these two men and the rest of the Lilly Endowment staff, initial research on the challenges facing pastors was completed. Then the endowment invested millions of dollars in the Sustaining Pastoral Excellence initiative. This book is one small contribution to the fruit of this investment. We trust that the church will be greatly strengthened in the coming years because of this initiative.

LIFE IN
PASTORAL MINISTRY

When do pastors receive mentoring and pastoral care?

Where do pastors pursue learning and growth?

How do pastors stay current in our rapidly changing world?

A FEW YEARS AGO, BOB WAS SITTING with a small group of pastors who were meeting together for the first time. In the midst of a lively conversation about ministry life, one pastor made the following comment:

I don't have anybody that I open up to about my life, my family or my ministry. I feel like a guy who is driving over the speed limit on a narrow mountain road without barriers. It's the grace of God I haven't driven off.

People hear pastors preach on Sunday morning and assume they have their lives together. But most of us don't understand what pastors think, feel and experience week by week. Take, for example, the pastor quoted above. A few years after he said this, Bob quoted him (anonymously) at a ministry gathering in this pastor's hometown. Afterward, an elder from this pastor's church came up to Bob. With his pastor standing behind him, the elder said, "Do you know what I remember from your presentation? It was that comment made by some pastor who said he didn't have anyone to talk to. I sure am glad it isn't that way in our church. Our pastor can really share with us."

His pastor and Bob exchanged knowing glances, sharing the secret that the words were his own. From our research, we have found those words to be true for most pastors. People in ministry rarely feel understood and seldom have anyone with whom they can openly talk about their experiences.

WHAT ENABLES PASTORAL RESILIENCE?

A denominational official recently made the following statement: "So many pastors today leave the church. Often they leave the ministry altogether. What does it take for pastors to remain fruitful in ministry for a lifetime?" This person was overwhelmed by the statistics of pastors leaving the ministry and by stories of people struggling with the idea of staying in the pastorate.

Ministry leadership is a tough but highly rewarding job. Many pastors love the challenge, but most find it much more difficult than they had anticipated. Some wonder what they have gotten themselves into. Like a recent seminary graduate who shared with dismay, "I never expected the church to be like this." Or a pastor of eighteen years who confided, "My experience in the ministry has been good. But I question whether I can subject my wife and family to this much longer." Statistics on the dropout rate of ministers vary.[1] But it is clear that conditions of ministry have changed in the past few decades and that too many local church ministers leave as a result.[2]

We probably qualify as ministry survivors. Bob has been involved in the church as a volunteer and a pastor for over forty years. Donald has served as a ruling elder in several local churches during the past twenty-five years. Tasha has been active in the church as a leader and staff member for over two decades. In addition, all of us train people for vocational ministry leadership.

Lilly Endowment, Inc., an Indiana-based foundation concerned about the health of the church, has been exploring this question of pastoral resilience for years. In one of their initiatives, called Sustaining Pastoral Excellence, the endowment invested over $84 million to support sixty-three projects that explore what it takes to thrive in ministry. The three of us have coordinated one of these grants, running research and facilitating continuing education for pastors designed to find some answers to this perplexing problem of pastoral survival.

What Is Pastoral Excellence? One of our Lilly-funded programs for researching resilience in the pastorate was called the Pastors Summit. At political summits, heads of state gather for several days to survey and collaborate on complex challenges. In a similar way, our summits were designed to be an emotionally safe place where pastors could share the difficulties of vocational ministry life. As we selected participants for the Pastors Summit research, we wanted pastors who demonstrated excellence in ministry. But how can you define ministry excellence? Our culture often identifies it by certain markers of *success*. These markers range from the numbers who attend worship services to the state of a church's finances to the popular programs a church creates and sponsors. As one pastor put it, "People judge our ministries by noses, nickels and noise."

Others, however, reject the idea of defining ministry excellence by these standards of success. They often counter by using the criteria of leadership *faithfulness*. Excellence is viewed as a pastor who remains committed over time. But we questioned whether the ability to "hang in there" and endure is a helpful way to judge ministry excellence.

As we worked on our selection criteria, we found some aspects of numerical success and pastoral faithfulness useful. But we felt that neither was sufficient to express the idea of excellence. After much discussion, we concluded a better measure was found in the idea of *fruitfulness*.[3] We came to believe that Christian leaders are to bear fruit by sharing their faith and nurturing the fruit of God's grace in their own lives and in the lives of others. Fruitfulness includes a measure of faithfulness and a measure of success—valuing both but preferring neither.

The Pastors Summit. To choose pastors for the summit, we asked trusted colleagues about pastors who exhibited fruitfulness in ministry. (See appendix A for the research selection criteria.) As a list emerged, we explored many questions concerning fruitfulness in their lives. We spent time talking with these pastors, their families, friends, church officers and outsiders. We knew that none of these pastors were perfect. Neither would they personally accept the term *excellent* to describe their ministries. But each of them was on a trajectory of fruitfulness in ministry and life.

Over a six-year period, we carefully selected and worked with seventy-three pastors in the Pastors Summit. The pastors represented twenty-six states from across the United States. Gathering in small groups, each cohort of pastors met together three times a year, often with their spouses, during each two-year program. We talked with participants and their spouses about their joys and challenges. In the earliest meetings, our staff developed the agendas. But the longer we met, the more freedom each cohort had to define topics and activities that they needed for furthering their ministry fruitfulness and tenacity to stay in the ministry vocationally.

While the summit groups began to bond by sharing their lives, our staff was actively involved in research. Each summit meeting was audio-recorded and transcribed, eventually creating about twelve thousand pages of material. This material was analyzed by our team, which constantly asked the question, "What does it take to survive and thrive in pastoral ministry?" Over the first five years, some answers came into sharp focus. Five subjects stood out as the foundations that enable pastors to sustain fruitful ministry with resilience. The following chapters explore these five themes. Before we look at them, however, we need to consider the uniqueness of ministry life.

SITTING ON A ONE-LEGGED STOOL

Ever heard jokes about pastoral work? We have heard them muttered by businesspeople after a worship service, by church members talking in grocery stores and even by pastors in denominational settings. These comments sound something like, "It must be nice to only work one day a week," or, "Besides preaching on Sundays and visiting folks in the hospital, what do pastors do?"

Good question. What is involved in pastoral ministry? Jackson Carroll is a scholar who has spent a lifetime studying American clergy. In his work, he identifies four core tasks of pastors: leading worship, preaching, teaching and providing oversight.[4] Carroll explains that pastors rarely handle these tasks as distinct activities. Rather, they blend together through much of the week. Researchers Gary Kuhne and Joe Donaldson conclude that pastoral work requires a great variety of complex skills and talents. They describe pastors' activities as "taxing, fast-paced, and unrelenting, often characterized by doing two or more tasks at the same time."[5]

On average, pastors work long hours. Carroll compared statistics on the average workweek of various professions with his own research of pastors. He concluded that pastors averaged more work hours per week than other managers and professionals.[6] He also found that the larger the congregation, the more hours the pastor works.

Peter Brain, an Anglican bishop in Australia, completed a survey exploring the amount of time congregational leaders expect their pastors to work. Then he compared these results to the actual time pastors spent in ministry. His survey showed that pastors work an average of fifteen hours per week more than their lay leaders realized.[7]

The late Peter Drucker, one of the leading management authors and consultants of the twentieth century, once told a pastor friend that he viewed church leadership as the most difficult and taxing role of which he was aware. This perspective was confirmed by one of our Pastors Summit participants, who has a master's degree in management and who left a successful real-estate development company to enter the ministry. He said bluntly, "The business world is much easier than the church."

One of the unique aspects of pastoral ministry is how it affects and defines all areas of life. Work, family and personal responsibilities blur together through the week, so that pastors have difficulty distinguishing when they are on and off duty. One summit pastor put it this way:

> Being a pastor is not just what I do—it is very much who I am. I live with that persona twenty-four hours a day, seven days a week, 365 days a year.

Another explained,

> I was an art major in college. I still love to work at the pottery wheel. But the people in my church have no idea about this area of my life. They only see me as a pastor, regardless of the time or place.

Still another pastor shared,

> Most people in our church have a life that is like a stool with three legs. They've got their spiritual life, their professional life and their family life. If one of these legs wobbles, they've got two others they can lean on. For us, those three things can merge into one leg. You're sitting on a one-legged stool, and it takes a lot more concentration and energy. It's a lot more exhausting.

The work of pastoral ministry may be summed up by two other comments. The first is from Jackson Carroll. After studying hundreds of pastors, he concluded, "Being a pastor is a tough, demanding job, one that is not always very well understood or appreciated. Pastoral work is more complex than that which transpires in the hour or so a week that many lay people see the pastor in action as she or he leads worship and preaches."[8]

The other remark is from a summit pastor, who explained,

The relentless nature of ministry means that fatigue is a constant companion of leaders in the church. While lay people joke about ministers only working on Sundays, the truth lies on the other side of the continuum. A pastor's work is overwhelming because it wears upon the body and soul.

FIVE THEMES OF RESILIENT MINISTRY

After seven years of studying our summit participants—their personal lives, marriages, families and ministries—we learned a lot about what it takes to survive and thrive in ministry. We spent hundreds of hours working through all of the data, pondering our notes and talking about our thoughts and reflections. Eventually our discoveries focused around five primary themes for leadership resilience in fruitful ministry:

- spiritual formation
- self-care
- emotional and cultural intelligence
- marriage and family
- leadership and management

Before we explore these themes in more depth, let's step back and look at them through the lens of two "big ideas." The first we learned is that while each theme can be presented as separate and unique, the themes should really be considered as a whole. Each is dependent on the others. They are like the strands of a tapestry woven into one piece. For example, we can't really talk about self-care without taking spiritual formation into consideration.[9] Similarly, we can't reference leadership and management without keeping marriage and family in mind.[10] The themes only stand together.

Second, consider the apparent simplicity of the themes. At first glance they don't seem exceptional or unique to ministry. When reading them, your response might have been, "Everyone needs to work on these areas." True enough. The unique nature of the themes, however, is how they speak into the lives and priorities of pastors and their families. As we look at them more carefully, ask yourself, *Why did this issue stand out as important for the strengthening of pastors?* We will explore this question and its implications as we look at each topic.

With these thoughts in mind, let's look at the themes and read what the summit pastors had to say about them. The next chapter will give an overview of the themes, defining what is meant by each and suggesting why it is crucial for enabling resilience in pastoral excellence. The following chapters will go into more depth, looking at key aspects of the themes and how they significantly affect pastoral life and ministry. The final chapter will explore the implications of these findings and what could be done in response to them.

QUESTIONS TO PONDER

1. Think of the people you know who are in vocational ministry leadership. How do others talk about these ministers and their jobs? How well do you think these ministers feel understood? What actions might help them feel more understood and supported?

2. How do you judge excellence in ministry? In what ways does the discussion of fruitfulness push your thinking about ministry success and faithfulness?

3. Before reading about the five themes, list as many topics as you can that would be important for leadership resilience in fruitful ministry work for a lifetime.

RECOMMENDATIONS FOR FURTHER READING

1. Richard Lischer. *Open Secrets: A Memoir of Faith and Discovery.* New York: Broadway Books, 2001.

2. Richard John Neuhaus. *Freedom for Ministry.* Grand Rapids: Eerdmans, 1979.

3. Susan Howatch. *Glittering Images.* New York: Ballantine Books, 1987.

2

THE FIVE THEMES
OF RESILIENT MINISTRY

Before you were called to be a shepherd, you were called to be a lamb.

Dr. Diane Langberg, psychologist, at a Pastors Summit gathering

EVERY YEAR MOST OF US GO THROUGH A series of checkups. We
have our annual physical checkups, during which doctors push, probe and
test to evaluate the conditions of our bodies. There are our annual financial checkups (otherwise known as income tax season), during which our
fiscal conditions undergo scrutiny. Then we regularly have planned (and
unplanned) conversations with our spouses, reviewing the condition of
our marriage and family. We also have annual reviews at work, looking at
the last twelve months' accomplishments and assessing future goals.

When an annual review is done for a pastor (which, unfortunately, is
rare), the topics for discussion usually focus on tangible issues that are vital
in the day-to-day operation of the church: worship, sermons, outreach,
education, finances, facilities, officer concerns, community issues and
counseling. Sometimes the conversation dips into personal life. Questions
like "How is your marriage?" "How are you doing financially?" and "How
are your kids?" may be asked at the end of the conversation.

While all of these questions are pertinent, they generally deal with surface concerns that don't probe the real issues that tear down or build up
pastoral resilience. As we shared in the introduction, after seven years of
studying our summit participants (including their marriages, families and
ministries), we learned a lot about what it takes to survive and thrive in min-

istry. Five themes, each with multiple factors, stood out as the keys for pastors to remain resilient in fruitful ministry for a lifetime. In this chapter we preview each theme, sharing why it is important for a lifetime of ministry.

THEME ONE: SPIRITUAL FORMATION

Over the years, we have had the privilege of seeing hundreds of people come to a faith commitment. In virtually all contexts where this has happened—from one-on-one meetings to large group gatherings—the new believer is instructed in the basics of spiritual growth. Spiritural formation can be compared to physical growth via nutrition and exercise. Spiritual growth is dependent on the care and feeding of the soul.

In our work with pastors, we have come to define spiritual formation as the ongoing process of maturing as a Christian, both personally and interpersonally. The key to this definition is the phrase *process of maturing*. It is a biblical expectation that all Christians, and especially leaders, be concerned about their own spiritual growth. This fits with the emphasis of Jesus when he said to his disciples, "If anyone loves me, he will keep my word, and my Father will love him, and we will come to him and make our home with him" (John 14:23).

With the same concern Paul encouraged Timothy to "train yourself for godliness" and to "keep a close watch on yourself and on the teaching" (1 Timothy 4:7, 16). Both Jesus and Paul understood that maturity is an ongoing process. No one ever "arrives" spiritually. We are all on a journey of spiritual growth.

It is easy to assume that pastors are always on a clear and intentional spiritual growth trajectory. After all, when was the last time you heard someone ask pastors how they were doing in their walk with the Lord? You might even think it rude to bring up the issue. Isn't it self-evident that pastors are attending to their spiritual formation? Sadly, the answer to this question is no. It is not unusual—in a place of safety—for pastors to share that they are hurting in their personal walk with the Lord. One summit pastor bluntly shared,

Look, I may be a pastor, but I'm an inch deep. My life is filled with incessant activity and little prayer. "Contemplation" is foreign in my vocabulary and nonexistent in my life.

Another important aspect of our definition of spiritual formation is that spiritual maturity involves both the *personal* and *interpersonal*. Pastors, like all believers, need to be involved in personal aspects of Christian growth like worship, prayer and Bible study. As discussed above, it is just as easy for pastors to neglect personal growth in Christ as any other Christian. At the same time, all Christians need one another. Jesus and the apostles never tired of stressing this need for community.[1]

This can present a problem for pastors, however. As paid leaders in the congregation, they can be viewed solely in terms of their role rather than as human beings who need others. They are rarely appreciated as persons with interests and relational needs. (An example is the pastor we quoted earlier who majored in art but lamented that few knew of that interest.) They are not looked at as fellow saints in the process of sanctification. As a result, pastors tend to be slow in opening up and sharing their lives with others.

Bob struggled over self-disclosure while serving in a pastorate. One Sunday afternoon he was helping a deacon set up for an evening activity. As they put up tables and chairs, the deacon suddenly asked the simple question, "How are you doing?"

When asked this question, Bob faced an ethical dilemma. He wasn't doing well at all. He was frustrated with the people in the church and was frustrated with his frustration. He was questioning his capacity as a leader and his own spiritual maturity. In a split second, he pondered the options: *If I answer honestly, how would this man handle my response? Would he continue to follow me? Or would he throw up his hands and say, "You're no spiritual leader! I'm out of here!" Do I tell him the truth or do I give him a superficial answer?* Bob decided to go superficial and lied. He said he was fine and then diverted the conversation.

We are *not* saying that pastors should share their personal struggles with everyone. We *are* saying that it is easy for pastors, fearing what people might think, to become isolated from others. By so doing, they fail to grow spiritually. As one pastor put it, "I have a longing to be shepherded by someone else, but a fear to actually ask someone into my life." Again, the themes all weave together: isolation is bad self-care *and* poor leadership as well.

Spiritual formation involves a growth in spiritual maturity that is generally reflected in lifestyle behaviors. Many biblical passages about the spiritual disciplines can be cited.[2] There is no doubt that a commitment to these kinds of activities is essential for spiritual development. Pastors struggle as much as laypersons to be motivated to engage in spiritual disciplines. But if pastors are the ones monitoring and encouraging others in this effort, where do they turn when they face similar struggles?

A few years ago we invited psychologist Diane Langberg to speak to a group of summit pastors and their spouses. In her talk she made this simple yet profound statement: "Before you were called to be a shepherd, you were called to be a lamb." When she said this, the entire room went silent. Everyone understood the tension her comment exposed. One of the pastors put it this way: "I realize that I have been forsaking my first love and making ministry an idol—that needs serious repentance."

This is the first thing pastors need to be aware of in order to survive for the long haul. They need to attend to their own spiritual growth. As we look at the tapestry of these themes, the next one may come as a surprise. It is the need for pastors to address their own self-care.

THEME TWO: SELF-CARE

The idea of self-care involves the pursuit of physical, mental and emotional health. While just as important as spiritual formation, self-care may initially sound selfish. After all, didn't Jesus say that those who follow him must give up all rights to themselves (Mark 8:34)? How does our Lord's call to self-denial square with the idea of self-care?

In truth, responsible self-care is actually a way to deny oneself. John Stott explains, "Becoming and being a Christian involves a change so radical that no imagery can do it justice except death and resurrection—dying to the old life of self-centeredness and rising to a new life of holiness and love."[3] The old life may have included slothful or obsessive activities such as inconsistent sleep habits, crazy work hours, poor or neurotic exercise, and an unhealthy diet. Self-denying self-care, on the other hand, may include getting to bed on time, saying no to work by setting aside periods for sabbath and sabbatical, getting responsible exercise, and eating a balanced diet.

Peter Brain defines self-care as "the wisdom to ensure, as far as humanly possible, a wise and orderly work that conserves and lengthens a pastor's ministry."[4] One of our summit pastors described his life in a simple but profound manner:

I feel like Frodo. In the *Fellowship of the Ring*, he's talking to Gandalf and says, "I feel like butter spread over too much bread." I just feel like I'm tired and running on fumes.

Having already explored the lifestyle of pastors in the introduction, this comment comes as no surprise. The idea of attending to self-care recognizes that pastors don't think about their self-care—but need to!

For example, at one Pastors Summit, we addressed areas of interest outside of work. One person responded: "Do I have a life outside the church? No. Do I have a hobby? No." Another put it this way:

I don't know that there's much I could talk about other than what I do functionally as a pastor and what's going on in the life of the church. That's a scary revelation to make.

We are not suggesting that all of the pastors in our study were one-dimensional workaholics. However, pastors can easily become so absorbed in their ministries that they fail to maintain a healthy equilibrium in their lives. As one of our participants said,

I am convicted that I need to be paying attention to (caring for) myself, not just for the church. I have been sacrificing myself for the work and really, this is not forming myself to Christ.

If you were surprised by this second theme of self-care, you may also be startled by the third area needed for pastors to build resilience in ministry. This theme draws together two ideas focusing on the understanding of self and others: emotional and cultural intelligence.

THEME THREE: EMOTIONAL AND CULTURAL INTELLIGENCE

Emotional and cultural intelligence are so closely aligned that we combined them under one heading. To understand how they influence pastoral life, however, we will look at each as a unique subset of the same theme.

Emotional Intelligence. Donald was sitting with a small group of pastors who had been meeting together for over a year. They were in an offsite location and had spent time getting reconnected with each other. The ensuing conversation included two comments that were telling about the role of emotions in the ministry.

> Well, you learn to play a game, to put on a mask, which then becomes a way you handle a lot of issues. You're suddenly the holy man that has to put on the holiness aura and have it all together. And that's going to come back and wipe you out. Wiped me out.
>
> ✦ ✦ ✦
>
> When I was in seminary, I was taught how to preach and how to exegete the Scriptures. I wasn't taught how to exegete people. . . . I didn't know that pastoring is dealing with people and their messiness.

These statements illustrate common pastoral challenges in the two sides of emotional intelligence (EQ, named in like manner to IQ for intelligence quotient): *EQ-self* and *EQ-others*. EQ-self concerns the ability to proactively manage one's own emotions. EQ-others concerns the ability to appropriately respond to the emotions of others.[5] The first comment—about pastors putting on masks—illustrates an EQ-self problem. The second remark—on exegeting people—displays the need for high EQ-others in pastoral work.

EQ-self is not easy. It is hard for all of us (pastors included) to identify our own feelings correctly, let alone to handle them wisely. One summit pastor observed,

> I'm increasingly seeing that I am not very aware of the emotional aspects of my personality. I see my weaknesses in this area reflected in the church I pastor. Our church is emotionally and relationally underdeveloped.

EQ-others is not any easier. It requires the ability to accurately discern what others are feeling and respond appropriately to them. Without this capacity, we tend to disregard others (whether we know it or not) while we push our own agendas. This is not a healthy way to lead!

As a pastor, Bob had worked for weeks to prepare a strategic plan. By the time he presented his ideas to the church elders, Bob was sold on the plan and believed it was the only way to precede. But the elders didn't buy it. They voted to postpone any decision. Afterward, one of them pulled Bob aside and said, "Your plan might be great. But you came across like a used car salesman, pushing your agenda. When we asked questions, you disregarded them as if they weren't important." The correction was clear: Bob needed to hear their thoughts and feelings and respond appropriately to them. His EQ-others was lacking.

Cultural Intelligence. In 2008, the U.S. Census Bureau announced that by midcentury, the United States will be much more racially and ethnically diverse. The report states: "Minorities, now roughly one-third of the U.S. population, are expected to become the majority in 2042, with the nation projected to be 54 percent minority in 2050. By 2023, minorities will comprise more than half of all children."[6]

The implications of this report are profound for the church. But it was not this information that signaled to us that cultural intelligence is an important factor for viable pastoral ministry. Rather, comments made by summit participants about their own experiences with cultural challenges prompted us to emphasize this topic.

What do we mean by cultural intelligence (CQ)? It is the ability to recognize and to adapt to different cultural contexts. CQ requires an understanding and appreciation of current contextual forces as well as the cultural background of one's self and others. It involves an awareness of ethnic, geographical, socioeconomic, educational and generational differences and the implications of these differences on one's perspective and behavior.

One of our summit pastors was born and raised in the southern United States. However, he was serving as a church planter in a western city. His church was actively reaching the unchurched in a very secular community.

Then two couples from the Deep South—my home turf—began attending our church. They griped to everyone how we weren't doing things right because it wasn't like "back home." The non-Christians dropped out. Tore our church up.

As we see in this story, cultural intelligence refers to all kinds of contexts. In order to lead effectively over the coming years, pastors must develop emotional and cultural intelligence. A primary training ground to develop these intelligences is found in the next theme of our research: the importance of marriage and family.

THEME FOUR: MARRIAGE AND FAMILY

This theme recognizes that to sustain the stresses in ministry, pastors need to focus on spiritual and relational health with their spouse, children and extended family. As one pastor put it, "The most effective way to develop a healthy church is for me to be healthy and maintain the health of my marriage." But the challenges embedded in this theme are significant. Who hasn't heard stories of spouses who felt they were in competition with the church? Or of children who share bitterly about being a "PK" (pastor's kid)? As one summit participant said, "I just feel that pressure sometimes to have this model home that everybody could follow and imitate. I'm not good at that."

One of the most significant lessons we learned early in the Pastors Summit research was the strategic role the spouse plays in ministry life. By "strategic role," we don't mean the functions a spouse may perform in the congregation. Rather, we mean the role spouses have in sustaining their pastor-partners in the work of ministry. One male pastor put it this way:

I know now more than ever that I cannot answer this calling without my wife. She is the only person in my life who will always be there for me in ministry.

It is easy for people in the church to assume that pastors naturally focus on the needs of their loved ones. As one summit pastor's wife shared, "People think that if you marry a pastor, you'll get pastored all the time." But this is far from true. Some pastors are so focused on others that they fail to be aware of how their spouses are doing. There was a general consensus among the married male pastors in our research that they needed to invest more time and energy into their marriage and family. One pastor stated simply, "My family gets the scraps."

Since Jesus taught that the world will know we are his disciples by the love we demonstrate toward one another, then the first place this should be visible is in the home (John 13:35). This, together with spiritual formation, self-care, and emotional and cultural intelligence, form a significant portion of what we identified as necessary for resilience in fruitful ministry.

By this time you may be thinking, *None of the themes you've mentioned thus far focus on the actual tasks of ministry.* True enough. While these first

four themes do touch every aspect of ministry life, none of them specifically describe any of the ministry tasks outlined by Jackson Carroll that we
reviewed in the previous chapter: leading worship, preaching, teaching
and congregational oversight.[7] It is valid to ask, "Don't these have a place
in resilient pastoral ministry?"

While the pastors we studied would affirm the place of these four ministry
task categories, one area stood out as critical for survival in the long haul.
Of the four, it is the area least discussed in the pre-professional training of
theological seminary. But it generally takes up more of a pastor's time than
any other responsibility. Carroll calls it "congregational oversight." In our
study, we named it leadership and management.

THEME FIVE: LEADERSHIP AND MANAGEMENT

The first chapter described the pastoral role as exceedingly diverse and
complex. Effective pastors require a great variety of skills. When it comes
to leadership and management, a massive study on the ministry catego-
rizes the tasks: sharing congregational leadership, building congregational
community, effective administration, conflict utilization and responsible
self-management.[8] Samuel Blizzard, one of the earliest researchers on pastoral life, reported that ministers allocate more of their energies to administering programs than would be anticipated in terms of training and their
own expectations. More recently, another research project identified "a
strong managerial dimension requiring significant amounts of time in the
pastor's weekly schedule."[9]

The responsibilities of leadership and management are rarely discussed in theological training. Indeed, pastors are generally surprised by
how much leadership and management is involved in their work. And
they must learn it on the job. As one person stated, "I never thought
about my calling as a leader until I was already in the pastorate." It seems
to us that these responsibilities of pastoral life are rarely discussed but
continually demanded.

In order for pastors to thrive in ministry, they must accept the fact that
they are leaders and managers. Business and professional literature de-
picts these roles as necessary but different in nature.[10] In general, the literature describes leadership as seeking adaptive and constructive change,
while management provides order and consistency to organizations. In

this book, we describe leadership responsibilities as *poetry* and managerial tasks as *plumbing*.

Leadership and management require different skills and abilities. As businesses or churches grow, these responsibilities are often separated into distinct roles. But as leaders of smaller businesses and churches know, they will always have both leadership and management obligations, even if they don't feel gifted for the work. An additional challenge is that most pastors dislike both leadership and management and would prefer delegating these responsibilities to someone else. As one summit pastor explained,

> What's my perfect job description? Preach, teach and spend time with my staff and elders. I'm so busy managing that I feel guilty doing relational things. I have this vision where I could maintain these close relationships and still keep the church moving forward if I had this guy—my own Ed McMahon—doing the stuff prohibiting me from doing what I want to do.

In his book *Good to Great*, Jim Collins says that a characteristic of great companies is an ability to confront the brutal facts.[11] Similarly, thriving ministries have pastors who have embraced the difficult facts that leadership and management skills must be learned and responsibilities must be accepted. One of our summit pastors described how he came to grips with this truth.

> When I got out of seminary, I didn't know what I was doing. I was so deficient in the area of leadership. If somebody mentioned a book on leadership, I bought it. I had to self-educate, and I'm still doing that.

Once pastors come to grips with the fact that ministry requires them to lead and manage, they must learn to confront the political realities and expectations embedded in these tasks. Expectations and demands for service are at an all-time high. Resources and time constraints constantly push against congregants' expectations. Disappointing people is a reality. Harvard professors Ronald Heifetz and Marty Linsky have summarized that "exercising leadership might be understood as disappointing people at a rate they can absorb."[12]

Similarly, pastors must learn to navigate the political realities of ministry. Yes, *politics* is a dirty word in the church. But ministry nearly always involves working with people, and people have divergent amounts of influence and differing interests. These differences lead them to act in certain ways when confronted with tough decisions.[13] The ministry involves negotiating with others, choosing among conflicting wants and interests, developing trust, locating support and opposition, timing actions sensitively, and knowing the informal and formal organizational sources of influence and action.[14] In short, Jesus might well have also said, "Where two or three are gathered together, there are politics."

A LOOK AHEAD

In this chapter, we have briefly introduced the themes discovered in our research with the Pastors Summit. In the following chapters, we will explore each of these themes—spiritual formation, self-care, emotional and cultural intelligence, marriage and family, and leadership and management—in more depth through the reflections and stories of the participants in the Pastors Summit.

The responsibilities of pastoral life are continual. The pace and demands of ministry can be relentless, often pushing even the most dedicated pastors to question their calls and evaluate their lives. It is time for all of us in the church to raise our understanding of ministry demands, review our expectations and make plans for building resilient pastoral excellence.

QUESTIONS TO PONDER

1. Do you know of a church that regularly reviewed the pastor for the sake of encouraging growth and effective work? If so, to what extent was the pastor's personal life assessed? If not, how would you conduct such a review?

2. In what ways have you successfully pursued spiritual formation? What roles did others play in your growth toward Christian maturity?

3. What "stories" do you tell yourself about self-care—what thoughts repeat over and over? What motivates you to prioritize the work required to pursue physical and emotional health?

4. Think of someone you know who seems to have high EQ-self (the abil-

ity to manage one's own emotions). How would you characterize them? Make a list of their characteristics. Do the same for someone you know with high EQ-others (the ability to appropriately respond to others' emotions) and someone with high CQ (cultural intelligence). How do the three lists compare?

5. Name several concrete examples of how spouses can play an important role in helping sustain their pastor-partners in the work of ministry.

6. Think of a recent conflict in your church. How were the skills of management and leadership expressed during that time?

RECOMMENDATIONS FOR FURTHER READING

1. Michael Todd Wilson and Brad Hoffmann. *Preventing Ministry Failure: A ShepherdCare Guide for Pastors, Ministers and Other Caregivers.* Downers Grove, Ill.: InterVarsity Press, 2007.

2. Jackson W. Carroll. *God's Potters: Pastoral Leadership and the Shaping of Congregations.* Grand Rapids: Eerdmans, 2006.

3. Dean R. Hoge and Jacqueline E. Wenger. *Pastors in Transition: Why Clergy Leave Local Church Ministry.* Grand Rapids: Eerdmans, 2005.

3

EVALUATING
SPIRITUAL FORMATION

How can I be intentional in my relationships (marriage, parenting, friendships)
when I'm not intentional in my relationship with the Lord? I simply don't make it
[time with God] a priority. I'm much more driven by the tyranny of the urgent.

A pastor at a Pastors Summit gathering

EACH OF US—DONALD, TASHA AND BOB—is the parent of two
children. We all found the early months of having a firstborn startling.
Nearly all of the baby's waking focus is on eating. We can't help but wonder
if the apostle Peter was reflecting on his parenting experiences when he
told his friends, "Like newborn infants, long for the pure spiritual milk,
that by it you may grow up into salvation" (1 Peter 2:2). In encouraging
God's people to obey the truth and pursue godly living, Peter likens their
need for God's Word to the infant's desire. We must "eat" to "grow in the
grace and knowledge of our Lord and Savior Jesus Christ" (2 Peter 3:18).

How do we pursue growth in the grace and knowledge of Jesus, that is,
in spiritual formation? How do we know real growth is occurring? In the
previous chapter, we described spiritual formation as the ongoing process
of maturing as a Christian, both personally and interpersonally. Every one
of us is on a growth continuum in our walk with Christ. No one has arrived. Instead, the Bible calls us to "work out" our salvation, "press on toward the goal," "be transformed by the renewal" of our minds and "grow
up in every way" into Christ.[1] The Scriptures describe phases of matura-

tion in spiritual life similar to physical maturation: a movement from be-ing "children" to "adults" and then "elders."[2] It is a given in the Scriptures that believers should grow in their spiritual lives.[3]

Holding a staff position in a church or ministry does not mean that a person has arrived at a place of mature spirituality (regardless of whether she or he has attended theological seminary). A factual knowledge of the Bible and theology does not equal spiritual maturity. In fact, many people preparing for the ministry abandon needed spiritual disciplines while in training. All three of us found it difficult to remain faithful in Bible study and prayer with the pressures of seminary exams and term papers. Simi-larly, author Kevin Harney has shared that while working with seminari-ans, he discovered that all had put aside Bible study from the rhythm of their daily lifestyle.[4]

People are often put into positions of responsibility before they are spir-itually mature enough to handle it. Each of us knows people with great "head knowledge" who don't have developed spiritual "hearts." For exam-ple, we each had classes with seminary professors who had long lists of degrees after their names but who consistently treated people in a gruff, unkind manner. This lack of interpersonal maturity did not seem to pro-duce fruit of the Spirit (Galatians 5:19-23). If we were to test some of their "fruit," as Jesus challenges us in the Sermon on the Mount, we would ques-tion whether they should be in influential roles (Matthew 7:15-20).

Unfortunately, laypersons often assume the spirituality of pastors and ministry leaders is mature and growing. However, it is not self-evident that pastors are attending to their spiritual formation. It is just as easy for pas-tors to neglect personal growth in Christ as it is for any other Christian. As one pastor from the summit put it, "People think I am closer to God than I really am." Another pastor has written, "It doesn't take many years in this business to realize that we can conduct a fairly respectable pastoral minis-try without giving much more than ceremonial attention to God."[5]

CHRISTIAN IDENTITY AND VOCATIONAL ROLE

Pastors need to be shepherded and nurtured in order to grow in their walks with the Lord, just like the rest of us. Foremost, this means they need to become secure in the love of the Father, practically working his love into the fabric of their lives and the foundation of their work. This security doesn't come by simply gaining knowledge of the truth. It is a lifelong journey in which, using a phrase from C. S. Lewis, we move "farther up and further in" in our understanding and appropriation of God's grace.[6] As one pastor from the summit expressed, "I want my faith to be separate from my career as a pastor: a faith that is authentic, not just a professional persona."

But gaining a healthy separation of our personal identities from our professional roles is a challenge, especially for pastors whose vocational tasks and Christian identity are so directly enmeshed.[7] The gospel clearly teaches us that our good works are a result of God's workmanship in us and are our response to his grace. But our fearful hearts and our performance-oriented culture, which increasingly views Christian practices as irrelevant, tell us the opposite: we are what we do.

When Bob was planting a church in Florida in his early years of ministry, his emotions fluctuated with the Sunday worship attendance. While he could articulate his belief in the love of the Father, it didn't penetrate how he felt about himself on Sunday afternoons. Then he moved to Pennsylvania, where he served on the staff of a large and growing church. The ministry was thriving. Bolstered by this experience, he again prepared to plant another church, telling himself that this time Sunday attendance would no longer be an issue. Secure in the Father? Not so easy when the worship services began! But at least this second time around he worked harder at understanding his feelings and sharing them with the Father and his friends. One step "farther up and further in."

Pastors often slip into the trap of building their identities around their roles and performance rather than being beloved children of God and co-heirs with Christ. Pastors need to pursue growth in their understanding of and feelings concerning God's acceptance. They also need to focus on their daily personal relationship with Jesus Christ. The sad fact is that, for most of us in ministry, our work for Christ comes before our relationship with Christ. We know in our minds that healthy ministry is an overflow of abiding in Christ. We know that godly leadership is an extension of one's relationship with God. But when push comes to shove, we usually put mission in front of relationship.

If the goal of ministry is seeing people transformed into the image of Christ, then the spiritual transformation of pastors is preeminent (see Colossians 1:28-29). As the Pastors Summit participants reflected on the theme of spiritual formation, they focused on two particular areas. First, they asked, "How can ministry leaders review and evaluate their spiritual formation?" Second, on the basis of this evaluation, they asked, "How can ministry leaders pursue their own spiritual formation?"

EVALUATING ONE'S OWN SPIRITUAL FORMATION

Pastors are constantly in evaluation mode concerning their sermons, involvement of laypersons, the worship service, outreach programs, discipleship initiatives, shepherding activities and the training of officers. The list could go on and on. But when it comes to serious reflection on their spiritual lives, pastors often fail to consider it. We planned the Pastors Summit schedule with one morning set aside for personal evaluation, usually starting with the topic of spiritual formation. Most of the pastors would return from this evaluation time dissatisfied with their spiritual lives. Here are a couple comments from their reflections.

I've seen patterns of anxiety and faithlessness through my reflection time. I've realized that my sleeplessness is anxiety. My devotional life is bad because I believe I have to take life by the horns. All of this reveals my lack of belief. I believe God is holding out on me.

What happens when I skirt my spiritual growth? I replace it with the "spiritual" tasks of pastoral life. So, for example, it is not unusual to find me substituting sermon preparation for personal worship and Bible study. "After all," I rationalize, "I will be meditating on the Bible." However, the sustained exchange of ministry duties for spiritual growth results in my becoming an "inch deep." The outcome is a spiritually dry, worn-out pastor with very little "left in the tank" for others. The "spring of water welling up to eternal life" has slowed to a trickle (John 4:14).

These responses correspond to what authors Jim Herrington, Robert Creech and Trisha Taylor call "soul neglect." They share: "We grow busier and busier to please more and more people. We spend more time in meetings than we do in prayer. We scarcely have time to read the newspaper, much less spiritual classics or devotional readings. We study Scripture, but we do it for other people to convey God's Word to them. Our own hearts are often thirsty for a word from God, but who has time? We faithfully minister to the spiritual needs of others and teach ourselves to be content with the leftovers."[8]

Ministry leaders collapse under the overwhelming pressures to ignore their own needs motivated by busyness, people-pleasing, the tyranny of the urgent and their own lack of priority on personal growth.

We asked our summit pastors, "What obstacles stand in the way of your fruitful, growing walk with Christ?" They focused on one primary issue: workaholism. Their workaholism largely stems from two sources: the belief that they never work hard enough (and that others work harder than they do) and the assumption that they are responsible for everything that happens in the church.

Diagnosing Pastoral Workaholism. "I work just as hard as you do, if not harder": this statement summarizes a common, heartfelt sentiment of the pastors. They were greatly concerned that, to the layperson, their flexible schedules make it look like they are goofing off. While studies we referenced earlier show that pastors work every bit as hard—if not harder—than other professionals, the anxiety that pastors carry of having to demonstrate that they are "earning their keep" is pervasive. One of the pastors put it this way:

One of the things I've been sucked into is the thought, "If I spend more time in prayer [in the morning], all the men that I'm working with who are already off to work, they're going to think, 'You know pastors. They are in control of their own schedule.' So I'm going to get up [and get to work] as early as they do." I feel guilty if I'm not at my desk doing something concrete by 8 a.m.

A few years back, Tasha felt burdened by anxiety that she might not be working hard enough. The combination of ministry responsibilities, a cell phone and a laptop made it so that work could follow her around all the time. To settle the matter, she began counting her work hours. She found that she had worked so much that year that it would take two months of vacation to bring expected time off into line with her work hours.

Another pastor felt this way even though he had examples of laypersons who saw things very differently. He explained:

There is a time clock within me that says you need to get to work. I had a mentor who held a significant position in a Fortune 500 company. He had to be at the office early and stay late. I remember talking to him about this struggle, and he said he'd give anything to have the freedom to stay home and pray. I have another friend who is a lawyer. He shapes his schedule to have time to pray and study. He's doing what I know I should be doing! It's convicting to see that when businesspersons have that opportunity, they take it.

Consider an insight into this workaholism gleaned from systems theory. Persons who study systems—such as families or organizations—talk about participants in the system who either underfunction or overfunction. Persons who underfunction do not carry their load of responsibility in the system. To compensate for this, other members of the system work hard to compensate—overfunction—sometimes with much complaint. Reflecting on this in church systems, Herrington, Creech and Taylor explain: "Many pastors live in an over-functioning position with their congregation. When they attempt to step back to become more intentionally equal in posture and more reflective, the congregation often engages in a variety of anxious behaviors designed (intentionally or unintentionally) to restore the pastor to the over-functioning position. They insist that the pastor change back!"[9]

Part of pastoral overfunctioning stems from the assumption that the success and failure of the congregation's life rests solely on the pastor's shoulders. This anxiety can be enhanced by congregants' comments about the work life of the pastor. Over time, pastors can develop mindsets that they never work hard enough or that the struggles of a congregation are always their responsibility. This creates unhealthy work patterns that leave no time for healthy spiritual formation practices.

Pushing Back Against Workaholism. What can be done about these pressures stemming from assumptions about pastoral work? We will explore this question in more depth in the chapter on self-care. For now, we will offer a number of practical steps. First, get the facts. Ministry leaders should do an audit of their schedules. Take one week and keep track of all that you do, including phone calls, interruptions and unexpected conversations. If you do such an audit a number of times over three months, you will get a good idea of how much time you are investing in ministry. It may be even more helpful to divide the working hours into categories.

Next, challenge your own attitude about how much time you actually are working. And have a conversation with a close friend or your spouse about your schedule and see whether your family thinks you work hard enough. Then, with prayer and courage, speak to trusted board members about your analysis and their priorities for your work. In this way, seek both to educate them about the problem and to gain support for needed changes to your work pattern.

A third idea is to ask people in your congregation about *their* work schedules. Discover when they get to work, what the rhythm of their work schedule is, how many nights they are at home and when they have time off. Compare their schedules with yours—not to see who works harder, but to understand the similarities and differences.

A fourth idea is to explore the perspectives of others in your church. Since pastors worry about what others think of their work habits, discover what others are actually thinking. It would be a good idea to visit people at their job sites. Not only would this give you a better understanding of their weekly experience, it would bless them to know you had that much interest in their lives between Sundays.

Fifth, consider educating the congregation on the pastoral life. Of course, this would need to be done subtly so it doesn't seem as though you are justifying your existence. We recommend several ideas. One is to ask members of your board (or broader congregation) to read portions of this book that discuss the pastoral lifestyle. Then create a conversation about this material. We know of one elder who, when learning about the pastoral lifestyle from an earlier booklet Bob wrote on the subject, declared, "This information must become mandatory reading in our officer training curriculum!"

Another idea is to share your pastoral experiences regularly with the congregation. Tell stories in your sermons about your experiences during the week. Or write a reflection on pastoral life for your newsletter. When Eugene Peterson was in pastoral ministry, he would write a quarterly article on the pastoral life to help his congregation understand his calling.[10]

Pastors can also help congregations understand their workload by sharing schedules and calendars. We know of one pastor who was consistently receiving critique from some in the congregation about her use of time. So for a period of time, she actually posted her schedule on the church website for open review. While this was a pretty radical way of addressing their concerns, after a few months of postings, the criticisms went away. Another pastor surveyed his congregation and computed their average weekly work hours. He then designed a contract with his board to limit his weekly work hours to that same average amount. Part of the board's job was to hold him accountable *not* to overwork.

Finally, and most importantly, pastors need to take steps to elevate the priority of their own relationship with God. For example, one pastor in the summit stopped to consider his lifestyle since entering the ministry. He reported that life was a blur since he had graduated from seminary, got a job, sold and bought a house, moved, had a baby the day his job started, had a second child, helped start a new church, filled in while the senior pastor was on sabbatical, and studied for ordination in his denomination. He shared:

> I haven't stopped. I mean, I don't even know what end is up. There's no wonder I'm so angry. There's no wonder I'm in a drought. Today while I read in 2 Corinthians, I saw that Paul was ministering out of a current experience of the grace and mercy of God in Christ Jesus. . . . I think today I realized I've been in a spiritual drought for two and a half years. . . . I've got to be the best, do the most. . . . Basically I've been ministering out of a place of drought, a posture of [false] strength and protected affections. I'm not going to make it in ministry long like this!

For pastors and ministry leaders to grow in resilience for a lifetime of fruitful ministry, they must pursue a vibrant relationship with God.

What is the impact of workaholism on the pastor's spiritual formation? A comment by Pete Scazzero in *Emotionally Healthy Spirituality* provides a helpful summative statement. "Work *for* God that is not nourished by a deep interior life *with* God will eventually be contaminated by other things such as ego, power, needing approval of and from others, and buying into the wrong ideas of success and the mistaken belief that we can't fail."[11]

QUESTIONS TO PONDER

1. As you think back over the past year, what evidences of spiritual growth can you find in your life?

2. What are some areas you desire to mature in during this coming year? What changes in your habits would it take to pursue this spiritual growth?

3. Who could help you assess your workload and expectations and look for places of overfunctioning?

4. To assess your tendency toward workaholism, consider the degree to which work is the source of your hope, joy, emotional energy, support and success. Are you ever satisfied with your work? Are you expecting more from your work than it can provide? Has it become an idol in your life? To what degree is work drawing you away from healthy self-care, friendships and family relationships?

5. In what ways could you help your congregation gain a healthier understanding of your work? How could you and your congregants deepen a commitment to every member being a minister and using their gifts?

RECOMMENDATIONS FOR FURTHER READING

1. Peter Scazzero. *Emotionally Healthy Spirituality: Unleash a Revolution in Your Life in Christ*. Nashville: Thomas Nelson, 2006.

2. Eugene Peterson. *Working the Angles: The Shape of Pastoral Integrity*. Grand Rapids: Eerdmans, 1987.

MEDIA WORTH EXPLORING

1. *Ratatouille* (2007), rated G. With the encouragement of friends, a rat named Remy realizes his calling as a chef in Brad Bird's brilliant, Academy Award–winning film. No one discovers his or her calling alone, just as no one matures alone. This film encourages consideration of how vocational calling and maturity grow interdependently.

2. *The Last Butterfly* (2000), rated PG-13. A famous French mime is forced by the Nazis to demonstrate their "kind" treatment of Jewish prisoners of war by participating in a propaganda play. During the course of this powerful film, the mime rediscovers his calling and recognizes his responsibility to "speak" the truth to the watching world.

PURSUING
SPIRITUAL FORMATION

How can I as a leader remain calm in an anxious context—especially when

a lot of the anxiety is being pointed at me? I just . . . kept coming back to

crying out to God and crying out for the calmness of his Holy Spirit,

for his peace, for the fruit of the Spirit to be reflected and again,

maybe that comes back to the spiritual disciplines.

A pastor at a Pastors Summit gathering

BOB VIVIDLY RECALLS THE TIME IN SEMINARY when a professor said, "Whenever you are preaching a sermon, I want you to envision me sitting in the back row of the church with my arms folded asking you the question, 'So what do you want me to *do* about it?'" In the previous chapter we saw how pastors often evaluate their spiritual formation. But how should they respond? What can ministry leaders do to pursue spiritual formation?

Over the centuries, hundreds of books have been written on developing the inner spiritual life, popularly called *soul care* today. Classics such as *The Imitation of Christ* by Thomas à Kempis and *The Practice of the Presence of God* by Brother Lawrence join with popular modern titles such as *Knowing God* by J. I. Packer, *Celebration of Discipline* by Richard Foster and *The Spirit of the Disciplines* by Dallas Willard. All of these books address our pursuit of maturity in Christ.

The insights of works like these are well worth serious consideration.

Here, however, we want to explore what the summit pastors said helped them the most. They identified four key practices for successfully pursuing maturity in their relationship with Christ: building rituals, maintaining accountability, growing through hardships and practicing spiritual disciplines.

BUILDING RITUALS

Healthy habits take time to build into our lives. Rituals are highly purposeful habits. In *The Power of Full Engagement*, authors Jim Loehr and Tony Schwartz explain the importance of consciously chosen rituals. "A growing body of research suggests that as little as 5 percent of our behaviors are consciously self-directed. We are creatures of habit and as much as 95 percent of what we do occurs automatically or in reaction to a demand or an anxiety. Rituals are precise, consciously acquired behaviors that become *automatic* in our lives, fueled by a deep sense of purpose."[1]

For believers in Christ, these rituals are not standardized expectations of a discipleship curriculum. Rather, within the provision of God's means of grace, different people need different formats and routines at different times in order to pursue formation.[2] As one pastor stated,

> There is no magic formula. [I pray,] "Lord, help me to discover the rhythms that will make my life fruitful for you." I've discovered some of those things and when I violate those rhythms, it doesn't take long before something goes wrong.

This is a matter of personal study. Each of us must explore the rhythms that make our life fruitful for God. These rhythms include the mental, physical, emotional and social aspects of our unique selves. For example, Bob worked with businesspersons for many years. Most of these women and men found they preferred a structured plan for spiritual growth. Then, for a period of time, he worked with a group of artists. He discovered that structured plans made some artists feel stifled and bored. He had to change his entire coaching approach concerning spiritual rituals in order to fit the rhythms of these people.

One evening during a Pastors Summit gathering, a pastor told us of his exploration of personal rituals. He shared:

How can I connect with God the best? I'm not best when I'm just sitting there praying. It's better when I am walking. I am much more consistent in prayer if I take a walk rather than sitting. Nevertheless, I feel the importance of a set time and place for reading and praying.

A word of caution: as you begin establishing new routines that you hope become rituals, this should not be approached like making New Year's resolutions. Learning is a process. Change does not occur by embracing a plan or instituting a five-step program. Rather, "those who achieve change commit to a process that provides simple guidance in the midst of the complexity of seeking personal transformation."[3]

We will come back to this idea of building rituals later in this chapter, as well as in the next chapter on self-care. Every healthy relationship incorporates ritual to sustain and grow it. Planning, practicing and evaluating our conscious and previously unconscious rituals are critical in the spiritual formation process of pastors.

QUESTIONS TO PONDER

1. Over the years, what rhythms have you developed that influence your walk with God? Which of these rhythms strengthen your spiritual life? Which ones undermine healthy spirituality?

2. What new rituals could strengthen your walk with God? How can you begin to incorporate these into your life? How could others help you build these rituals into your life?

MAINTAINING ACCOUNTABILITY

As we have shared, our working definition of spiritual formation is the ongoing process of maturing as a Christian, both personally and interpersonally. Much of what we say in this chapter focuses on the personal. Yet the interpersonal is also a critical component of growing in Christ. Pastors are very aware of this fact. Most of them can quickly cite passages on the body of Christ, such as 1 Corinthians 12 and Ephesians 5. They know the "one another" passages sprinkled throughout the pages of the New Testament. And yet study after study shows that most pastors are lonely. This contradiction—an understanding of the need for others and the tendency to be isolated—was discussed by many of our summit participants. One described it this way:

Spiritual growth requires that we recognize our need for one another—even be "weak" with one another! We pastors often urge others to develop these relationships. We even plan ministry activities to promote relationships, such as small groups and neighborhood fellowships. However, when it comes to our own lives, we are often fearful to "let down" and acknowledge our need for others.

Finding and forming intimate friendships, in which "iron sharpens iron" (Proverbs 27:17), is often a frightening and elusive challenge for pastors.

Allies or Confidants? Where can pastors find helpful, accountable relationships? In the book *Leadership on the Line*, Ron Heifetz and Marty Linsky make a very helpful distinction we will use often in this book. They write of the relationship difference between allies and confidants. *Allies*, they state, "are people who share many of your values, or at least your strategy, and operate across some organizational or factional boundary."[4] They go on to say that allies "*cannot* always be loyal to you; they have other ties to honor." *Confidants*, on the other hand, "have few, if any, conflicting loyalties. They usually operate outside your organization's boundary, although occasionally someone very close in, whose interests are perfectly aligned with yours, can also play that role."[5]

Pastors are constantly working with allies. Everyone from members of the ruling board to kids in the youth ministry share a unique bond with the pastor. On the whole, they share the pastor's values and operate within the organization of the church. Yet pastors are always calculating—consciously and unconsciously—whether these allies in the congregation could or should be party to their more personal concerns. Could they be trusted confidants who would honor such increased responsibility with loyalty and integrity? Mistaking an ally for a confidant could lead to conflict and serious breaks in trust.

A simple but common example of this relational calculation concerns money. Suppose a pastor shares with a friend, who happens to be on the church finance committee, that she has just purchased a wide-screen TV. The friend might think, *I'm glad she got that TV; we must be paying her well. I need to remember that when we are talking about salary increases next year.* The friend is now pulled between the confidence of the pastor's purchase and the interests of the finance committee. In later budget decisions, the pastor might easily feel that the personal information is used against her.

Now we apply this distinction between allies and confidants to the area of mutual accountability. To whom can pastors go to get pastored? Who is safe for pastors to talk with about struggles and sins? As one person in the summit put it,

---

If I'm sick and tired about what is happening in my church and considering leaving, do you think I'm going to talk to an elder about it?

No way. Yet pastors, just like the rest of us, need others to help them navigate life and pursue maturity.

One pastor shared about safety in spiritual accountability. This pastor was excited when one of his best friends from seminary transferred to a church in his area. He looked forward to connecting with this friend and renewing the accountability they shared while in school together. For over a year this pastor reached out to his friend, yet this person put off getting together. When they finally met for coffee, the friend shared why he had been slow in responding. "You are on the local shepherding committee for our denomination," the friend explained. "If I told you how I was doing, you would be required to report me. And I can't risk losing my job. So I can't tell you how I'm doing."

Allies for Accountability. While pastors must be careful how and with whom they share their lives, we don't want to give the impression that allies cannot be helpful in providing spiritual accountability. Pastors can find significant help and encouragement from fellow staff members or other friends in the congregation. Bob was blessed and surprised recently in a conversation with the pastor of a large congregation who is leading his staff in spiritual formation. Four days a week, this staff meets together at 9 a.m. for a brief time of worship. At another time during the week, staff members pair off to share a time of mutual confession and repentance. Donald has experienced similar mutual encouragement on several local church and ministry staffs.

Sadly, trustworthy accountability like this is infrequent on church staff teams. We have rarely heard of or experienced such healthy, trusting relationships within the same church staff. Tasha has served in several church and ministry positions over the last twenty years, but she has never experienced significant healthy accountability toward spiritual growth within the team. Bob has also served on numerous church staffs and as a senior pastor. The only time he was ever given support and structure for spiritual formation was when he served as a youth ministry intern in the 1970s! How could he lead and serve in so many dynamic places where the shepherds were not mutually encouraging each other in their walk with Christ? As one of the summit pastors put it,

---

There is a longing to be shepherded by someone else, but trepidation that if we were to actually ask someone into our life, that person might ask us something that we weren't really interested in talking about.

Accountable relationships are necessary for spiritual growth. Pastors need brothers and sisters who are confidants: persons who "can provide you with a place where you can say everything that's in your heart, everything that's on your mind, without being predigested or well packaged."[6]

QUESTIONS TO PONDER

1. Who in my life have I been able to talk to about anything, without concern for the repercussions?

2. Who understands my work and world, such that I would not feel like I had to explain myself to them, but also speaks the truth in love to me?

3. What potential confidants can I name from inside my church system and from outside of it?

4. Who stimulates me to grow spiritually? How can I wisely steward my time with them?

GROWING THROUGH HARDSHIPS

A few years ago we attended a seminar led by Russ Moxley, former senior fellow at the Center for Creative Leadership. From repeated research studies, Moxley became convinced that the most important element of marketplace leadership training concerns how persons learn through hardships. The center's research summarizes the lessons learned from hardships in four categories: self-knowledge with a clarifying of values, sensitivity and compassion toward others, limits of personal control over circumstances, and flexibility.[7] These lessons are not only relevant to leadership but also to spiritual growth.

Hardship, affliction and suffering are given little space in most spiritual formation books and discipleship courses. Only in the classic *The Imitation of Christ* by Thomas à Kempis are afflictions a regular topic. Yet the value of hardships referenced above informs us that growth toward Christian maturity often results from them. Indeed, the Bible demonstrates that hardships are surprisingly common ways in which God develops us spiritually. Take, for example, James 1:2-4, in which the brother of Jesus tells us to count it all joy when we meet trials, because this testing of our faith produces steadfastness, making us complete. Or Romans 5:2-5, in which Paul explains a process that begins with suffering, produces character and ends with mature hope. In 2 Corinthians 12:7-10, Paul states that his own thorn in the flesh caused him to learn God's grace and exhibit God's power.

Perhaps the most striking passage concerning growth via hardship comes in Hebrews. Here the author makes this profound statement: "Although he [Jesus] was a son, he learned obedience through what he suffered" (Hebrews 5:8). Jesus' suffering provided experiential learning toward obedience in the fullness of his humanity. Just as we learn the bitterness of a pill by actually tasting it, so Jesus learned the cost and work of obedience by his suffering, though always without sin (Hebrews 4:15). Indeed, the hallmark of Jesus' life was suffering; he was "a man of sorrows, and acquainted with grief" (Isaiah 53:3).

In his commentary on Romans 8, John Stott elaborates on the place of hardships in the spiritual life of believers when he says, "Caught in the tension between what God has inaugurated (by giving us his Spirit) and what he will consummate (in our final adoption and redemption), we groan with discomfort and longing. The indwelling Spirit gives us joy, and the coming glory gives us hope, but the interim suspense gives us pain."[8]

The afflictions we experience now can greatly increase our longing for final redemption and our passion to be with God. In addition, as we follow Jesus Christ, we become more like him through our hardships.

Throughout the centuries, God's people have reflected on the ways God shapes his people for his purposes through hardships. For example, the prophet Isaiah reflects on God's use of the defeat of Israel as "his strange work . . . his alien task" (Isaiah 28:21 NIV). How many of us have sat back, in the midst of confusing and distressing situations, wondering what God is doing? While we may never discern his purposes in a particular situation, we often gain deeper insight into God's plans over time.

One pastor shared how hardships have helped shape his understanding of God's agenda. When entering the ministry, he assumed that the most important priority was what he could accomplish for God. He discovered that God's plan had as much to do with *who* he was becoming as it did about *what* he was accomplishing. He explained:

> We start a journey into service with God without conceiving his purpose or the pain necessary to reveal it. His work, I have found, had much more to do with my own heart than I knew. I wanted him to work through me; he wanted to work in me. This dynamic has been the most painful and fruitful in my life.

Hearing this, another pastor responded that it was through crises that he grew into a deeper personal honesty and understanding of God's grace. It was a process, he said, not unlike the one recorded in Genesis 32 in which God wrestled with Jacob:

> This is the process God has taken me through: getting to the end of myself to the point where I am freed into authenticity, honesty and ultimately into grace. I do notice that it practically takes a crisis, though. I always want to slip back into performance-oriented manipulation of myself and others. God does the whole Jacob thing—repeatedly "touching my hip," so to speak. Brokenness, weakness, struggle with sin, receiving grace.

Yet another participant reflected on how the pastorate is a context in which this experience of spiritual growth through hardships is accelerated.

> The "pressure cooker" of being in the pastorate brings up issues more quickly than in others' lives, and what a blessing that is! I want maturity and growth and never considered that the pastorate facilitates this in a different way than, say, [the vocation of] a typical parishioner.

In order for spiritual growth to occur via hardships, a couple of things are necessary. First, pastors need to slow down enough to reflect on their experiences. Ted Ward, mentor to a generation of Christian educators, is famous for saying, "Anything worth doing is worth doing poorly . . . the first time . . . and better the second time."[9] His comment underlines the fact that learning requires the disequilibrium that comes through failure.

But failure isn't usually appreciated in the ministry. The disequilibrium and pain that often come with failure and with hardship are useless if we don't learn from them. Taking the time to pray, reflect and consider what God is doing is hard work. And the hectic lifestyle of most pastors does not lend itself to such reflection and space for learning. The discipline to stop and consider what God is accomplishing through hardships is critical for spiritual growth.

Russ Moxley, the speaker who referenced hardships as the most important element in leadership development, made another striking observation. He said that hardships are only useful when persons experiencing them have support systems that sustain them emotionally and that encourage them to reflect on the experience. "Hardships often evoke powerful and painful emotions, and an inability or unwillingness to face and reflect on this pain prevents learning."[10]

Vulnerability in safe relationships makes learning possible. Therefore, it is not surprising that the isolation and loneliness of ministry often turns hardships into damaging experiences rather than ones of growth. Intimate relationships are necessary for spiritual growth. Besides providing accountability, they also offer the emotional support and objective perspective to sustain us and to help us grow through hardships.

QUESTIONS TO PONDER

1. How has God used hardships to develop you spiritually? How and with whom did you process the hardships? What are you continuing to learn from them?

2. Consider a recent experience of failure. What did you do to cope with it? How did it deepen your walk with Christ?

3. Who provides you with emotional support and a mature perspective when facing hardships?

PRACTICING SPIRITUAL DISCIPLINES

Many excellent studies on the role of spiritual disciplines in spiritual formation are available.[11] The books we have explored on this subject list anywhere from ten to sixty-two different disciplines for Christians to consider.[12] In this section we will highlight five spiritual disciplines of greatest concern and interest to the Pastors Summit participants: reflection, prayer, sabbath, repentance and worship.

Before we look at these disciplines, we need to consider how challenging they can be to implement. As noted in the previous chapter, most pastors suffer from workaholism. Their lives have no room for new challenges. For most of us, just the mention of spiritual disciplines makes us feel a sense of failure in our Christian walk.

Change requires loss. Making room for new practices requires ceasing old activities. In addition to the hard work of changing priorities, successful life change usually requires a strong commitment to a learning process. The process consists of a repeated cycle of gaining information, taking steps to put new ideas into practice, and reviewing and evaluating the results (successes and failures). Then we have to make adjustments to the practice, which are followed by new reviews and so on. It is not easy to replace old habits with new, healthier rituals. We need to extend grace, humor and freedom to fail to ourselves as we seek to implement change.

Reflection. Reflection is the discipline of pausing and considering what you are thinking and feeling, as well as what you have been doing and saying to others. Intentional reflection is a required part of any learning process.[13] An ounce of reflection can lead to a pound of learning, so we often refer to reflection throughout this book. While we did not find it listed in the classic books on spiritual disciplines, reflection is most akin to meditation—a discipline that usually refers specifically to reflection on Scripture and on God's works.[14]

Reflection is a broader term that encompasses the idea behind biblical commands such as "consider," "remember" and "think." For example, when Jesus encourages his followers to "consider the lilies," he is calling them to reflect on creation and ponder how God cares for them (Matthew 6:28). Or when the disciples think his warning about leaven refers to bread, Jesus chides them, saying, "Do you not yet perceive? Do you not remember . . . How is it that you fail to understand?" (Matthew 16:9-11). Jesus expected them to mull over the implications of his feeding miracles and grasp the implications. When Paul encourages the Philippians to "think on" what is true, honorable, just and so on, he is calling them to do serious reflection and to consider the implications on their lives.

Most of the summit pastors openly acknowledged that they rarely took time for self-reflection. They did not routinely ruminate on their lives: what they were thinking, feeling, doing and saying. When asked, "When is the last time you reflected?" many said they had no idea. They did, however, recognize their need for this discipline. One pastor explained, "If we live an unexamined life, we're going to continue to think that what we are thinking is right." And another shared, "Nobody else is going to encourage me to take time to reflect. People won't bear down on me saying, 'Did you reflect today?'"

After significant conversations during the summits, we often took time to revisit what we had just talked about and to consider how it applied to our lives. In the middle of one of these reflections, a pastor blurted out:

I'm quick to take what I hear and apply it to someone else. I think, "That'll preach . . ." Not very reflective. 1 Timothy 4 talks about watching yourself and watching your doctrine. My reaction is to think about how to use something rather than allowing it to impact my own heart.

Without critical self-reflection, pastors easily fall into a trap of only thinking about how they can use recent experiences and ideas in their teaching and preaching.

How can pastors build reflection into their lives? While it can take place in spontaneous moments or occasional relational appointments, we have found that quality reflection requires intentionality. It doesn't just "happen" in the midst of daily demands. As cultural intelligence authority David Livermore urges, "We must learn to reflect in the midst of action and create space to step aside from our constant movement in order to contemplate, reflect, and prepare for future action."[15]

Our summit pastors discussed a variety of ways to create space for reflection. Some find setting aside daily time to journal works well. Others believe that a scheduled conversation with a confidant fits them best. Many feel that a regular time and location to do the work of reflection are helpful. Still others require a change of environment to look at things from a fresh perspective. We each should experiment to discover what works best for us.

Heads up: we are becoming countercultural when we commit to reflection. This discipline cuts across the deeply held patterns of Western society. But it is important if we are going to gain critical distance from the busyness that people call "normal." "The goal is to look closely at our thoughts and to ask ourselves how we understand new situations," Livermore writes. "Make the invisible influence of culture more visible."[16] One summit participant shared that Bernard of Clairvaux wrote that it is laziness to remain active and not to spend time reflecting before God.

Pastor and author Peter Scazzero, one of our summit special guests, summarizes the tension between action and reflection this way:

> Emotional health and contemplative spirituality call us to *reflection* so that we might listen to God and to ourselves. . . . Martha and Mary represent two approaches to the Christian life. Martha is actively serving Jesus, but she is missing Jesus. . . . Mary, on the other hand . . . is "being" with Jesus, enjoying intimacy with him, loving him, attentive, open, quiet, taking pleasure in his presence. . . . In every generation, Christians have written on the balance of Mary and Martha in our lives. They all sound the same theme: the active life in the world *for* God can only properly flow from a life *with* God. God has a unique combination of activity and contemplation for each of us.[17]

This tension between action and reflection will always be in motion. Think of a coiled spring, not a teeter-totter; there is no place of resting balance. Each day calls for both action and reflection to different degrees. Scazzero does suggest an order of priority, however. Our Christian *doing* must flow from an outpouring of our *being*. Our doing must be an overflow from the grace and love of God in our life with him.

Prayer. Everyone knows it is important for Christians—especially pastors—to pray. Richard Foster comments in his classic book *The Celebration of Discipline,* "All who have walked with God have viewed prayer as the main business of their lives."[18] At the same time, we also know intuitively what the Puritan Thomas Goodwin shared: "That our fallen nature is actually allergic to God and never wants to get too close to him. Thus our fallen nature constantly pulls us away from prayer."[19] This reluctance to pray was echoed by many in the Pastors Summit. One of them summarized his feelings about this saying, "Why is prayer so hard? I'm not going to accuse you, but I'll accuse myself—prayerlessness is just plain arrogance."

It is shocking to realize that, in our experience of reviewing job descriptions for pastors and ministry leaders, not once have we seen prayer—or any of the spiritual disciplines, for that matter—as an expectation on the list of responsibilities. Pastor and author Eugene Peterson has written, "Among the considerable demands on my time not one demanded that I practice a life of prayer. And yet prayer was at the very heart of the vocation I had entered."[20]

Bob grew up under the ministry of Richard C. Halverson, former chaplain of the United States Senate, who used to comment, "When the disciples interrupted Jesus while he was praying, they asked him, 'Lord, teach us *to* pray,' not 'teach us *how* to pray.' The challenge of praying is to start praying!"[21] Regular, faithful prayer requires intentionality and practice, just as all of the disciplines do.

In addition, the challenge of prayer must be considered in light of the performance-focused, workaholic nature of ministry. Eugene Peterson comments about the current situation: "For the majority of the Christian centuries most pastors have been convinced that prayer is the central and essential act for maintaining the essential shape of the ministry to which they were ordained. . . . Have conditions changed so much in our age that prayer is no longer fit to be the formative act? Have developments in theology shown other things to be central and prayer at the periphery? Or have we let ourselves be distracted, diverted, and seduced? I think we have."[22]

One summit pastor acknowledged,

We say prayer is the work and not just the preparation. And we nod our heads. I have nodded my head for twenty-five years. But I allow the pressures of work to detour me from the real work.

Our culture and ministry work environment will provide us no help in remedying our lack of prayer. With the triple challenge of parishioner demands, cultural expectations and our own sinful tendencies to turn from God, we are left in a rather helpless state and must cry out like the disciples, "Lord, teach us *to* pray!"

The pastors of the summit acknowledged that neither the sinful reluctance to pray nor the pressures of work responsibilities should keep pastors from the discipline of prayer. It becomes a conscious decision simply to pray, whether we feel like it or think we are good at it. One pastor summed it up well for the whole group.

It just hurts not to be good at important things like prayer. I recently read this phrase—I want to say it's by Brother Lawrence—who said, "I decided I was never going to be good at praying, so I'm just going to start not being good at praying. I'm just going to start to pray." For a performance person, that's freeing: just to say, "I'm not going to be really good," and just do it. It won't be something to write a book about. But the thought that Christ meets us there, not when we get good, but when we're not—doesn't that define grace?

Developing a prayer life is much like developing the habit of exercise. If pastors start slowly by devoting a few minutes to prayer every day, they can build up their "prayer muscle" gradually over a period of weeks. One pastor shared,

---

I began praying for ten minutes, and initially it felt like an eternity. But after a while, I discovered that I was praying for longer periods without even thinking about it.

Of course, the apostle Paul's call to "pray at all times" means that prayer also becomes a daily and ongoing conversation.

In summary, we offer Eugene Peterson's powerful exhortation to pastors about prayer: "The pastoral work . . . begins in prayer. Anything creative, anything powerful, anything *biblical*, insofar as we are participants in it, originates in prayer. Pastors who imitate the preaching and moral action of the prophets without also imitating the prophets' deep praying and worship so evident in the Psalms are an embarrassment to the faith and an encumbrance to the church."[23]

Our summit pastors experienced the guilt and grief of feeling like failures and impostors in this area of prayer. But the summit gatherings didn't leave us there. We followed a learning process of scheduled time for prayer, discussions about creative practices, leaning on each other for accountability and support to pursue change. Building healthier habits in the discipline of prayer is challenging yet vital work for resilience in ministry leadership.

Sabbath. The root idea behind the word *sabbath* is simply, "Quit. Take a break. Cool it."[24] It's like receiving the gift of a snow day each week.[25] But it is more than a "day off," which Eugene Peterson calls a "bastard Sabbath."[26] As a summit pastor said, "There is a difference between a day off of work—where you may be running errands, mowing lawn, etc.—and a sabbath day." Yet for many pastors, the idea of taking a sabbath (let alone a day off) is foreign. Reflecting on his service in a number of large churches, Bob recalls that for each staff team he joined, the standard lifestyle pattern of the leaders was to work seven days a week. This is the norm, rather than the exception, for many in ministry. Peterson sadly comments, "It is diagnostically significant that of all the commandments not one is treated with such contemptuous disregard by pastors as this one. . . . We conscientiously catechize our people on the fifth commandment and without a blush flaunt our workaholic sabbath-breaking as evidence of an extraordinary piety."[27]

However, the summit pastors did not associate their workaholism with *piety,* but with the cultural and congregational pressure to overfunction and to prove themselves successful and hardworking.

What does it mean to intentionally practice the discipline of sabbath? Pete Scazzero describes it as a humble act of trusting God. "At the heart of the Sabbath is stopping to surrender to God in trust. . . . We imitate God by stopping our work and resting. . . . I give up control and trust God to run his world without me. . . . [It] is our means as the people of God to bear witness to the way we understand life, its rhythms, its gifts, its meaning, and its ultimate purpose in God."[28] Far from our culture's view of personally earned leisure, this view of sabbath calls us to surrender and witness to the Lord of life.

Finding a way to celebrate the sabbath is a challenge with a pastor's schedule. Experimentation is necessary. A summit pastor shared,

---

I've needed to adjust when I take my sabbath. Right now on most weeks I take a half-day sabbath on Saturday from noon to four, and then another half-day on Sunday afternoons. Then I take Monday as my day off work.

Other pastors find taking a midweek day for sabbath works best. One pastor stated that he refused to take his sabbath on Mondays. He felt so lousy after Sunday that he didn't want to have his sabbath on that day.

Perhaps more difficult than working out scheduling issues for a sabbath is the challenge for pastors to help their congregation understand the need of a day of rest. This is one of the many places in which the rhythms of pastoral life are different from those of others in the congregation. Because parishioners don't experience this lifestyle, many are simply not aware that pastors don't experience sabbath on Sunday. Add to this the expectation that pastors should be working when others in the congregation are at work, and you have the expectations to push pastors toward workaholism. The result? Many pastors never take a break. This is both disobedient and unwise.

How should this be countered? We suggest the place to start is a conversation with church leaders about pastoral life and the layperson's expectations. One of Eugene Peterson's quarterly reports on the pastoral life provides a helpful sample of how this conversation might sound.

> One of my tasks is to lead you in the celebrative keeping of sabbath each Sunday. But that is not a sabbath for me. I wake up on Sunday morning with the adrenaline flowing. It is a workday for me. Monday is my sabbath, and I need your help observing it. I need your prayers; I need your cooperation in not involving me in administration or consultation; I need your admonitions if you see me carelessly letting other things interfere with it. Pastors need pastors too. One of the ways you can be my pastor is to help me keep a weekly sabbath that God commanded.[29]

Repentance. More often than not, the idea of repentance is found within the broader discipline of confession. Confession includes repentance before God and before our brothers and sisters for any and all sin. This may include confession of "hidden sins" to a friend, as James commands when he says, "confess your sins to one another and pray for one another" (James 5:16).

But in the context of the summit, the needed discipline of repentance went beyond, as Dallas Willard writes, letting "trusted others know our deepest weaknesses and failures."[30] Specifically, it referred to times when pastors need to acknowledge how their attitudes, words and actions are rebellious against God and hurtful to fellow believers. This process begins, according to Adele Ahlberg Calhoun, when we "invite God to come right in and look at our sin with us."[31] Then it means going to those we've hurt, acknowledging our failure and seeking their forgiveness.

For example, during one summit, after a period of reflection and repentance focused on the health of our marriages, one pastor shared this about his experience:

There were some things I identified about which I needed to repent— some patterns into which I had fallen—and I was not being reflective about what was going on. A lot of it related to things I needed to say to my wife. I was undermining our relationship without intending to do so. . . . I was pursuing bad habits to compensate. I feel like I've been really liberated.

There is another role that pastors must fill in the area of repentance— that of being the congregation's "chief repenter." Jack Miller describes this pastoral responsibility as requiring the "courage first to teach your own heart and then to teach others that there are only two ways to stand before God: either as a contrite publican or as a self-righteous Pharisee (Luke 18:9-14)."[32] When one summit pastor shared, "I believe the congregation has a right to expect a level of godliness from their pastor," another pastor quickly responded, "And that godliness is modeling repentance and faith. Godliness is not 'I have it all together.'"

One pastor described how he modeled being the "chief repenter" when he realized his anger regarding the way some church members failed to fulfill commitments. He repented to the church members involved in both a letter and face-to-face conversations. This led to a peaceful resolution of a conflict that had spread beyond their relationships and into the congregation.

This is an example of the repentance described by the summit pastors. They affirmed the need to exercise the discipline of repentance in private and in public. They strongly desired to grow in this discipline in order to "walk in the light" and to demonstrate that God's grace is made perfect in weakness so that all the glory might be God's and not their own.[33]

Personal and Corporate Worship. We believe godly leadership is an extension of the leader's relationship with God. We also believe that God calls us to a personal, ongoing relationship with himself before he calls us to mission. Therefore, nothing is more important in the life of a pastor than the discipline of worship.

In John 4:23, Jesus taught that the Father seeks people who worship him in spirit and in truth. This verse is emphatic about God desiring that his people be worshipers. Therefore, for all Christians, but particularly for pastors, worship is a top priority of life. Ministry leaders cannot afford to be so busy doing things *for* God that they don't take time to be *with* him, especially in personal worship. As one pastor shared,

So much of it comes back to that notion of the importance of personal worship—do I believe in John 15, where Jesus says I can't do anything apart from God?

Intentionality is the key for growth in the discipline of worship, which can be a personal priority regardless of the variety or consistency of time and location. A summit pastor shared, "If I am not before the Lord in personal worship time, then ministry will be my master." Another acknowledged, "If I lose the perspective of dependence on God, I find myself running and working instead of worshiping."

Many of the pastors in the summit struggled with this discipline and needed more structure and creative ideas for their personal worship. As the pastors brainstormed about it together, they found help from a number of ideas. For example, one pastor shared how to use the corporate worship plan to structure daily worship.

One day as I was planning our Sunday worship, I asked myself, "How often do I structure my personal worship around the elements I plan for corporate worship?" I realized how sloppy my personal worship had become. Now I take our worship bulletin and use it as an outline for my private worship during the week. And I teach my congregation to do the same thing.

Other pastors talked about the importance of music in their personal worship. One said,

When I think of personal worship, what I do is listen to CDs and sing, and go through hymns or just meditate. Without these, it just becomes very mental.

Agreeing, another responded, "Music almost always works to bring calm to my heart. What I do is play my guitar and sing to the Lord."

Another encouraging idea for personal worship came from a conversation with author Pete Scazzero. Scazzero shared how he had been trained to have a daily quiet time and yet how, within a couple of hours after that time, he would easily forget that God was active in his everyday affairs. So he incorporated the use of the Daily Office in his own personal worship. The Daily Office consists of short liturgical formats of worship used morning, midday and evening.[34]

Regardless of the arrangement, all of the summit pastors affirmed the importance of personal worship and the necessity of investing thoughtful time in the planning of this discipline for their own spiritual health as well as the health of their ministries.

One would think, with the time and energy pastors invest in corporate worship, that worshiping with others would be one discipline they wouldn't need to work on. The experience of the summit pastors, however, was quite to the contrary. For these pastors, the corporate worship experience in their own congregations was more a time of work than of worship. Whether it is wondering about things like the temperature of the sanctuary, the dynamics of the sound system, the quality of the music or the logistics of the offering (let alone the quality of the sermon), pastors can become absorbed in details that rob their sense of freedom to worship. As one pastor poignantly shared:

> Worship used to be one of my favorite things to do before becoming senior pastor. . . . I think one of my chief issues right now is learning how to worship and celebrate the love of my Father in the midst of the activity in the service. I'm thinking during the entire service about what's happening and what isn't happening. Then I'm flat-lined for the rest of the day.

Summit pastors found that two things decrease their anxiety during the service: preplanning and confidence in the ability of others helping to lead the service. But there were no simple solutions to the challenge of engaging in worship. One pastor reported,

> I told my elders that when the service began, there wasn't anything I could do about the details and that I was simply going to "let go and let God."

But even he discovered that his cavalier statement was betrayed by the fact that on Sunday evening or Monday morning, he was making a list of what needed to be corrected at the next worship service!

One pastor shared steps a colleague had taken to experience freedom in corporate worship.

A friend of mine will get his sermon done by Saturday at lunch, spend the afternoon with his family, then every Saturday night he goes to a big church in the area and he worships there. He says that it prepares him to preach more than doing more studying. His heart is prepared there. He is not known there. He just shows up. Sometimes he only sits there through the music; other times he stays for the sermon.

While attending another church might not be the answer for everyone, most pastors discovered that talking about this problem with their staff or elders was helpful. First, it allowed them to share the struggle and to find support from understanding friends. Second, these friends could brainstorm together about the particular challenges found in the worship services. The result was that the pastors would not feel like the only ones concerned about the details. Third, in some instances a staff member or elder would say, "Pastor, this morning you let *me* worry about what is going wrong." While this wouldn't remove all of the anxiety, pastors would be able to mentally download concerns onto the shoulders of fellow leaders.

One team of elders actually mandated that their pastor be freed from all responsibilities in worship at least once every other month. This pastor was to sit with family and simply enjoy the service. After a few times of doing this, the pastor was able to start to relax during these morning sabbaticals from leading worship and focus on worshiping.

QUESTIONS TO PONDER

1. Where could you create some intentional space in your work day to stop and reflect on how you are feeling and what you are doing?

2. To what extent is prayer considered one of your job responsibilities? How can you invite others to help you heighten this aspect of your job?

3. Consider several creative ways to trust God by taking a sabbath. Choose one new idea with which to experiment.

4. In what areas might God be granting you the role of "chief repenter" as you lead your congregation?

5. What activities help you to worship personally? When are you truly able to fully engage in corporate worship? How can you increase these times?

CONCLUSION

We began these two chapters on spiritual formation by stating that when a person holds a staff position in a church or ministry, it does not mean that they have arrived at a place of mature spirituality. Pursuing spiritual maturity is a lifelong calling for every believer. This is especially the case for those who lead in ministry.

But pastors often slip into the trap of building their identity around their role rather than their relationship with the Lord. So they must regularly consider their *walk* with God over and against their *work* for God. The pursuit of spiritual formation includes many facets. We have focused on themes highlighted by the summit pastors, which include developing healthy rituals, pursuing accountability relationships, growing through hard life experiences, and practicing the spiritual disciplines of reflection, prayer, sabbath, repentance and worship.

In closing, we are reminded of the challenge put forth by Dallas Willard in *The Spirit of the Disciplines*. Willard writes, "Now you have studied a number of ways in which we can be with Jesus and with his Father. It is time to take what you have learned and make your own specific plan for your life with them. This will come down to what you do on Sunday, Monday, Tuesday, Wednesday, Thursday, Friday, and Saturday. More importantly, it will come down to what you do *not* do, to how you will manage to step out of the everlasting busyness that curses our lives."[35]

The next chapters on self-care will focus on how we can better "step out of the everlasting busyness" so that we can run the race God has for us with endurance.

RECOMMENDATIONS FOR FURTHER READING

1. Dallas Willard. *The Spirit of the Disciplines*. San Francisco: HarperSanFrancisco, 1988.

2. Adele Ahlberg Calhoun. *Spiritual Disciplines Handbook*. Downers Grove, Ill.: InterVarsity Press, 2005.

BURNING ON, NOT BURNING OUT

SELF-CARE I

Self-care is never a selfish act—it is simply good stewardship of the only
gift I have, the gift I was put on earth to offer to others. Anytime we can
listen to true self and give it the care it requires, we do so not only for
ourselves but for the many others whose lives we touch.

Parker Palmer, *Let Your Life Speak*

THE IDEA OF SELF-CARE MAY SOUND SELFISH. But taking the time
to do responsible self-care is actually a way to deny oneself. Self-denying
self-care can include things like

- getting to bed on time
- saying no to work by establishing sabbath, sabbatical, vacation and
  days off
- building in regular exercise
- maintaining a nutritious diet

Peter Brain defines self-care as "the wisdom to ensure, as far as humanly
possible, a wise and orderly work that conserves and lengthens a pastor's
ministry."[1] He proposes, "The reason for self-care is not so that pastors can
become indulgent hypochondriacs, always concerned about their own welfare, or even to avoid the twin ravages of growing older and the fatigue of
hard work and pastoral concern." Instead, Brain asserts, "Self-care means
understanding the meaning of positive health and working toward it."[2]

In the Pastors Summit, we grew to describe self-care as the *ongoing development of the whole person*, including the emotional, spiritual, relational, physical and intellectual areas of life. As one participant shared, "Pastors can only encourage people over the long haul when they themselves are moved, inspired, spirited. That means self-care."

WHY DO PASTORS NEGLECT SELF-CARE?

Many in ministry quote Christmas Evans, a famous Welsh preacher from the early nineteenth century, who supposedly said, "I'd rather burn out than rust out in the service of the Lord." One of Evans's contemporaries, James Berkeley, is said to have retorted, "I admire the bravado. It sounds dedicated, bold, and stirring. However, when I view the burnt-outs and the almost burnt-outs who lie by the ecclesiastical road, the glory fails to reach me. Is there not a third alternative? In Acts 20:24, Paul stated, 'I consider my life worth nothing to me, if only I may finish the race and complete the task the Lord Jesus has given me.' Herein lies the model I choose to follow. I want neither to burn out nor rust out. I want to finish out the race."[3]

Author Dave Gibbons, a twenty-first-century pastor, agrees with this critique. He says, "It's about burning on, not burning out. I don't know if many of us can finish well unless there's some type of rhythm of rest and restoration and relationship in our lives."[4]

As we began to dig into the research on the condition of pastors in our Western culture, we were surprised by the results.[5] For example, one study shows that 76 percent of clergy were either overweight or obese, compared to 61 percent of the general population. And a survey of Lutheran pastors referenced problems with depression.[6]

Another study cites that the low pay and high expectation of ministry creates a unique avenue for stress to take hold in the life of clergy.[7] In his book *Pastor as Person*, Gary Harbaugh states, "Nutrition, physical exercise, and other forms of self-care were at lower levels [for pastors] than for the general population."[8]

Why don't people in ministry seem to value self-care? Several reasons become apparent. First, the pastoral role itself places expectations on clergy that can become unrealistic. David Mosser says, "Pastors face pressures and expectations in their organizational role in the church arising from the clergy's unique combination of spiritual, personal, and professional roles."[9] And G. Lloyd Rediger explains, "The clergy role is *sui generis*, for it is the only profession that wraps personal identity, professional identity, and religious all in the same package."[10] If we combine the expectations of this role with the fact that most pastors are people-pleasers, we can understand how the ministry can feel like a never-ending treadmill of trying to satisfy others whose expectations cannot be met.

A second reason that pastors may not value self-care is that they don't view it as an "ethical imperative."[11] For example, psychiatrists use two terms describing how those in the caring professions are affected by their work: *compassion fatigue* and *secondary stress disorder*. These terms name the truth that caring for others drains physical, emotional and spiritual energy from caregivers.[12] When pastors don't recognize the impact ministry has on their lives, they seek to press through difficult circumstances without taking responsible steps for their own health or recovery.

A terribly tragic accident occurred in Bob's congregation years ago. A single adult was accidently shot in the head by a neighbor. Bob spent hours sitting in the hospital with the victim's family, and then led the memorial service and also counseled the neighbor who shot the woman. These activities, layered on top of "normal" work responsibilities, took a toll that he didn't recognize or acknowledge. He was dealing with secondary stress disorder, but neither he nor those with whom he worked ever recognized it.

A third reason that pastors may not value self-care may be that they "spiritualize away" their need for it. We suspect this is the mindset behind the "burnout" comment from Christmas Evans above. However, this dualistic perspective—separating the spiritual from other aspects of life—permits those of us in ministry to take self-denial to an extreme. By doing so, we neglect Christ's commandment to love the Lord with all our heart, mind, soul and strength, and to love our neighbors as ourselves (Mark 12:30-31).[13]

In talking with the leaders of another program on sustaining pastoral excellence, we learned that it is also commonplace in the Korean culture for pastors to spiritualize away self-care. The story of one Korean pastor intrigued us. He said that in order to earn respect, he had to "overwhelm" laypersons with his spirituality and godliness. That is, he had to outdo everyone else in the church with his practice of spiritual disciplines. But in so doing, he ended up neglecting his own health, emotional well-being, marriage and family.

Ministry leaders need to consider self-care as, in Peter Brain's words, "a way of ensuring that we will remain effective in the great work God has given us to do."[14] With this perspective in mind, self-care becomes another manner by which pastors actually care for others. Gunderson and Pray state that they "spend a lot of time with clergy and laypersons, sometimes focusing on their individual health and sometimes on their communities' health. It turns out to be the same subject."[15]

Self-care is a holistic concept that explores how five aspects of one's life are interwoven: the emotional, spiritual, social, intellectual and physical. A pastor in the summit shared how these are integrated in his life, saying, "I have an irregular heartbeat, which coincides with times of emotional lows and spiritual doubts." We have found these five aspects of self-care, used by a number of authors, to be a helpful outline for discussing the complex challenges of ministry leaders' lifestyles.[16]

QUESTIONS TO PONDER

1. What is your current pattern of rest, restoration and relationship around work?

2. What would help you value self-care more, even in the midst of extreme expectations, exhausting work and spiritual-sounding excuses?

3. How do you assess your current health in each of the five life areas: emotional, spiritual, social, intellectual and physical?

SHOULD I LEAVE OR STAY? CALLING AND SELF-CARE

We believe spiritual self-care is synonymous with spiritual formation: the ongoing process of maturing as a Christian both personally and interpersonally. This has been the theme of the last two chapters. But here we discuss an area of spiritual formation for ministry leaders that uniquely coincides with emotional self-care—that is, how they handle their sense of calling to the ministry.

One surprising discovery we made in the summit was the continuous questioning by pastors of their call to the particular ministry they were serving. This seemed to be a nearly universal experience. This review usually was not about their personal call to the pastoral vocation. Rather, it was focused on whether they were serving at the right place for that time. One summit pastor described, "I find myself going through loops: *I'll stay here. I need to leave. I should stay here. No, I'm leaving.*"

Another pastor, deeply moved by the revelation that most of the others struggled with this issue, asked,

---

I'm wondering how you . . . deal with the day-to-day, week-to-week reviewing of your call. I know that, inevitably, when I'm not getting the results in ministry—numbers, money, affirmation, people standing there hugging you and telling you how you have changed their life—how do I process it when that's not happening?

No easy solutions came out of our times together. A consensus did emerge, however, around a number of ways to manage these concerns and put them in perspective. First, Paul's comments about learning contentment were often referenced. In Philippians 4:11-12, the apostle Paul writes from a prison cell, "I have learned in whatever situation I am to be content. I know how to be brought low, and I know how to abound." How did Paul learn contentedness? By being brought low and by abounding. Without these extreme experiences, Paul wouldn't have learned contentedness.

As we saw in a previous chapter, hardships play a critical role in spiritual formation. So during the summit, we discussed the way God shapes his servants through the difficulties of questioning their call. This helped the pastors see how God was teaching them about contentedness. One shared,

---

I keep waiting for the "next" season to be smooth. I'm coming to realize that this is not going to happen. I'm learning contentment in my current context.

People experiencing hardships need a support system to sustain and encourage them. So it is no surprise that the pastors often referenced important relationships they leaned on during such times of placement uncertainty. One shared,

There have been several times in my life when I was asking, "Okay, what's next?" Those are the times I felt like I was on the rocks. I felt like, "Am I the right person for this situation?" I personally have never found it profitable to go there unless I open that up to some other trusted people. I can't get an answer on my own.

Another said,

When doubting your call, whom do you talk to? I must have someone I can trust and to whom I can be accountable. Someone who understands my struggles, prays with me and holds my burdens. God has blessed me with a particular pastor-friend, and some other pastors who are not so close but are really good friends in the city. That has been a source of strength.

The most common person our pastors turned to for support and insight was their spouse.

Who do I talk to? My wife. Because there have been a few times when I've been ready to leave the last couple of years. And she said, "We haven't been called somewhere [else]." When I came to [our current church], it was clear to both of us. And there have been times when she's been like, "We need to get out of here." And I've said, "No, it's not time." But mostly it's her telling me it's not yet time. We have really been committed to be in agreement.

While these two coping methods—learning contentedness and processing questions with trusted partners—do not remove calling uncertainties, they do give comfort in the midst of ambiguity. First, they help pastors see things from God's point of view. God is working his purposes out, and he is teaching his servants contentedness. The author of Hebrews explains, "For the moment all discipline seems painful rather than pleasant, but later it yields the peaceful fruit of righteousness to those who have been trained by it" (Hebrews 12:11). Second, these two coping methods remind pastors how much they need the wisdom and encouragement of others. No one should process these questions alone. We all need allies who will listen with compassion and speak the truth in love.

QUESTIONS TO PONDER

1. In what ways have you learned contentment through struggling with ministry placement calling?

2. To whom can you go for help in processing questions and concerns about calling?

WHO AM I? IDENTITY AND SELF-CARE

The first line of John Calvin's famous book *The Institutes of the Christian Religion* says, "Nearly all the wisdom we possess, that is to say, true and sound wisdom, consists of two parts: the knowledge of God and of ourselves."[17] As we talked with summit pastors, we discovered that they often had much more knowledge of God than of themselves. So one of the things we did was to explore our identities. We looked at the four identity issues of personality, family of origin, distinctions between role and person, and comparisons to others.

How Am I Wired? Personality. Several of our pastors learned about their personality preferences via the lens of the popular Myers-Briggs Type Indicator (MBTI). While every personality profile has its limitations, we found that many appreciated the help they received from this tool. We laughed as one pastor, who called himself a "people-pleasing approval suck," learned that this was not unusual for his personality style. Another pastor said,

---

I've avoided these profiles for two reasons. First, I don't like the idea of being boxed into a type. Second, I didn't think using instruments like this had a biblical framework. I was wrong on both counts.

During the summit, all of the pastors took a newer personality profile called the RightPath 4/6, together with an instrument called the RightPath Leadership 360.[18] The Leadership 360 was completed by twelve or more friends and associates of each pastor. Each person rated the summit participant in key areas of leadership attitudes, behaviors and skills.

A significant majority of our participants had never received such honest, straightforward comments from others (except from their critics). Most learned that they were much harder on themselves than were the raters on their 360s. The use of this tool gave them new insights into who

they are and how they relate to others. Their overall reaction to these instruments was enthusiastic.[19] One pastor, who had been anxious about using these materials, simply said, "It is freeing to finally come to peace with
my temperament."

It was a powerful experience for the pastors to compare the report of
their personality style with the responses of others in the 360 survey. One
pastor discovered a clear disparity between his personality style and the
way he functioned with others. Exploring this disparity, he began to realize how growing up with an alcoholic and abusive father had impaired
some of his natural abilities. As a result, this pastor is still on a journey of
exploring the implications of his family of origin in his leadership.

How Did Relatives Shape Me? Family of Origin. The term *family of
origin* refers to our nuclear family—those persons with whom we lived for
at least the first eighteen years of our life—as well as extended family of
current and past generations. While some people use their family of origin
as an excuse for the way they act as adults, the truth is that our experiences
in childhood and adolescence profoundly shape our identity. As Pete Scazzero explains, "While we are affected by powerful external events and
circumstances through our earthly lives, our families are the most powerful group to which we will ever belong. Even those who left home as young
adults, determined to 'break' from their family histories, soon find that
their family's way of 'doing' life follows them wherever they go."[20]

Scazzero points out that the Bible indicates the brokenness in one generation is often passed on to at least three or four generations.[21] He later
states, "Every disciple has to look at the brokenness and sin of his or her
family and culture. . . . All families are broken and fallen."[22] Since every
family is dysfunctional to a certain extent, family patterns can be carried
like unwanted baggage into adult life.[23] These painful memories from the
past that we carry with us can often lead to sinful patterns of living. While
the Scriptures encourage us that these patterns can be broken, they usually
need to be recognized, acknowledged and worked on for such change to
take place.[24]

One exercise that summit participants found very beneficial in identifying family baggage was developing and exploring a *genogram*, or family
diagram. Each person in the summit developed a family diagram that
traced a number of generations.[25] (Appendix D provides a description of

how to draw and explore a genogram. This appendix also provides many interview questions that can help you learn about the systemic impact of one's family on one's emotional health.) We found at least three reasons that these family diagrams were helpful.

First, by looking at multigenerational dynamics, we can move from focusing on specific individuals in our past (particularly our parents) to a more objective and well-rounded perspective of the influences in our lives. Second, since all families develop myths of what really took place in the past, the family diagram enables us to look more objectively at what happened and how people behaved. Finally, family diagrams help us consider possibilities for the future.[26] For example, Tasha was fond of a particular branch of relatives who used humor well to combat stress and conflict. She now consciously uses this familiar method to manage her larger family-of-origin pattern of responding with anger.

A few years ago, Bob was listening to a friend give a talk about the impact of her childhood on her adult life. She pulled a volunteer from the audience and asked him to hold a piece of baggage. She continued to add luggage throughout her presentation, and the poor fellow was eventually loaded with garment bags, suitcases and other travel gear. Finally, to top it off, the speaker asked him to walk across the stage carrying all of this baggage. Although each of us laughed at his predicament, the point was driven home: it's hard to function while you are weighed down with baggage.

What's Left If I Quit the Ministry? Role/Person Distinctions. The pastoral life can be so absorbing that pastors have difficulty distinguishing when they are on or off duty or even who they are when they are not pastoring. Congregants have the same difficulty, often thinking of their pastor only in terms of her or his vocation rather than as a whole person. Unlike other professionals, pastors never seem to be "out of uniform."

Because ministry is as much about the person as it is about the task, it is easy for those in ministry to have their personhood absorbed by the task. This problem is not unusual for anyone in a visible leadership role. Heifetz and Linsky explain, "It is easy to confuse yourself with the roles you take on in your organization and community. The world colludes in the confusion by reinforcing your professional persona. Colleagues, subordinates, and bosses treat you as if the role you play is the essence of you, the real you."[27]

Listen to various summit pastors as they express this confusion over roles versus personal identity.

I base a great deal of my own personal sense of self-worth on my preaching. Take away my teaching, my illustrations, my gift to connect with people—what's left? I'm afraid there's nothing there if these things are taken away. All I am is my ability to do this or that.

✛ ✛ ✛

I want to be the type of pastor who doesn't get so wrapped up in my role that I lose sight of my foundational identity as a follower of Jesus Christ.

✛ ✛ ✛

I don't even want people to call me "Pastor," because being a pastor is what I do; it is not my complete identity.

Authors Donald Hands and Wayne Fehr confirm this concern about the role challenge, saying, "The crucial point for the clergyperson to consider is this: Do I have a personal life and unique relationship to God? Or am I totally defined by the ministry that I carry out to others?"[28]

What steps can pastors take to differentiate between role and identity in the pursuit of emotional and spiritual self-care? First, ministry leaders should maintain the disciplines of their own personal relationship with Christ as distinct from their ministry responsibilities. If they work at keeping their walk with Christ fresh (spiritual formation), distinction between self and role becomes clearer. As one summit pastor commented,

---

Things get less muddy as I engage with God; things fall into place more. I seem to have a better sense of how to spend my day and what to focus on and what not to do. I don't know how to explain how it happens, but I just know it [does]. [Still] I have to re-remember it every single day.

A second step that ministry leaders can take for healthy role/person distinction is to develop friendships outside of their ministry context. We explore the unique challenge of friendships later. But for now, we will make a simple point: it is often easier to be yourself with people who do not view you as their pastor or ministry leader. Tasha observes this experience with doctor of ministry students, who are all in ministry leadership positions. Since none of them serve at her church, they seem very free and easygoing in class and close to unruly at times, enjoying humor and banter as peers even as they pursue their unique passions for research.

A third way to develop selfhood in distinction from vocation is to pursue hobbies and other interests outside ministry responsibilities. Ministry leaders are generally not good at this. As recorded earlier, one summit pastor admitted,

> I don't know there's much I could talk about other than what I do functionally as a pastor and what's going on in the life of the church. That's a scary revelation to make.

One pastor had seriously considered pursuing a science research career before attending seminary. He told us how he still spent time in the library reviewing science journals to keep current on issues of interest. He valued this as an important element of his personal development. As a side benefit, he surprises people who expect that, as a pastor, he would be ignorant of issues in science. Another pastor, a highly trained musician, formed a band that does occasional gigs in local bars. Of course, these unusual stories may not have encouraged the other pastors. This leads us to the next identity self-care challenge: comparisons.

How Do I Measure Up? Comparisons. This final identity issue explores the commonplace practice of comparing ourselves to others. One pastor stated, "We often base our identity on how well we're doing and we do this by contrasting ourselves with others." Another confessed,

> I marginalize many whom I think are incompetent, and feel superior to them, then compare myself up to those whom I idolize and feel inferior.

During one summit meeting, the pastors had an extended conversation that focused on one pastor's negative comparison of himself to another pastor, whom he called a "rock star" due to the other pastor's charisma and congregation's rapid growth in size. The conclusion of the summit discussion was insightful. A friend corrected the pastor's sharp critique of himself:

> You probably have much stronger pastoral gifts than [the rock star] does, so your church might not grow as large because you need to have more contact with what's happening and a broader scope of the whole fellowship.

In response, the pastor who had been comparing himself said,

I'm just starting to come to grips with my desire to be in contact with everyone. I want to be able to deliver the message, "Sure, I've got time for you." I don't think having the kind of relational connections I have could be done in a larger church. It would require a different person. I want to be the best leader I can be, and for me, maybe that means I will never be the pastor of a large church. But the difficulty is actually becoming comfortable with that.

That was a healthy response to comparison: learning to understand and accept one's personality, strengths and struggles. We can only be who God has made us to be and offer the gifts he has built into our lives. The apostle Paul confronted the temptation to build identity by comparison. He discovered that his opponents in Corinth were trying to establish their credibility by showing how much better they were than he was. He responded bluntly, writing, "When they measure themselves by one another and compare themselves with one another, they are without understanding" (2 Corinthians 10:12).

QUESTIONS TO PONDER

1. If you haven't taken a personality profile or 360 survey lately, consider doing so in order to learn more about your strengths, struggles and how others experience your leadership. Invite those who work with you to join in this self-care work.

2. What are the broken family patterns of living that have become baggage in your life? What are you doing to change them? What are the healthy patterns you can be thankful for and enhance?

3. When are you free to be fully yourself without your ministry leadership role? In what ways are you developing your hobbies? In what ways are you tending to your relationship with Christ and with those outside your ministry in order to pursue self-care?

4. Pause to confess to God any comparisons to others that you have made and to thank God for who he has made you to be.

HOW DO I MANAGE MY FEELINGS? EMOTIONS AND SELF-CARE

For years, Christians have debated the topic of emotions. The three of us recall how, as young Christians, we were told that we should put the facts of Christianity first, exercise faith in those facts and then force our feelings to follow in submission. This well-meaning formula seeks to steer believers away from a life vacillating on mood swings that propel doubt—which is, as James writes, "like a wave of the sea, carried forward by the wind one moment and driven back the next" (James 1:6 Phillips). This simplistic formula is problematic and unhelpful, however, for emotional self-care.

First, emotions need to be acknowledged and then managed. As Scazzero writes, "To feel is to be human. To minimize or deny what we feel is a distortion of what it means to be image bearers of our personal God."[29] In addition, when people refuse to acknowledge their emotions, they often become a victim of them. As counselor Norm Wright explains, "The worst possible manner of dealing with our emotions is to deny or ignore them. Our bodies are structured to respond automatically to emotional stimulation. The energy that is generated when we feel an emotion must find a healthy outlet. If it does not, it will find expression in some unnatural manner."[30]

Our society's difficulty in dealing well with emotions only strengthens this point. Daniel Goleman points out from his extensive research, "The rhythm and pace of modern life give us too little time to assimilate, reflect, and react. Our bodies are geared to a slower rhythm. We need time to be introspective, but we don't get it—or don't take it. Emotions have their own agenda and timetable, but our rushed lives give them no space, no airtime—and so they go underground."[31]

In addition, emotion will always affect the way we interact with others. If pastors do not recognize this, it will impede both their ability to maintain healthy relationships as well as their leadership capacity.

Early in her first church staff position, our friend Christine attended a missions committee meeting. The senior pastor became upset during the meeting when people spoke against a project he liked. He pounded his fist on the table and blared, "That's not the way it's supposed to be!" Then he walked out of the room. Everyone sat in stunned silence for a few moments, then continued the discussion without comment on the pastor's actions. In about ten minutes, the senior pastor came back and reengaged, not saying a word about the outburst. When the meeting adjourned, Christine left wondering when this pastor would explode next. The church environment was not emotionally safe.

Healthy self-care requires emotional management. This is affirmed by the apostle Paul who said, "Be angry and do not sin; do not let the sun go down on your anger" (Ephesians 4:26). With these few words, Paul shows that the management of feelings includes both the ability to name and acknowledge feelings ("be angry") as well as the capacity to responsibly handle those feelings ("do not sin . . . do not let the sun go down on your anger").

Our limited purpose in this section is simply to demonstrate some specific ways in which emotional management is needed in the self-care of pastors. Numerous books on skill development for emotional management are available, and it would be impossible here to explore even a small number of effective methods.[32] Instead, we will describe the most challenging emotional self-care issues and suggestions that came up in summit discussions.

What About Feelings of Frustration, Depression or Dryness? Of the many emotions that pastors candidly discussed during summit meetings, these three stood out: frustration, depression and dryness. The frustration concerned handling the expectations placed on the pastors. One expressed,

---

We can live with all the frustrations of ministry. But those are compensated when we see the spiritual returns—when peoples' lives are being changed. But when the balance goes the other way, the seesaw goes in the other direction and the frustrations exceed the returns, understandably we begin to ask questions like, "Is it worth it?"

A second common emotional response was depression. Depression can be very complicated, with roots that go much deeper than a response to immediate circumstances.[33] Regardless of the reasons, it was commonplace to find pastors struggling with these feelings. One admitted,

---

I'm not in a good state. I kept thinking, "I wouldn't mind if the Lord took me home." I'm not thinking of sucking a gun or anything, but when those thoughts cross your mind, you go, "Whoa! I'm losing it."

We were encouraged to see how many pastors found significant relief from depression simply by having an opportunity to talk about it during summit gatherings. These times provided a uniquely safe place with people who had faced similar ministry leadership challenges. Also, a number of participants were encouraged to seek professional counseling and medical support in order to responsibly address these concerns.

A third feeling that many pastors expressed was an overall sense of emotional dryness. Here is how one pastor put it:

My relationships and ministry are presently taking place from a place of drought. Outwardly I present a posture of strength and competence. But I am using a lot of energy protecting and guarding my affections. No wonder I am tired, on edge, angry and restless.

While such dryness may have spiritual roots, issues of poor self-care were also an issue. These comments on dryness often came after the extended time set aside for personal reflection. Most pastors were functioning at a pace that prevented them from examining their lives and acknowledging their emotions. When they were given the time to do this, the truth of their emotional condition quickly came to the surface.

How Do I Gain Healthy Emotional Space? One idea from our readings and discussions that the summit pastors found transformative is the concept of differentiation. Differentiation is "the ability to remain connected in relationship to significant people in our lives and yet not have our reactions and behavior determined by them."[34] When we talked about this idea, most pastors admitted that it is easier to talk about it than to do it.

Differentiation is the capacity to hear and empathize with parishioners' frustrations while not necessarily agreeing with their analyses or taking the attacks personally. It is the ability to care for church members while not taking responsibility for them or their emotions.

Differentiation is a tricky concept for pastors who genuinely want to care for others. As one participant shared,

When pastors assume responsibilities that belong to others, they can become overwhelmed and fail to depend on Christ as well. But the metaphor of shepherding must mean something more than setting an example. I believe it takes a great deal of wisdom to know where responsibilities start and stop.

Nevertheless, the pastors agreed that the self-care management of emotions requires an ability to have what used to be called an attitude of *disinterest*. This doesn't mean a lack of care and concern (*un*interested); rather, it means the capacity to be engaged (interested) without being absorbed or aligned with the interest. This is differentiation.

How do we learn to do this? Edwin Friedman, a Jewish rabbi who wrote on emotional systems in religious congregations, stressed that differentiation is a lifetime process rather than a goal to be achieved.[35] The pastors with whom we worked said that two things helped them in this process. First, regular prayer helped: talking with God about particular people and situations while seeking to see things from God's point of view. Second, regular conversations with safe people who could provide a more objective perspective also helped.

QUESTIONS TO PONDER

1. What have been your levels of frustration, depression and dryness this past year? What activities and relationships help you manage them well?

2. Who can you safely talk to about your emotions and the impact of ministry leadership on how you're feeling?

3. Think of a current conflict with someone in your ministry. What might it look like to practice differentiation with them, moving toward them while not having your response determined by them?

DO I WANT TO BE A STAR? MINISTRY IDOLATRY AND SELF-CARE

In the previous chapters on spiritual formation, we explored the problem of workaholism and how it stands in the way of pastors having a fruitful, growing walk with Christ. So it is no surprise that an underlying motive for workaholism—ministry idolatry—would surface as an issue in pastoral emotional self-care. Peter Brain describes ministry idolatry as "drivenness to perform and succeed in the name of Christ." And to show that this drive isn't new to our generations, he quotes Robert Murray McCheyne, a Scottish preacher of the nineteenth century, who said, "God gave me the gospel and a horse [speaking of his body]. I've killed the horse, so I can no longer preach the gospel."[36]

One summit pastor poignantly confessed this idol, sharing,

We [pastors] idolize our work. The church is our idol. It's what we do for a living. I reflect all the time on why the Israelites chose a cow to worship. Cows were their livelihood. So we idolize what we do for a living.

Another pastor said,

I'm anxious that I'm not the effective pastor or person I want to be. I fear that most of my life will be regarded as stubble.

Still another admitted,

Pastors—myself included—are notorious in running flat out to care for our congregations while we abuse, neglect and torture ourselves into depletion. I speak for myself when I say I rarely have time to read Scripture for my own personal well-being.

One of the most memorable stories shared during a summit was a lesson a participant learned while watching the *Oprah Winfrey Show*. This pastor said,

Oprah told how she talked to a close friend and said, "I want to be an actress." Her friend replied, "No. You don't want to be an actress. You want to be a star. Being an actress is only a means to becoming a star." And as I was sitting there thinking about that, it was as if the Holy Spirit whispered, "Do you want to be a pastor, or do you want to be a star? Are you in the pastorate because you want to be a star?"

On hearing this, one of the others exclaimed, "Would you shut up! That's too convicting. What you just told me is that I'm addicted to the narcotic of public acclaim."

In a very real way, the response of that last pastor—calling public acclaim a narcotic—is accurate. Bryan Robinson, who has written widely about workaholism, states, "Workaholism is an obsessive-compulsive disorder that manifests itself through self-imposed demands, an inability to regulate work habits and an overindulgence in work—to the exclusion of most other life activities."[37] Bestselling authors Jim Loehr and Tony Schwartz comment on Robinson's words: "Unlike most addictions, workaholism is often admired, encouraged and materially well rewarded. The costs are more long term. Researchers have found that those who describe themselves as workaholics have significantly higher than average incidence of alcohol abuse, divorce and stress-related illnesses."[38]

These comments correlate with an article from the *Journal of Clinical Psychology*, which states that Protestant clergy have the highest overall work-related stress and are next to the lowest in having personal resources to cope with the occupational strain.[39]

How are pastors to cope with stress and break the pattern of work idolatry? In the next chapter, we will look at areas of social, mental and physical self-care. A number of great ideas will be found there that address workaholism. However, in this section we are looking at the emotional and spiritual areas of self-care. One of the dominant coping responses of the pastors was a method D. Martyn Lloyd-Jones called "preaching truth to yourself."[40] That is, take passages of the Scripture and directly apply them to the challenge.

An example of how one pastor copes by "preaching to himself" focuses on the stress of performance anxiety around preaching. Pastors tend to be anxious before preaching and hypercritical afterward. One of our participants emailed us a series of texts he uses to preach truth to himself about this stress. It is well worth contemplating.

First, I go to Psalm 127. "Unless the Lord builds the house, those who labor, labor in vain." Few texts have been more meaningful to me than being reminded it is the Lord who builds the house. In a workaholic culture, this becomes a confession of faith for me as I go to sleep the night before I preach: to know that all of my work is ultimately a gift of grace.

Next, I remember Genesis 28. Jacob mistakenly felt like he had to kick, fight and scratch for the birthright and blessing, even after it had been promised to him *en utero* (via God's word to Rebekah). It is profound that as [he is] a fugitive on the run, while asleep, God comes to him "down the ladder" and promises grace upon grace.

Third, I remember Matthew 20:1-16—Jesus' parable of the workers in the vineyard. How often I feel like the guy working in the field all day, only to watch others get the same blessings for only an hour of work. But in the economy of grace, *all* of us are the worker who has only worked one hour, with a product equivalent of my five-year-old "helping" me mow the lawn.

Then there is 1 Kings 19. Elijah was running for his life after a great "performance" on Mt. Carmel. He is lamenting, "I alone am left." But God, the Creator of the universe, fixes him a meal and reminds Elijah, "I have my seven thousand left; I'm at work; I'm getting it done; so get back in the game, it's not all on you."

And, of course, Ephesians 2:8-10 must be remembered. God has prepared the works I'm to do beforehand—no more, no less. In our culture, unless you're extraordinary, heroic, successful, you're crap. Who wants to get a C and be called "average"? But this passage gives me comfort that God has saved me by grace and given me works to do by grace. He asks me to do the works he has especially prepared for me to do: no more, no less. He merely asks me to do the work he has given me to do, by grace. Praise God for the ordinary, average Christian man or woman.

Then lastly, when I'm trying to deactivate my obsessive tendency to over-study (and under-sleep) for Sunday, the single verse that begins to decompress me is in 1 Corinthians 15: "By the grace of God I am what I am" [1 Corinthians 15:10]. The gospel to me on Saturday night sounds something like this: "By the grace of God, I have what I have tonight. Lord willing, next month, next year, maybe next decade, if/when I preach this text again, I'll have more because I'll know Jesus more and I'll actually be more. But today, *by the grace of God*, I am what I am and I have what I have from God's Word. So I'll go to sleep by grace alone, through faith alone, in Jesus alone.

QUESTIONS TO PONDER

1. What aspects of work do you tend to value too highly?

2. What results do you tell yourself you are gaining by working too much? What are the real costs in your life?

3. What Scripture passages can you use to preach truth to yourself about work idolatry?

In this chapter we have discussed why pastors tend to ignore issues of self-care. Then we explored the unending pastoral self-care issue of ministry calling, and the three emotional self-care challenges of identity, emotional management and ministry idolatry. Reflecting on these issues and spending time with God and his Word provide a great help toward healthier self-care in these areas. The next chapter continues the discussion of self-care with the focus on the social, intellectual and physical aspects of our personhood.

PACING OUR LIFESTYLES

SELF-CARE II

One of the ironies of our time is that many people who serve in caring
professions experience poor health. Perhaps the most ironic of all is the
strikingly below average health of clergy. Age for age, clergy have significantly
greater incidences of chronic disease, heart and GI tract conditions, and stress,
which is a bit embarrassing for a group preaching about life every week.
Clergy today have, on average, a pattern of health that is
significantly worse than the average American.

Gary Gunderson and Larry Pray, *Leading Causes of Life:*
Five Fundamentals to Change the Way You Live Your Life

ALL THREE OF US ARE SPORTS ENTHUSIASTS. While Tasha isn't into watching professional sports, she loves to jog and to hike mountains. As Bob exercises on the treadmill, he loves to watch baseball (Go Cards!) and football. Donald is passionate about all of his beloved Pittsburgh teams. But one thing we've all noticed: the best athletes carefully pace themselves in order to last. And this idea of pacing applies to more than just physical exertion. The social and intellectual areas of life need to be regulated as much as the physical. In this chapter we will explore self-care in the three vital areas of the social, intellectual and physical aspects of our lives.

HOW ISOLATED AM I? SOCIAL SELF-CARE

Every human being needs relationships. At the time of creation God declared, "It is not good that the man should be alone" (Genesis 2:18). Even people with the most introverted personalities need others with whom they can share their lives. So pastors, as persons created in the image of God, need to be in relationship.

All leaders—and pastors in particular—can experience deep loneliness. A summit participant shared, "I've found that the times in my life I've been isolated the most are when I'm a senior pastor." Another assessed, "I am dangerously isolated." In order to counteract the loneliness of ministry leadership, pastors must be intentional in developing relationships. One participant shared,

> I realized I could not live alone, and that God would never design any member of his kingdom to live alone. So I've created a system of friends.

Everyone in the summit agreed that there is, as one person put it, "a certain loneliness of the pastor, and it goes with the territory." This person continued,

> We have to be careful not to cultivate loneliness. It's possible to begin isolating ourselves from relationships so that we can kind of construct our world the way we want to see it instead of the way it really is. We need each other as mirrors and reflectors to see the way we really are.

Indeed, relationships of all varieties are vital to ministry health. Building friendships for social self-care requires discernment, however. Below we will explore the different pastoral challenges for social self-care that were prominent in the Pastors Summit research.

Are They Allies or Confidants? We explored the distinction between allies and confidants in chapter four on spiritual formation. But we must bring it up here again, because a failure to understand the difference between allies and confidants can create devastating social damage and breaks in trust. Recognizing this distinction is the starting point for pastoral social self-care. As we previously observed, Heifetz and Linsky suggest that allies are people who share many of our same values but who *cannot* always be loyal to us due to some relational or organizational ties.[1] In contrast, confidants "have few, if any, conflicting loyalties. They usually operate outside your organization's boundary, although occasionally someone very close in, whose interests are perfectly aligned with yours, can also play that role."[2]

One pastor clearly made this distinction between allies and confidants by saying,

---

I meet with some folks on Friday mornings. I know my limits of what to share. I have one friend I get with less often with whom I can share *anything*.

To mistake the Friday morning friends for confidants could result in sharing private matters that result in conflicts and broken friendships.

How Many Friendships Do I Have? A second way to look at relationship development is to recognize there are varied levels of friendships. In *Friends and Friendship*, Jerry and Mary White suggest that we view friendship with four levels: acquaintances, casual friends, close friends and intimate friends.[3] They explain that *acquaintances* are people with whom we have transient relationships but who we never intend to pursue as friends. Most people make five hundred or more acquaintances each year.

Level two describes *casual friends*. These are people we see regularly in the normal course of living and with whom we occasionally initiate social contact. They may number from twenty to a hundred or more. Casual friends may include neighbors, coworkers, former classmates and relatives.

Level three friendships are *close friends*. These may include people at work, church or other contexts who we see and to whom we talk frequently. They tend to remain close for many years, regardless of age or distance. The number of close friends may range from ten to thirty active relationships, while up to thirty could be inactive. Due to popular social media, the boundaries between casual and close friends can be more blurred and quite flexible. Allies could fit into either the casual or close friend categories.

Finally, *intimate friends* make up level four relationships. Most likely, these friends would all be confidants. They "are the few people to whom we pour out our souls, sharing our deepest feelings and hopes."[4] The Whites suggest that, on average, most people have four current and active intimate friends. But the number can range from only one person up to perhaps six.

Failure to distinguish between these varied types of relationships has hurt many pastors. As one pastoral couple shared, "We've often felt the brunt of unfounded criticism through email, a call or a conversation. It hurts, especially when it comes from someone we've thought safe."[5]

Another pastor shared of an experience that marked his ministry. During seminary, he was interning at a church and grew quite close to a family in the congregation. As this friendship developed, he began to receive criticism that he was "making favorites." He reacted to this criticism by vowing, "I'll never have any friends in the churches I serve." He stubbornly kept this vow, with the result that he has experienced deep loneliness throughout his adult life.

Can I Have Significant Friends Within My Ministry? This question was discussed in every summit group. A handful of participants were disturbed by the idea that pastors couldn't find their social needs met in their own congregations. One of them stated,

---

It seems like the reality is that pastors and their spouses can't get their body life from the congregations they're responsible for. Is that the case? Does it betray the very body life and image that we're trying to teach our church for pastors to say, "I'm going to be connected to the body *outside* of my congregation"?

Other pastors flatly reported they were unable to make friends in their church. One explained, "I know tons of people; I have many acquaintances, but probably only one friend, and he isn't in the church." Another agreed, "I'm hungry for deep relational connectedness at church, but it's hard to get past the 'pastor' barrier." And another pointedly asked, "Can I honestly be a friend with someone in the church? What happens if they leave or I leave?"

These comments demonstrate the common failure to distinguish between allies and confidants or the varied levels of friendships discussed above. But one pastor did nuance this distinction more carefully by sharing,

---

I think we have a vital body life and great connections within the church [allies]. But there are deeper things, things too great for them to bear. It's helpful to have someone not associated with the situation [confidants]. But we do have great connections with those in our church.

What this pastor shared became the consensus of the summit participants. Generally they found many casual and close friends in the church (allies).

Only three of the pastors in our whole study had a confidant in their congregation.

What About Other Ministry Staff? In general, we found that summit pastors often found very good, close friendships with other members of church staffs. This was reflected in a story one participant shared, about two staff members who felt safe enough to be brutally honest.

Two folks on our staff came into my office one day. They didn't knock on the door; they just came in and sat down. I said "What's up?" and they said, "You know, we love you, and we minister alongside you. We're watching you, and you look to us like a person who's dying."

With the support of these ministry partners, this pastor took the necessary steps to address the issues that had created his crisis. Another pastor in the summit was facing some intense resistance to an initiative he was spearheading in the church. He acknowledged, "There were times when I thought, 'Maybe I'm not called.' I mean, it was pretty shaky there for a while." Then he shared the importance of a staff friendship:

What really kept me hanging in there was one of my ministry directors. We get together every week. And he pumps me up every week and reminds me of how now, for the first time, our church was really doing ministry. . . . He says, "God has used you to do this stuff."

Other pastors, however, shared how they had to be careful to set proper boundaries in an "ally" relationship. They could not assume that a healthy, working relationship meant they could honestly share everything. As one person sadly confessed,

---

My spouse and I were having dinner at the home of another staff couple. I openly shared a personal frustration I was experiencing. In the next day or so my associate told my frustrations to another staff member, and problems snowballed.

How Do I Find Safe, Intimate Friends? Pastors are often unsure what to look for in a confidant. One shared,

---

Our struggle is feeling connected at a surface level with many people but at a deeper level with *none*. You can't be deeply connected when you have different people over every Sunday, or when you are only with a family during a crisis and then moving on to the next thing.

Another reasoned,

We're looking for safe situations where we can get honest feedback and then evaluate without feeling threatened that our job is on the line (because it's our elders) or our reputation is on the line (because it's our denominational gathering).

One place pastors generally do *not* feel safe is their local denominational meetings. As one Presbyterian put it,

I think presbyteries see themselves first and foremost as judicial bodies and not as pastors of the pastors. They've got the "court" thing down pretty good. The "congregation" thing? Not really. . . . There're no relationships of trust.

We've heard similar comments from Baptists, Episcopalians and pastors from a wide variety of other denominations. How does one find trustworthy relationships? It starts with lots of time, patience and energy for initiating. It requires an effort that is easy to forfeit under the pressing needs of the moment. But it is possible. Here is the story of what one participant did when he was called to a new church.

When I went down [to my new pastorate], I thought I better find somebody who'd tell me the truth. I sought [an older pastor] out, and he was very kind to do it. We met once a month. I'd drive two and a half hours to his church and meet for two hours. He would tell me his own struggles. He was very open about his own mess.

Another pastor wrote us an email saying,

I see the need for a "community of grace and truth" in my life. However, being at a new church in a new city, it is difficult to know how to find such a community. Do you have any thoughts on how I might find that or tips for what to look for?

We responded with the following, which comes from our experiences and research.

The difficulty you are finding is, unfortunately, normal. It takes work to find authentic community for pastors. Here are some thoughts.

- For some, community can only be found (at least initially) in a virtual community—friends from seminary or other life contexts that you can talk with on the phone, email or Skype. (But beware of using Facebook or Twitter—they are open for the world to see.)

- Get a copy of the book *Safe People* by Henry Cloud and John Townsend.[6] Read it with your spouse. Talk about it together. Write down the characteristics you would want in a safe friend.

- Sometimes you can find confidants in denominational meetings —but in the experience of the pastors we've worked with, this is very rare.

- In seeking out confidants (or maybe allies, with which you have an 85 percent or better agreement in interests), take one step forward by sharing something honest, then two steps back to evaluate and see how they handle things. It takes time. Don't assume this relationship will work based on initial reactions or responses. See how these people handle information and trust over a few weeks or even months.

- Some other ideas of where to find friends:
  - people in other churches
  - retired pastors or pastors from other denominations
  - members of an AA group or other support groups
  - members at the gym where you work out
  - college alumni gatherings
  - fellow enthusiasts on the golf course
  - again, one step forward, two steps back

- Working in the church means that most relationships are dual relationships. A dual relationship is one in which you serve multiple roles in the life of another person. One moment you might be their friend; the next, a counselor; the next, a spiritual mentor; the next, the hired minister being evaluated by this person on a supervisory committee. Yikes! It's hard to find confidants in this kind of context.

- Make this a matter of prayer and a project you are talking about with your spouse. It will take time. Find enjoyment in the people God is putting around you even if it feels superficial. Recognize there are various levels of friendships. That is okay. Give yourself time. Keep asking God for community.

What About a Peer Group? This final relationship concern has to do with involvement in a peer group. Earlier we shared that the Pastors Summit was funded by the Sustaining Pastoral Excellence project of Lilly Endowment, Inc. The Pastors Summit is only one example of numerous pastoral peer groups developed by participants in the Lilly initiative. Research shows the profoundly helpful impact participation in such peer groups has had on pastors and their congregations.[7]

Key characteristics of peer groups include the freedom to self-select into a group that provides anonymity and safety, a trained facilitator, a degree of structure and a focus on spiritual practices. The Lilly initiative research indicates that pastors who participate in peer groups benefit in many ways.

- They strengthen their ability to deal with conflict in their congregations.
- They enhance their understanding of ministry skills.
- They improve in emotional health.
- They develop better self-care habits.
- They experience church growth.
- They find a place of relational safety and support in the group.

In a recent Lilly report, one young New England pastor shared how much participation in a peer group meant to her. "I was exhausted. But there was no time or place for reflection. Where can clergy go? I couldn't talk to anyone at the church, and none of my friends outside of ministry understood." Once she heard about the peer groups sponsored by her denomination, she eagerly accepted the invitation to join. "I was feeling pretty needy," she reflected, recalling the first session she attended. "They were great—so supportive and willing to help me deal with everything that was going on in my life. It really helped me navigate that year."[8]

Participants in the Pastors Summit shared similar enthusiasm for their peer group experience. Here are some of the comments they made about their involvement.

- "Learning and positive change occur most deeply in the context of relationships."

- "It was a treat having freedom from being 'on' all the time and to be able to share with mutual understanding about our lives and work."

- "The Pastors Summit was about our health, not the health of our church."

- "My summit group is the only place I can be myself and laugh from my gut."

One other comment sums up the profound impact of summit participation. This pastor shared,

---

I don't want to lose this, because I don't have this anyplace else. I hope that if I veer off, you all will come and get me. Because I don't know who in the world, literally, will come and get me if you don't.

The basic structure of a peer gathering shares some characteristics with other effective small groups. But there are a few unusual best practices for pastors that we discovered through our study. First, there needs to be intentionality in participant selection. As one participant put it, "To benefit from a group, you've got to be hungry for what it provides."

Second, and perhaps surprisingly, these groups must have a designated leader who is *in* the group but not *of* it. The facilitator cannot be one of the participants the group is meant to serve. We agree with Roy Oswald, who explains, "In the absence of strong leadership at the center of most groups, the trust level usually doesn't develop . . . we need to hire someone to be a pastor to us when we gather as peers to review our lives."[9] Third, groups need a dedicated time and location, and participants must have a strong commitment to attend. Because pastors often don't know how to practice good self-care, they generally allow the pressures of the moment to intrude on calendar commitments. All must regularly attend if a peer group is to be effective.

Fourth, the pastors must agree to "unplug." This means that cell phones are turned off and iPads or computers are not brought into the room. Fifth, groups must not be open-ended. A commitment should be made for a specific period of time. At the end of the time, the experience should be evaluated, and participants should determine whether they wish to continue in the group. For example, summit cohorts committed upfront to meet three times per year for two years.

Finally, we learned that it was important to find a way for spouses to be involved in the peer group. Some of our groups had spouses come periodically. Others had a spouses group that met simultaneously with the pastors group. The different cohorts of spouses simply chose different commitment levels for involvement based on their felt need and stage of life.

Peer group meetings are one highly effective way for pastors to find the relational support necessary to stay in ministry. While they are not the only method, research and practical experience tell us they are a great way to provide relational self-care. In appendix E, we provide a detailed list of best practices for forming and facilitating such groups from our years of planning and facilitating Pastors Summit cohorts. The participants gave thorough input and feedback on the gatherings as the program progressed. So this is really a summary of practices that pastors think meet their needs best.

The social self-care of pastors is not an easy topic. Every pastor has a unique personality with strengths and struggles in relationships. And every context has relational opportunities and danger zones that need to be understood. What we have shared here from the summit pastors can provide a starting point for a lifelong exploration of this subject.

QUESTIONS TO PONDER

1. How do I describe my various friendships? Who are true confidants to whom I can tell anything?

2. To what extent are my needs for connection with others met?

3. Who can I talk with about forming a peer group?

AM I MENTALLY SHARP? INTELLECTUAL SELF-CARE

Two areas stood out in the Pastors Summit discussions regarding intellectual self-care. The first understandably had to do with keeping one's mind fresh with opportunities to reflect, learn, and explore creatively and imaginatively. The second focused on the establishment of boundaries and the use of time to mirror personal values and priorities.

How Do I Keep Learning? Pastors constantly deal with ideas. The weekly demands to teach and preach push them to stay current with cultural concerns as well as be grounded in biblical and theological understandings. It is very possible, however, for pastors to fall into intellectual ruts and to not be renewed in their minds.

One way the summit pastors experienced intellectual renewal was in dedicated times of reflection. We talked about reflection when we explored spiritual formation, but it also plays a vital role in self-care.

We've already learned that the taxing, fast-paced lifestyle of ministry does not naturally lend itself to contemplation.[10] Working reflection into the daily rhythm of pastoral vocation needs to become an intentional commitment. As one pastor commented after a two-hour reflection time on life priorities and scheduling,

---

I've got to make time for this—it doesn't just happen. If I live an unexamined life, I'm going to continue to think that what I am thinking is right.

In addition to reflection, when it comes to intellectual self-care, we must add opportunities for informal, nonformal and formal education. *Informal education* accounts for the daily, unintentional and unstructured learning and growth we experience through leisure reading, interacting with others and having new experiences that stretch us to see things differently. Informal learning happens without a designated teacher and outside of a school environment. For example, one objective of the Pastors Summit was to offer pastoral couples opportunities to see and experience new things. Hiking a mountain, taking a cruise with friends and conversing informally over a meal are some examples of the informal learning options we had together.

The term *nonformal education* describes more structured, intentional times for learning. Before each summit meeting, the pastors were given a new book to read. Then we had planned conversations around that material. Often guests were invited to a summit as content specialists. For example, Steve Garber, director of the Washington Institute for Faith, Vocation, and Culture, was asked to meet with summit groups. The prereading was Wendell Berry's novel *Jayber Crow*. Steve guided the discussions around the ways that Jayber's service as a barber modeled the pastoral vocation. When considering that conversation, one pastor ruefully remarked,

This is one of the first times I've sat in a group and talked about a book other than the Bible since I was in seminary.

Formal education is a structured and certified plan of study that usually takes place in an educational institution. While the Pastors Summit did not involve formal education courses, many of the summit alumni have responded to their experience by enrolling in classes. The unique experience of relationship-based educational experiences in the summit caused them to reconsider what they want from formal educational venues. As one pastor put it, "The Pastors Summit has shown me that what I desire is continuing education in the context of trusted relationships." This desire for relationship-based continuing professional education has pushed many seminaries to restructure their programs in order to feature small groups, or cohorts, which remain consistent throughout the degree program.

Does My Calendar Mirror Personal Values? The second area of intellectual self-care is the responsibility pastors must take to establish boundaries on their use of time. It is easy for the pastoral lifestyle to become one of reaction and response to circumstances rather than a studied plan based on personal values and priorities.

We had a number of excellent conversations in summits around the topic of schedule boundaries. The pastors recognized that parishioners often place undue expectations on their time. For example, during early days of a church plant, one pastor got a call from a woman who was afraid she had overextended in buying her house. He realized that his response would send a message to her and the church regarding his boundaries. So he gently but firmly said, "Monday is my day off, and I'm not a financial counselor."

At the same time, pastors have a corresponding problem: they often *want* to be seen as the one with answers for everybody's problems. As one pastor put it,

I think the biggest challenge with boundaries for me is not other people asking me things. It's me. It's my ambition to be the answer man instead of pointing others to the answer. It hurts.

Yet as another shared,

The bottom line is, there's no easy way to say no and set boundaries. We
have to live out our priorities. And by doing so, pastors will have to do things
that cut across the grain of many—they will have to disappoint people.

Another insightful participant put it this way:

If we don't develop the ability to look someone in the eye who has a
genuine need and say "no," we're dead. I mean, to be in situations where
you can look someone in the eye and say, "I am not the answer to this
need." And to have that person look back and say, "The pastor is so un-
compassionate, uncaring." To face that criticism and maintain our boundary—if we can't do it, we're dead.

Below we explore four categories crucial for time commitments in mental self-care. These include home and office schedules, days off, vacations,
and sabbath and sabbaticals.

Home clock versus office calendar? It is no surprise that summit discussions often centered on the struggle of maintaining boundaries to protect
the family from ministry demands. One time, a pastor just threw his hands
up in the air and bemoaned, "My family gets the scraps. What can I do
about it?" We will look carefully at this topic in the chapters on marriage
and family. Right now we simply flag its importance in this discussion.

We will only emphasize one point here regarding the need for wise
boundaries between home and office. Pastors must face the brutal fact that
they have made vows—marriage vows and dedication or baptismal vows—
to commit time and energy to their marriage and family. One older pastor
counseled, "Listen, you only get one shot at the time you have with your
spouse and kids. Don't blow it by responding to everyone else's whims."
And another pastor shared,

I would come home every day thinking about work. I had a five-year-old,
a three-year-old and a one-year-old. And my body would be at home, but
my head would still be back with a student, with the book I was supposed
to be writing, with what I was going to be doing in church during the
weekend. And she [my wife] could just see that I wasn't really there. She
finally grabbed me by the short hairs and said, "There is only one human

being on this planet who can be a father to these children. And there is only a certain window of time in which you can be their dad."

A weekly day off. For many years a standard seminary homiletics text was John Broadus's *On the Preparation and Delivery of Sermons.*[11] How ironic that so many pastors forget Broadus's exhortation to take a day off. Broadus explained, "Every pastor should have a day off. Since he works strenuously on Sunday, he should have a day during the week which may be used for rest, recreation, meditation or uninterrupted study. A day's recreation will return a pastor to his parish invigorated and ready for work."[12]

As we shared before, Bob has served at a number of multistaff congregations. When he started at one church, only three out of six pastors took a day off. On moving to a different congregation, he was surprised to discover that he was the only pastor on a staff of nine who took a dedicated day off! And the reason he took a day off every week was not because of his own wisdom. For three years during college, he had served as a youth intern. Russ Cadle, the youth pastor for whom he worked, insisted that everyone take a day off every week—with no exceptions. This ritual was so ingrained in his experience that it was already a part of his "pastoral rhythm" before he was ordained.

Unfortunately, most of the pastors in the summit were highly irregular in taking time off. But many of them reconsidered it when they heard each other's stories of feeling run-down and constantly tired. Roy Oswald identifies this problem precisely when he writes, "The research on burnout generally agrees that chronic fatigue and apathy develop from being overly committed and involved in our work. The literature on stress states that there are only so many life changes that we can endure. A clear coping strategy is to remove ourselves from an agitated, changing environment and take some time for ourselves. Yet, because the role of religious authority is often ambiguous, we clergy have difficulty knowing when we have done enough and can take time for ourselves. It often seems more prudent to do 'just one more thing' before taking time out."[13]

The ambiguous nature of pastoral work makes the need to take time off even more pressing. Oswald recommends that pastors have one day off a week as personal time and a second day for sabbath. While many pastors may scoff at this as unthinkable, those who do set aside a separate sabbath day would be wise to consider at least another half-day for personal use. Establishing a routine of taking days off is a healthy, life-giving ritual.

Vacations. The pattern of pastors overworking carries over to the way that they handle their yearly vacation time. Most of the pastors we worked with rarely took their full vacation each year.[14] Unfortunately, this pattern is often unconsciously promoted by members of the congregation. For example, one person shared that he felt "trapped" by the current circumstances of his ministry. He felt pressure from people who would make comments like, "I brought visitors to church last Sunday and you weren't preaching. How come?" Another pastor said,

---

One of the great frustrations is everyone telling us, "You need to get some time away," and "You need to make sure to take your vacation time." There's always a caveat, though. They want me to do this as long as it means I don't miss their meeting or their activity. It is impossible to leave and not miss something. I've been learning that *getting* time away is *taking* time away. That is, I just have to bite the bullet and get out of town, knowing that I'll miss someone's special something.

Wise self-care requires ministry leaders to take large enough breaks to become fully refreshed. A younger pastor shared some wisdom he received from a mentor about vacations.

I had a preacher tell me once, "Don't die to find out that the people can do without you. I guarantee that they will do without you. So you need to learn to take time so God can refresh you and do other things with you.

Sabbath and sabbaticals. Experts on energy management affirm that humans need to cease labor and rest. Jim Loehr and Tony Schwartz point out, "We live in a world that celebrates work and activity, ignores renewal and recovery, and fails to recognize that both are necessary for sustained high performance."[15] In contrast, they say, "The richest, happiest and most productive lives are characterized by the ability to fully engage in the challenge at hand, but also to disengage periodically and seek renewal."[16]

It is beyond the scope of this study to explore the biblical and theological obligations of sabbath-keeping. It is our belief, however, that God rested after the completion of his creative acts and has called his people to demonstrate their trust in him by enjoying times of rest. More discussion on sabbath as a spiritual discipline can be found in chapter four.

The discussion of how and when pastors can take time for sabbath may never be resolved. Some feel that their Sunday activity, as work done for the Lord, fulfills sabbath expectations. Others view Sunday as a work day and believe they need other time for sabbath.[17] Regardless of one's view, the summit pastors thought that most pastors get so caught up in the busy activities of the week that they fail to enjoy any sabbath time. But sabbath rest is necessary for mental and spiritual health. One pastor, who formerly suffered a debilitating illness, agreed, saying,

---

As I look back on it, I think it was a "hard gift" getting deathly ill. . . . I was out eight weeks. I was the only pastor—there was no one else on staff— and the church didn't die. Experiencing the severe limits of my illness makes me know I just can't do as much. And so I have to embrace my limits and say, "Okay, I can't do as much." Now, as I walk out and look at creation and see all of these beautiful things that are blooming and blossoming, I've come to realize I didn't do anything to make it look like this. All of this was happening while I was asleep last night. God is at work while I rest. I can only do so much. So I hear you guys say, "How could I take a sabbath?" And I think, "How could you *not*?"

If the idea of taking a weekly sabbath is radical, then the suggestion of taking a sabbatical, or extended study leave, might be essentially unheard of. Yet a pattern of work and renewal is built into God's design for our world, not only in the seven-day week but also in longer cycles. The notion of a sabbatical rest is rooted in the creation story (Genesis 2:2-3). It is also established in the Levitical law (Leviticus 25:3-4). Farmers were instructed to allow their fields to rest after six years of productivity. This activity of a sabbatical rest allowed time for the earth to rehabilitate itself and gave the people who depended on the land an opportunity to trust in the Lord for their provision. People take sabbaticals to renew their minds for future work.

Even though there are sound theological and practical reasons for sabbaticals, many ministry leaders never consider them an option, let alone a requirement for healthy self-care. One reason for this may be a lack of understanding and support from the congregation.

When talking about sabbaticals, one summit pastor stated, "My church is full of professional people and they say, 'We only get a few weeks off, so you need to suck it up!'" Another one explained, "Most of my elders don't understand the dynamics of pastoral ministry. The idea of taking sabbatical to them sounds desperate." Of course, these other professionals fail to recall all the study time, professional development, peer collaboration and conferences that are built into their work. These forms of professional growth and renewal are not built into most pastors' calendars.

While the granting of sabbaticals is a blessing, there can be pitfalls. One summit pastor shared his bad experience.

I took a sabbatical, and I learned how *not* to do it. It was a miserable experience. I took six weeks. Some of that was speaking, some of it was vacation and I had an additional four weeks for renewal. But it just wasn't long enough. Six weeks was too short and not very thought through. I had a big agenda, and it took me about two weeks to find out that it was stupid. I was able to recover, but it wiped me out. I will never do that again.

Sabbaticals must be carefully planned. Generally they should last at least two to three months. The first two weeks should be considered a time of decompression from normal activities. Then the bulk of the sabbatical should be designed to provide rest, study, experimentation and reflection. This can include travel and may involve meeting with leaders in other congregations. But pastors should not take on speaking engagements or other activities that match their normal routines or feel like regular work. The final two weeks should be a time of "ramping up" to pastoral life again. This may include returning to the congregation for worship and reconnecting with parishioners. We also recommend that pastors do not preach until they have returned from their sabbatical for at least two weeks.

Many churches encourage their pastors to take regular sabbaticals, because they view it as a short-term investment for their long-term strength. Though the sabbatical should provide a measure of rest, it will not correct a working environment that fosters burnout. The wise use of vacations, study leaves and sabbaticals, along with careful accountability for time and work boundaries, are needed to create a situation in which pastors can thrive.

QUESTIONS TO PONDER

1. Where do you have space and time for reflection and learning? How could you create more?

2. In what areas would you like to pursue professional development? What would you hope to learn?

3. Compare your home and work calendars and weekly schedules. To what degree do they reflect your priorities and values? Who can help you bring them into better alignment and build healthier boundaries?

4. Who can you start talking to about sabbaticals and the possibility of taking one?

WHAT RECHARGES MY BATTERIES? PHYSICAL SELF-CARE

In "Which Way to Clergy Health?" Bob Wells reports, "Although data is limited, research indicates that some of the most critical issues facing clergy appear to be in the areas of weight, mental health, heart disease and stress."[18] Alan Taha, who did his doctoral work on clergy physical self-care, agrees, stating, "The physical issues that cause pastors to struggle show no signs of abating." Indeed, one study found that "76 percent of clergy were either overweight or obese."[19] Ministry leaders generally have poor physical self-care.

Occasionally pastors make reference to Paul's comments on the priority of godliness over bodily training as an excuse for poor physical self-care.[20] In reference to this verse, Taha comments, "The value in bodily training is not dismissed completely. Paul found some value in it."[21] And Kathleen Greider writes, "We have a responsibility to develop a constructive relationship with our bodies through which we become knowledgeable about its powers and vulnerabilities. From this point of view, exercise is no more optional for care of the body than food or sleep."[22] Further, pastors who dismiss physical self-care need to be reminded of Paul's statements that the body should be offered as a living sacrifice, that it is a temple of the Holy Spirit and that believers are called to glorify God in their bodies (Romans 12:1; 1 Corinthians 6:19-20).

Pastors in the summit would agree with David Wells, who asserts, "They must avoid the cult of health, beauty, and fitness so prominent in our day, with its near exclusive emphasis on looks and physique."[23] At the same time, comments from our pastors emphasized that poor physical health translates into less effective ministry. One said,

> I'm discovering that if you don't treat your body well, you can have plenty of gospel inside you and have plenty to share with people. But how can you do it when you're not physically fit?

And another emphasized, "If you don't take care of the body, then a lot of other things are going to get messed up."

Taha draws a number of important conclusions from his study of best practices in pastoral physical self-care. First, he says pastors need to increase their level of physical activity. "Each of the participants [in the study] were not content to sit throughout the day. While aerobic exercise contributed to their fitness levels, they also walked and moved often during their daily activities."[24] He continues, "Overcoming the inertia of old, unhealthy ways is how to start a physical self-care regimen."[25]

Second, Taha suggests that pastors seek peer support in their exercise routines. He shared, "Having people who needed them to participate helped each of the pastors to continue their physical self-care activities with regularity. In addition, they found both relationships and relief from the stress and challenges of ministry."[26]

Third, Taha explains that awareness of problems and changes in nutrition habits are important elements of physical self-care. He says, "Poor diet can compound physical problems and reduce physical activity through weight gain."[27] Finally, in his conclusion, Taha asserts, "Physical self-care seems to engender ministry fitness by relieving stress, improving sleep quality, and providing the resource of physical health to the ministry endeavor. To honor the body as 'the temple of the living God' certainly enriches one's capacity for service, increases well-being, and models care of God's gift of life."[28]

QUESTIONS TO PONDER

1. What stories do you tell yourself about your current state of physical health?

2. What is one bad habit that you would like to replace with a new routine toward better physical health?

3. Who can help you pursue that new routine?

4. When was the last time you had a complete physical examination? Why?

CONCLUSION: LIMITS AND RHYTHMS

Self-care requires limits and rhythms. It does not come easily. It begins by recognizing that we are finite creatures who rebel against the reality of our limitations. This rebellion is fueled by a culture that often pretends there are no limits in this life. But more fully embracing our limits allows us to accept what God is doing in our lives and ministry. Reflecting on this in a journal entry, one pastor wrote,

---

I want a growing church. I and my elders are praying and working hard to grow it. But right now God has not given us growth. Can I accept this as a gift from him? He knows what is best. He knows my limits and the limits of my church.

Limits are linked to life rhythms. Certain rhythms—like sabbath, exercise, friendship and contentment in calling—create patterns of healthy living. Life rhythms can be discovered by reflection: considering what patterns have worked well for health and others that haven't. We are creatures of habit. By recognizing and building on healthy habits and rhythms, we can work on establishing good self-care. Healthy rhythms can also be strengthened by reviewing our deeply held values, defining precise behaviors that reflect these values and working on them. With the support of others, these behaviors can become habits.

Developing life rhythms toward self-care does not come naturally, nor are they often supported by those around us. In *A Soul Under Siege: Surviving Clergy Depression*, C. Welton Gaddy recounts his own journey facing poor life patterns and self-care. He instructs pastors to "take care of yourself and your family. No one is going to watch out for the best interests of yourself and your family like you." He warns pastors not to expect churches as employers to set sensible limits. Instead, he writes, "employers and peers frequently support a person's senseless work habits by affirmation and praise."[29]

Self-care is an important but neglected aspect of pastoral life. In these two chapters, we have explored why pastors neglect self-care. Then we surveyed our Pastors Summit research findings by dividing them into life areas that need intentional self-care efforts. Self-care is not *selfish*. It is a necessary part of staying involved in fruitful ministry for a lifetime.

RECOMMENDATIONS FOR FURTHER READING

1. Peter Brain. *Going the Distance: How to Stay Fit for a Lifetime of Ministry*. Kingsford, NSW: Matthias Media, 2004.

2. Henry Cloud and John Townsend. *Safe People: How to Find Relationships That Are Good for You and Avoid Those That Aren't*. Grand Rapids: Zondervan, 1995.

3. Kent and Barbara Hughes. *Liberating Ministry from the Success Syndrome*. Wheaton: Tyndale, 1988.

4. Gordon MacDonald. *Ordering Your Private World*. Nashville: Thomas Nelson, 2003.

5. Tom Rath and Jim Harter. *Wellbeing: The Five Essential Elements*. New York: Gallup Press, 2010.

MEDIA WORTH EXPLORING

1. *Enchanted April* (1992), rated PG. Four women experience rejuvenation as they discuss love, relationships and their lives amid the breathtaking beauty of an Italian island. The film illustrates the power of reflective conversation in the context of God's restorative creation.

2. *The Straight Story* (1999), rated G. Seventy-three-year-old Alvin rides his tractor hundreds of miles in order to mend his relationship with his estranged brother Lyle. His determination to make things right between them is both inspiring and instructive when considering the centrality of healthy relationships to our well-being.

UNDERSTANDING EMOTIONAL INTELLIGENCE

When I was in seminary, I was taught how to preach and how to

exegete the Scriptures. I wasn't taught how to exegete people. . . . I didn't

know that pastoring is dealing with people and their messiness.

A pastor at a Pastors Summit gathering

DAVID IS A PASTOR WE HAVE GOTTEN TO KNOW over the past few years. Although he was not involved in the Pastors Summit directly, we've been talking together about the five themes for some time. Recently he contacted us, sharing this story:

> You know about Sam, who has always been a difficult person and who often fails to see things from differing points of view. Recently he told me that he wanted to return to the elder board, forgoing the reelection and training that are required for everyone, regardless of their past service. I brought this up to the elders, and they were unwavering on the policy.
>
> I set up a time to meet with Sam. He became frustrated over the policy and attacked me, saying that the policy had somehow changed. I explained to him that he had voted for the policy when he was on the board. He was very frustrated, personalizing it as though I, or the board, was seeking to keep him off.
>
> It is only by God's grace I didn't get emotionally hijacked by Sam. I remained calm and did not feel the need to appease his concerns. I lis-

tened, reaffirmed the policy and let him know that I respected him. Later I was able to have lunch with Sam and brought up the difficulties he had with the policy. I reaffirmed that it was not reflective of any personal issues and that he had voted for it. I explained to him that the purpose of the training was to promote the functioning of our board, highlighting gospel dynamics, emotional health and getting people up to speed on what is going on. He responded that he would not be able to serve as an elder given how much time was involved.

It is clear that Sam did not like the policy placing requirements on former elders returning to the board. The deeper issue in this story, however, has to do with Sam's emotional intelligence (EQ): his ability to manage his own emotions and to appropriately respond to the emotions of others.[1]

David identified this problem when he said, "Sam . . . has always been a difficult person and always wants to get his way." Later David related, "[Sam] attacked me . . . he was frustrated, personalizing it . . . he dodged talking about anything in a deep way." Obviously, working with Sam is a challenge for David in many ways and requires David to muster his EQ in order to respond graciously.

For years, the business world neglected the topic of emotions, writing them off as "soft skills" that were trivial compared to the task of getting things done.[2] Many in the marketplace now, however, recognize that emotions do matter, even for a company's success and the bottom line. Researchers and consultants David Caruso and Peter Salovey write, "We believe that to ignore their role, to deny the wisdom of your own emotions and those of others, is to invite failure as a person, as a manager, and as a leader."[3]

Author Daniel Goleman, one of the leading authors on emotional intelligence, underlined the importance of EQ by sharing the story of a research project that began in the 1950s. Eighty Ph.D. students in science at the University of California, Berkeley, went through an intensive battery of IQ and personality tests. They also had exhaustive interviews with psychologists, who evaluated them on such qualities as emotional balance, maturity and interpersonal effectiveness.

Forty years later, when these former students were in their seventies, researchers tracked them down again. They evaluated each person's career success based on their resumes, assessment by peers in their field and sources like *American Men and Women of Science*. The conclusion drawn from this analysis was that issues of EQ—the capacity for self-awareness, self-management, social awareness and relationship management—were about four times more important than IQ in determining professional success and prestige for these scientists.[4]

Christians have long debated the value and role of human emotions.[5] Over the last thirty years, theologians and Christian counselors have acknowledged the role of emotions as a critical, God-given aspect of our personhood, which is made in the image of God.[6] Pete Scazzero summarizes their conclusions, bluntly saying, "Emotional health and spiritual maturity are inseparable."[7]

Many of the participants in the Pastors Summit recognized that emotional maturity has never been part of their discipleship agenda. When this issue was addressed, one of them shared,

---

I'm trembling inside. . . . I feel that I'm an emotional and spiritual infant leading a large church. I'm in danger of crashing and losing a lot if things don't change.

Another reflected, "I'm easy to get along with because I'm nice. But I am really very out of touch with my emotions."

DESCRIBING EMOTIONAL INTELLIGENCE

Emotional intelligence can be described as the ability to proactively manage your own emotions (EQ-self) and to appropriately respond to the emotions of others (EQ-others).[8] EQ-self is not easy. It is hard for any of us (pastors included) to identify our feelings. However, without the ability to *understand* our emotions—as well as our strengths, limitations, values and motives—we will be poor at *managing* them and less able to understand the emotions of others.[9] Our EQ-self directly affects our EQ-others.

EQ-Self. One summit pastor shared this story about how out of touch he had been with his emotions and how it affected a volunteer in the congregation:

I had a watershed moment some years ago. . . . One Monday morning, a very godly woman from our church came in to see me. She was one of the people involved in projecting the words for hymns in the worship service. She came in and told me, "I can't do this anymore." And I thought, *What's going on in your life? What's wrong?* And she said, "I just can't do it because you look so mad when I don't do something right. I just can't take it." I was totally unaware of it. I was sure she was wrong. But I asked my wife, "Is she right?" And she said, "Yes, she is." She was the first person who had the courage to tell me. That was deeply convicting to me. What was coming across from me was displeasure. I was communicating, "You're just not doing a good job." And yet she was willingly serving, and she was doing a good job. It just wasn't perfect.

There are a number of things to notice from this story about EQ-self. First, the pastor was not in touch with his feelings of displeasure toward this woman's performance. His emotions were in full operation, but he wasn't aware of them and therefore did not manage them.

Second, he was also clueless that his emotions were visible in his facial expression; to at least two other people, he looked "so mad." The pastor was wearing his feelings and was totally unaware that he was communicating them. Yet this woman picked up on his nonverbal cues, came to her own conclusions and responded to them.

Third, the pastor went to a trusted friend (in this case, his wife) to discover whether the woman's interpretation was valid. Even though he was not in touch with his own feelings and did not understand what he was communicating, when he received feedback, he did not negatively react to the critical interpretation. Rather, he went outside of his own frame of understanding to explore whether this woman's perspective accurately reflected what he was projecting.

This story tells us a great deal about EQ-self. It shows us that when we lack self-awareness, we are at a loss to manage our feelings. It also demonstrates that "emotions are primarily signals about people, social situations, and interactions. The events that call forth emotions are typically interpersonal actions."[10] Further, the story identifies how important it is to gain a better understanding of the ways we make others feel. Finally, it shows how we often need outside feedback to heighten and to clarify our self-awareness.

EQ-Others. The skill to appropriately respond to the emotions of others (EQ-others) is not any easier. Like EQ-self, it has a two-part challenge. First, it requires discerning accurately what others are feeling; second, it means responding to those feelings well.

We have a friend who serves on the staff of a church that faced a very messy conflict. One staff member had criticized another in a public email. Our friend sought to intercede. She went to the offended party (who was very angry) and sternly charged him to remain calm and not respond to the email at the moment. Then she went to the offending person, seeking to help him understand the impact of his email.

As it turned out, the offended party was upset by our friend's stern admonition. So our friend went to this person, listened carefully to his offense and asked forgiveness for being too strong with him. He was so grateful for her repentant attitude that he initiated a conversation about the circumstances behind the conflict. She, in turn, was able to offer him some constructive insights that he was prepared to receive.

Our friend demonstrated EQ-others. She was attuned to how her staff partner felt in the moment and responded appropriately. Through active listening and a repentant spirit, she was able to turn the emotional mood from anxiety to hope.

Developing EQ. Human emotions are part of what it means to be made in the image of God. As a result, the expression of emotion is one aspect of human personality. And as the personalities of individuals develop, emotional intelligence progresses as well. While there are many factors that influence this development of EQ from childhood into adolescence and then into adulthood, none has as much influence as one's family of origin. As Jim Herrington, Robert Creech and Trisha Taylor state, "The family is the fire in which our level of emotional maturity is forged. . . . Since we learn from our family how to relate, we carry these same behaviors directly into the work system and congregation of which we are part. So does everyone else who is part of the system."[11]

Author Pete Scazzero shares that even his new birth in Christ did not immediately transform the influence of his family of origin. "While I was now a new member of Christ's family, almost everything I had learned about life had come from my original family. The issue of discipleship now was how to do life Christ's way. Learning how to pray, read Scripture, participate in small groups, worship, and use my spiritual gifts were the easy part. Rooting out deeply ingrained messages, habits, and ways of behaving, especially under stress, would prove far more complex and difficult. . . .

The gravitational pull back to the sinful, destructive patterns of our family of origin and culture is enormous."[12]

The good news we saw in the previous chapter on self-care is that the Scriptures teach we are not irrevocably consigned to repeat the sinful behaviors of our family. We can grow and change, especially if we take the time to identify and address patterns within our family systems. In reference to EQ, this potential for growth and change is affirmed by Goleman, who explains, "Emotional intelligence is not fixed genetically, nor does it develop only in early childhood. . . . [It] seems to be largely learned, and it continues to develop as we go through life and learn from our experiences—our competence in it can keep growing."[13]

At the same time, we must keep in mind that the flip side of this potential for EQ growth is also in play. Just because a person has grown up physically and intellectually, or even in some aspects appears spiritually mature, doesn't necessarily mean they have grown up *emotionally*. It is possible that a mature adult can be an emotional adolescent. As Goleman declares, "Out-of-control emotions can make smart people stupid."[14] And Pete Scazzero discovered that "a person can be deeply committed to contemplative spirituality, even to the point of taking a monastic vow, and remain emotionally unaware and socially maladjusted."[15]

Later we will explore practices that develop emotional intelligence. At this point it is important to stress that emotional intelligence is not static. We can grow—and have setbacks—in understanding and managing our own emotions, as well as reading and responding to how others feel. As one of the pastors in the summit explained,

---

I embraced this paradigm [of emotional health] five years ago. Through counseling and developing close relationships, I began experiencing emotionally healthy spirituality. However, the stress of ministry has pushed me and our marriage away from practices of emotional honesty, reflection and dialogue. I am also very prone to blame my failures on my schedule, my wife and my parishioners. I definitely can feel the difference when we take time to cultivate our marriage, when I participate at home, when I say "no" to things that are not a priority and when I contemplate and pray.

QUESTIONS TO PONDER

1. How do you feel about emotions? What would help you value them more as part of bearing the image of God?

2. How quickly and accurately are you conscious of your emotional state?

3. When your emotions suddenly change, to what degree are you able to manage them? When do they rule your behavior?

4. Who could give you honest feedback on how your emotions are showing?

5. In what ways has your EQ grown or diminished this past year? Why?

MINISTRY LEADERSHIP REQUIREMENTS FOR EQ

How is emotional intelligence affected by serving in ministry? Pastoral ministry requires learning about ourselves and how we function in various environments and under various circumstances. As one summit pastor put it,

> You have to know who you are and how others are different. How can you manage yourself or work with other people if you don't know how everyone is unique?

Vocational ministry nearly always involves working with people. People have interests that lead them to act in certain ways when confronted with situations in which they must make a judgment about what to do or to say. The ministry, then, involves negotiating with others, choosing among conflicting wants and interests, developing trust, locating support and opposition, being sensitive to timing, and knowing the informal and formal organizational ropes.[16]

Most people, however, enter the ministry with little experience understanding themselves or others, especially in the area of emotions. One pastor said bluntly, "I love the ministry, but I can't deal with the people." Since our summit participants were selected for "ministry excellence," it was surprising how many of them bemoaned their own lack of emotional maturity.[17] For example, another shared,

> The benefit of this cohort is learning to deal with emotions. I don't know how to deal with my own or others' emotions, so it has not become part

of our discipleship agenda. We leave it to the therapists. . . . Up until now,
I have not had any idea of how to make emotional maturity a part of discipleship—one reason being my own lack of emotional maturity.

These comments reflect the great need for emotional intelligence in
ministry leadership. It is interesting that a national survey result of what
employers want in entry-level workers reads much like the skills congregations desire in pastors. Employers listed characteristics such as

- listening and oral communication skills

- adaptability and creative responses to setbacks and obstacles

- personal management, confidence and motivation to work toward goals

- group and interpersonal effectiveness, cooperativeness and teamwork,
  skills at negotiating disagreements

- effectiveness in the organization, wanting to make a contribution

These skills are relational rather than technical in nature. And they are
all abilities founded in emotional intelligence. Yet in order to develop such
skills, pastors are required to learn emotional intelligence on the job, in the
day-to-day struggles of ministry. And the pastoral ministry has unique
demands that make this EQ training difficult.

During the summit meetings, pastors discussed many topics that mold
the development of emotional intelligence. Four problems and two challenges stood out from our conversations as vital areas for ministry leaders
to work on. The four problems, discussed below, are people-pleasing,
emotion-faking, lack of reflection and conflict avoidance. The two most
significant challenges go hand in glove: listening and expressing empathy.

The Problem of People-Pleasing. People-pleasing is the willingness to
deny one's own feelings, priorities, values or convictions in order to try to
make others happy. As one pastor expressed this problem,

I will ultimately let go of everything that is good for me to please others—
I'm far more driven by the fear of man than anything else.

Several other pastors admitted to their people-pleasing habits. A story
from a church planter's experience illustrates this.

We were having a hard time finding a good location where our church plant could meet. We were meeting in the music classroom of a school on the edge of town—a location that was out of the way and hard to find. I found a good space in the heart of town. Before signing the contract, another tenant mentioned that the town had an ordinance we might want to check into. Churches could not meet within a certain distance from establishments that served alcohol. In my gut I felt, "This is important." But I was being pressed to find a new location by our leadership team, so I disregarded my thoughts and feelings and signed the lease. About nine months after meeting in this space, we were called on the carpet by the town council for violating the ordinance.

Later in the conversation this pastor acknowledged that his concern for pleasing the leadership team negated his impulse to stop and reflect on what his "gut" was telling him. By doing so, he lost the opportunity to reflect on his feeling, to respond more wisely and to mature in his emotional intelligence.

The Problem of Emotion-Faking. When pastors pull away from their day-to-day routines and ponder their lives, many realize how often they deny their feelings and assume an unflappable "pastoral persona." As one described it,

Well, you learn to play a game, to put on a mask, which then becomes a way you handle a lot of issues. You're suddenly the holy man that has to put on the holiness aura and have it all together. And that's going to come back and wipe you out. Wiped me out.

Another pastor said, "So many thing are coming at us and we take so many hits that if we allowed ourselves to feel, we wouldn't get anything done." And another responded, "I don't want to be weak. I don't want to be needy. I don't want to come across to you as needy."

This tendency to fake it cuts across the most important aspect of emotional intelligence: learning to identify our own feelings and respond appropriately. "Self-awareness means having a deep understanding of one's emotions," explain Goleman, Boyatzis and McKee. "Without knowing what we're feeling, we're at a loss to manage those feelings."[18]

What happens when feelings are denied, repressed or covered over by a superficial veneer of "having it together"? When pastors lie to themselves about the way things really are, personal energy is drained away. One pastor admitted,

> I feel like I'm running a forty-yard dash with a sprained ankle. I don't have time to feel. I've got to go to the next thing. And you know, you just get tired.

And another commented,

> What's scary is year after year, if we deny our pain and our losses, we become less and less human. We become like empty shells with the painted face for Jesus. But inside we're empty, and our churches are filled with people who are empty inside.

This is a call for EQ growth.

The Problem of Lack of Reflection. In previous chapters we noticed that a lack of reflection due to busyness can affect spiritual formation and self-care. Understandably, this lack also undermines the development of emotional intelligence. As one pastor mused,

> I wonder if not really knowing how I'm doing is an indicator of how I'm doing. . . . You are all talking about this idea of emotional intelligence and it struck me: I don't know how I'm doing. Maybe I'm just too busy to think about it.

Another pastor acknowledged,

> I can't sleep, can't concentrate. It sounds like depression and probably is. I don't concentrate well. I have a chronic anxiety after the last two years. I'm always anxious about something. I've got all this conflict.

These pastors are working at such a fast pace that they had not reflected on how they were doing until they came to a summit gathering. We know ministry leaders work long hours and that their lifestyle is "taxing, fast-paced, and unrelenting, often characterized by doing two or more tasks at the same time."[19] As a result, they do not take time to reflect on what is happening. A pastor spoke of how the pressing responsibilities of the moment kept him from developing self-awareness.

I had been working on a major seminar for over a year. This included studying the topics I would be presenting as well as recruiting other speakers. It also involved developing publicity for the seminar and recruiting participants, not to mention training a volunteer team to work on registration, refreshments, small-group leadership and behind-the-scenes logistics. Oh, and did I mention the need to write materials for the program? When the program was over Saturday night, everyone said it was a complete success. I was exhausted—mentally, physically and emotionally. But I had to teach Sunday school the next morning to a class of 150 people. And the next week I was scheduled to preach. Reflection on the experience? Are you kidding?! I had too much to do.

Reflection is the discipline to stop and consider what we are thinking and feeling, as well as what we have been doing and saying to others. Growth in emotional intelligence requires the discipline of reflection. But meaningful reflection only happens when we slow down and make time to do it. In the next chapter, we describe several concrete exercises for the practice of reflection toward EQ development.

The Problem of Conflict Avoidance. Most pastors do not like conflict. As one of them insisted, "We view conflict as an anomaly, a problem, an intrusion." There is no question that conflict is messy and that the outcomes from it are impossible to determine. We invited Alfred Poirer, senior pastor of Rocky Mountain Community Church in Billings, Montana, and author of *The Peacemaking Pastor*, to come and talk with us about conflict in the church.[20] From great experience, he commented, "There are so many pastors who have said, 'I am not going to try to resolve this conflict, because I can't control the result, so I'm not going to do anything.'"

Avoiding conflict will inevitably result in a failure to face and address emotions. And by not addressing them, those emotions can begin to control us. Sure signs include the following:

- We try to avoid people on Sunday mornings.
- We don't open emails.
- We won't respond to telephone calls.

- We wish the problems would go away.

- We try to isolate ourselves from reality and the pain that might take place.

But as Jeremiah warned Jerusalem, "You can't heal a wound by saying it's not there!" (Jeremiah 6:14 LB). And in order to grow emotionally, we must face and address conflict.

Our friend Cindy used to be part of a worship ensemble at her church. While she admittedly wasn't very good on the guitar, she enjoyed playing with the group and even jamming together on free nights. The organization of the ensemble was pretty loose. So she didn't think about it much when she wasn't told about rehearsals for a few weeks. But the result was that she was excluded from playing on the following Sundays. After about a month of missing practices, however, she finally asked the worship director, "Why haven't I been told about the practice sessions?"

"Oh, a number of us felt you were holding us back musically, so we decided not to tell you about the rehearsals," he bluntly reported.

"Why didn't you talk with me about it?" Cindy responded.

The music director replied, "We thought it might hurt your feelings."

Needless to say, the avoidant behavior of this staff member and others in the ensemble actually caused deeper hurt to Cindy than an honest conversation about her musical skills would have.

The Challenges of Listening and Expressing Empathy. A crucial component of EQ-others is the ability to listen. Author Donald Phillips comments, "Listening itself is so critical in leadership that any leader who is not a good listener will be a failure."[21] But listening is hard work. One pastor said,

I realize that I don't listen well. I tend to think I know where we ought to go, so I think my job is to go about persuading people. So people don't feel I listen to them as much as I should.

And another pastor said,

Listening is really hard—emotional nakedness makes me feel uncomfortable. I want to run and hide. I want to stuff it and not deal with it.

In order to properly respond to others, we can't *assume* we understand what they are thinking and feeling. Bob can remember arguments he had with his wife, Janet, that went far into the night, only to realize (around 2 a.m.) that he didn't really understand what Janet was saying in the first place! A similar experience of misunderstanding happened to one summit pastor in a congregational meeting. He explained,

> The chair of the building committee was presenting plans for a new education wing. One person in the congregation stood and asked a question about the youth ministry. I assumed this person was against the building proposal. So I stood up and launched into a defense of the youth ministry and why we needed the addition. It turned out that I misread the questioner. She was actually supportive of the ministry and only wanted to learn more of what it was doing.

Getting so caught up in our own agenda that we fail to hear what others are thinking or feeling is easy. But for pastors, it is critical to hear what some have called "the song beneath the words."[22] As one pastor emphasized,

> We could say we love our people. But if we don't know how to find out about their lives, without being artificial about it, we will never connect with them in a way that causes them to feel loved.

Active listening includes the capacity to empathize with the one to whom we are listening. Empathy is the ability to hear and to relate to the feelings of the one to whom we are listening. It also includes the willingness to understand and seriously consider the other's views and objectives, especially when those perspectives differ from our own.

Sarah, a friend of ours who works on the music staff of a church, shared how she developed a new ensemble made up primarily of single adults. After working with this group for a number of months, she asked the pastor if they could present a selection in the worship service. With his agreement, they prepared a piece. At the Friday night rehearsal, the pastor quietly sat in the back of the sanctuary, listening to the group practice. The next morning he told Sarah, "That selection isn't going to work with my sermon." When Sarah explained how hard she had worked with the group and how excited they were about singing in the service, he responded, "That's not my problem. They aren't singing that song in the service." His lack of empathy created a disruption that eventually led a number in the ensemble to leave the church.

Unfortunately, the lack of emotional intelligence demonstrated by this pastor is not unusual. Determined to get what he wanted, he failed to hear Sarah's perspective or to demonstrate any level of concern for her feelings and the interests of the people with whom she worked. He may have been accurate in believing that the musical selection was not a proper fit for the worship service. But the way he stated his views and the lack of care he demonstrated toward Sarah and the ensemble created great feelings of hurt and distrust.

As we consider listening and empathizing as ministry leaders, it may help to think of relationships as the connective tissue of the church. The capacity to listen in such a way that people feel understood conveys the message that they are valued. When pastors fail to demonstrate an understanding of and respect for what others are saying, and especially for what others are feeling, those people will question whether they are appreciated or desired in the congregation.

CONCLUSION

Emotional intelligence involves the dual capacities of EQ-self and EQ-others. In this chapter, we discovered that emotional intelligence plays a critical role in the resilience of pastors to minister for the long haul. We identified a number of common EQ struggles for those in ministry: people-pleasing, emotion-faking, lack of reflection and conflict avoidance. Similarly, we found two significant EQ challenges for pastors: listening and empathy. In the next chapter, we will dig deeper into this subject, looking at specific ways to grow our EQ.

QUESTIONS TO PONDER

1. In what roles and with whom are you currently feeling the pressure to please people and deny your own priorities and values?

2. In what situations do you tend to put on your unflappable pastoral persona? Why? What might be a healthier way to manage your emotions in those situations?

3. Describe how you are currently doing emotionally with as much detail as possible. What new things about yourself become evident?

4. What are methods you use to avoid conflict? How do the signs of conflict avoidance play into your current relationships?

5. To test your EQ-others and to practice empathetic listening, try describing to another how you think they are feeling and then ask them if you are right. Be prepared to follow with a sensitive response and "How can I help?"

8

DEVELOPING EMOTIONAL INTELLIGENCE

The key to learning new habits lies in practice to the point of mastery.

Daniel Goleman, Richard Boyatzis and Annie McKee,
Primal Leadership: Realizing the Power of Emotional Intelligence

IT IS ONE THING TO KNOW ABOUT emotional intelligence. It is another thing to put it into practice. We are reminded of a friend in ministry who has read numerous books on EQ and has even been a trainer on the topic. But when he faced a crisis at work in which he had to listen carefully to coworkers and manage his own reactivity to the circumstances, he failed miserably and hurt others.

Jim Loehr and Tony Schwartz, authors of *The Power of Full Engagement*, explain, "The performance demands that most people face in their everyday work environments dwarf those of any professional athletes we have ever trained. . . . Great athletes spend about 90 percent of their time practicing in order to perform 10 percent of the time."[1] Our ministry friend lacked practice on those EQ skills.

What, then, are the practices that pastors need to develop in the area of emotional intelligence? We will focus on the three key areas that summit pastors identified as most helpful: prayer and worship, exercise, and reflective work. Although some of the topics below have been presented in previous chapters, here they will be specifically applied to the development of EQ for ministry leaders. After exploring these EQ practices, we will briefly discuss congregational EQ and Jesus and EQ.

PRAYER AND PERSONAL WORSHIP FOR PERSPECTIVE

In the chapter on spiritual formation, we learned that prayer and personal worship are both important and difficult for pastors. While prayer and personal worship are significant disciplines for our spiritual formation, they also benefit us with clarity, perspective and emotional calm. We learn to rest in God's love as we focus on his sovereignty over all things and his care for all of his creatures and all of their actions (Zephaniah 3:17). You might remember this pastor's comment from earlier:

> Things get less muddy as I engage with God; things fall into place more. I seem to have a better sense of how to spend my day and what to focus on and what not to do. I don't know how to explain how it happens, but I just know it [does]. [Still] I have to re-remember it every single day.

Another pastor shared how prayer and worship played a critical role in the management of his emotions.

> In the midst of a panic attack, I have to believe that God is in control and pray. God created me with my emotion. He is sovereign over my emotion, and I can cry out in the midst of that and say, "I'm really anxious, and there's nothing I can do, and I want to give it to you."

What we learned from the summit pastors is that the regular, disciplined ritual of daily prayer and worship allowed them to gain perspective on their emotions, which furthered their ability to manage them in the midst of the turmoil and challenges of the day. Prayer and personal worship help develop EQ.

PHYSICAL EXERCISE FOR EMOTIONAL RECOVERY

We saw in the self-care chapter that regular exercise is an important habit. Another benefit of exercise is the role it can play in the management of emotions.[2] Loehr and Schwartz point out that exercise not only sustains one's physical capacity but also provides mental and emotional recovery.[3]

Pastoral ministry naturally comes with emotional strain. Psychologists have coined the term *compassion fatigue* to describe how caring professionals are personally affected by their work. The work of caring and empathy "extracts a cost under most circumstances."[4]

A regular exercise routine provides an important level of relief from the emotional stress that comes with ministry leadership. In addition, physical breaks and light exercise, such as walking around the block or taking the stairs rather than an elevator, also help to relieve the emotional pressures of caregiving and work performance.[5]

We asked a number of pastors how exercise had influenced their ability to handle their emotions. Here are some telling examples.

I used to run in high school, college and even my first year of seminary. Then I quit when responsibilities crowded out the time. Over the last six months, I began running again. I found that when I am upset after a meeting or mad over an offhanded criticism, when I run, those feelings just seem to melt away.

✤ ✤ ✤

I have discovered that I am calmer, that I have a more positive attitude through the day and that I am able to deal with difficult relationships with a better attitude.

✤ ✤ ✤

I have found in the ministry that I cannot afford *not* to exercise. It is the one time, other than my daily prayer and meditation on the Scriptures, that I feel a significant release from the pressures of the day.

REFLECTION PRACTICES FOR EQ

As we saw in previous chapters, reflection plays a vital role in spiritual formation and healthy self-care. The same is true for emotional intelligence. Six specific EQ reflection practices came out of the Pastors Summit experiences and discussions.

Slowing Down to Feel. It is a rare thing for people in Western cultures to deliberately slow down their lifestyles in order to reflect. When we do slow down—usually during a vacation or sickness—we often discover how helpful it is. Sometimes this is followed by a vow to consciously assume a more unhurried lifestyle. But as pressures build and expectations push, soon we find ourselves back in a hectic and unreflective pace once again.

Goleman and his associates state, "The process of slowing down . . . is one we don't see enough in organizations, but that nevertheless is critical."[6] One of the summit pastors described slowing down as "being aware of what is going on inside of you and being able to name those things, not when you are at the verge of collapse, but as you are moving along."

We have all heard of pastors who have succumbed to moral failures. In a conversation about these problems, one participant attributed them, at least in part, to the failure to slow down enough to be aware.

We need to be attentive to what is going on emotionally that leads to inappropriate behaviors. It's not enough just to say to yourself, "Stop doing that!" Instead, we must look deeper.

During a pastoral couples discussion, one spouse shared,

Most of our friends are super-intense about their ministries. Everything is serious. So it is hard to unplug when we are with them. We have found a couple of places in our city—particularly the botanical gardens and the art museum—are places we can go, get away from the daily pressures, take a deep breath and consider what we've been facing.

Journaling. We briefly referenced the discipline of journaling in our chapter on spiritual formation.[7] This activity has long been encouraged as a "way of processing the hopes, fears, longings, angers and prayers of our heart. It can be the place we sound off before God so we don't sound off in an inappropriate way to others."[8] Psychologist Diane Langberg encouraged members of the Pastors Summit to journal, asserting, "Feelings need to be articulated in a safe way. Words allow us to manage feelings rather than being engulfed by them."

Biological research backs this up. EQ researchers Caruso and Salovey reference the work of James Pennebaker, who claims that people who write about their feelings are able to lower their blood pressure and heart rate. They write, "Other researchers have discovered that writing about emotions has a positive impact on our immune system and how we cope with difficult situations."[9]

Here are some journaling practices that promote emotional maturity and EQ development.[10]

- Write for at least twenty minutes a day. Consider developing the helpful ritual of journaling at the same time each day.

- Write without stopping—unplug from people and other distractions to focus on your journal.

- Keep on writing without editing your thoughts. Don't worry about what you say or how you say it.

- Use a book, notebook or word processor to keep your thoughts together in the same place.

Journaling allows us to freely express our feelings and consider how they relate to the experiences of our daily lives. It is one of the most effective methods of accomplishing disciplined reflection. As one of the summit pastors concluded,

---

I used to journal—probably did it for about ten years. It was so healthy and therapeutic for me. And that's one thing I've been thinking about doing again.

Accurately Identifying Emotions. One of the earliest researchers on emotional intelligence was Peter Salovey. Together with coauthor David Caruso, he stressed the importance of identifying—naming and acknowledging—our emotions. "The first step in managing emotions is to be aware of them and accept them," Caruso and Salovey write. "Neither to suppress feelings nor to vent them but to reflect on them, integrate them with our thinking, and use them as a source of information and inspiration for intelligent decision making."[11]

Caruso and Salovey point out three main cues to identifying emotions in ourselves and others.[12] The first is facial expressions. They claim, "If you can focus on a few key principles of emotional expression—focusing on the mouth, eyes, and nose is an especially effective way to ascertain what a person is feeling—you can greatly increase your accuracy of decoding emotions."[13]

In order to learn what you communicate nonverbally through facial expressions, you might need to enlist the help of your spouse or a friend to give you feedback. One of the things that has mystified and enlightened Bob in his married life is when his wife asks, "Why are you looking at me like that?" Early in their marriage, Bob would get angry when Janet said that. But over the years, he has learned that he often gives messages that he doesn't want to send through facial expressions. He has discovered how very valuable his wife's insights regarding his nonverbal messages are.

A second way of becoming aware of emotions is to observe the pitch, rhythm and tone of people's voices. Most likely you have been with someone who has gotten excited. Their pitch often goes up, and they may talk faster and louder as they express their enthusiasm. Similarly, if someone is discouraged, they may lower their tone and speak softly. Consider the differences in pitch, rhythm and tone between fans speaking at a sporting event and friends speaking at a funeral. This comparison immediately clarifies the dramatic difference emotion plays in verbal expressions.

Finally, a third way of identifying emotions is by someone's posture. Again, consider friends at the sporting event over against the funeral. At the sporting event, fans may stand throughout the entire game, waving their arms in excitement. At a funeral, people often have drooped shoulders, bowed heads and an unusually slow pace. One summit pastor shared,

---

When I became aware of these emotional cues of the face, voice and posture, it really helped me understand what emotion I was conveying and how others were feeling.

These three cues are a good place to start identifying emotions. Yet many of us have a very limited understanding of the variety and intensity of emotion. A checklist of adjectives describing varied emotions can be very helpful, so we provide a sample list in appendix C. To try it, make a list of your emotions from the past hour. Then go to the appendix and mark all the words in the list that describe the emotions you felt. How do the two lists compare? How well could you name those emotions? Some use this list at the end of the day, considering their circumstances and how they felt. Others keep the list in their journal so that they can identify the feelings they may be writing about. Still others use it as a "test-retest," exploring how their feelings may have changed from one point of time to another.

Discovering how to better identify emotions deepens the learning process. Many use their journals to record what they are discovering about themselves and others. One friend of ours keeps an audio diary on her smartphone, recording her reflections on situations she has faced or persons she has met.

Exploring Family Genograms. In the first chapter on self-care, we looked at the impact of our family of origin. And as you can imagine, exploring one's family background is very important when working on emotional intelligence. This is often done by constructing a family diagram (also called a *genogram*). A genogram is a visual description of behavioral systems in a family over time. It is a helpful tool for leaders to "see" the family system to which they belong and how their family of origin has influenced their leadership, both positively and negatively. These diagrams generally go back at least three generations. Appendix D provides a description of how to draw and explore a genogram.

Appendix D also provides many questions for "interviewing" the genogram, in order to learn about the systemic impact on one's leadership and EQ. We encourage people to interview their genograms, asking questions to explore any number of categories and emotions. This makes it easy to see patterns of behavior in the family tree. Listen to how the summit pastors and spouses who worked on their genograms responded to the experience:[14]

Doing the family diagram was hard work. I am beginning to realize that I avoid conflict or pain by "doing more," like my dad. Like my mom, I stuff emotions—sadness, anger. I can also be passive-aggressive and use sarcasm, which my children often call me on.

✣ ✣ ✣

Being led into our family history is very helpful. There are things my spouse and I have talked about before—suicide, divorce, affairs, alcoholism and depression. We have acknowledged those as sins of the generations in our families. But how to look at these things in a helpful way was not something we have really understood how to do. I can see that it could take a long time to make real sense.

✣ ✣ ✣

I am beginning to realize that I follow a long history of faithfulness and commitment *without* connection and intimacy. I don't know how to connect intimately with those closest to me. I've never seen it modeled and it is not normal, in my experience. I don't want faithfulness without intimacy: not with God, my marriage or my children. I have no idea how to deeply and emotionally connect—how to truly love.

✣ ✣ ✣

It's very humbling and mind-boggling to think that God put me in my particular family with all of its sinful patterns, conflicts and breakdowns in relationships in order to shape and mold me into a useful servant for his church and kingdom. I normally don't think of using all of these weaknesses as resources. . . . I'd rather avoid them and think that I'm "past" that phase of my life.

✛ ✛ ✛

I always kind of scoffed at looking at family of origin as psychobabble, and I haven't ever done it. Today was the first time I have tried to do it, and I can see it does impact me.

✛ ✛ ✛

I came from a very stable, loving Christian family. And I praise God for that. But one of the results is we just don't see what's happening with us. We see what's happening with everybody else. But we never talk about what's going on with us. So I may battle depression, my brother may battle depression and my father may battle depression. But we don't talk about it.

The impact of identifying emotional patterns from our family backgrounds can be quite profound—at times even overwhelming. It is important to discuss these discoveries and how you want to manage them. If you are married, this could begin with your spouse, who has his or her own family story to share. You may also want to bring a close friend, a partner in ministry or a counselor into the conversation. An important thing to consider is that exploring family genograms is not for the purpose of blaming or attacking others. All families are broken and fallen. There aren't any "clean" family diagrams.[15] We review our family diagrams so that we may grow in our own self-awareness and learn how to identify and respond to the emotions of others.

Differentiating in Order to Connect with People. Emotional reflection leads to the work of differentiation, which we looked at in chapter five on emotions in self-care. There we described differentiation as "the ability to remain connected in relationship to significant people in our lives and yet not have our reactions and behavior determined by them."[16] Family therapy pioneer Murray Bowen coined this idea of differentiation as an important aspect of maturity in families. There is a tension in every family between "togetherness" and "separateness." Some families are bound so tightly together that the members have difficulty functioning as individuals. Other families are made up of members so separated from each other that they function as autonomous units.

Differentiation describes the work toward a healthier relational tension in which members of a family (or any other system such as a church, a small-group Bible study or an office team) can be relationally connected with each other, yet maintain their own beliefs, goals and values, even when others in the system pressure them to change. In order to differentiate, we must be able to understand our emotions and how they are influenced by relationships with others. Conversely, in order to reflect on our emotions, it is necessary for us to differentiate.

It is easier to describe differentiation than to do it. One pastor in the summit shared,

> When I am sitting down with someone, I find myself asking, "What do they think of me as a pastor?" Instead of listening to them and being emotionally engaged, I'm in my own little world. It's all fear of man. I need to be living out the gospel. I need to separate from my own emotions and be available to them.

Another pastor agreed, saying,

> Differentiation is the hardest thing for me. It is so difficult for me to actually uncover who I am: What do I really want? What do I really like? It's frequently easy for me to be a chameleon in stressful or intimidating situations. Being able to say what I want is difficult to determine with any degree of confidence.

Another expressed the challenge of differentiating after being criticized by people in the church. He explained,

> Pastors are the most tangible representation of God. This means congregants often take out their frustration on pastors. It leaves them feeling like a punching bag for congregants when they experience disappointment in life and/or with God. Pastors need good differentiation to withstand this over time.

Differentiation involves not being afraid of others, not avoiding them and not being overly influenced by them. It means remaining connected to people with different opinions, yet not forming our beliefs or making our decisions based on the voice of our parents, the voice of a church officer or even the voice of our spouse. It takes work, and that work includes times of reflection on our emotions. Of course, total differentiation can never happen. We are whole persons, and our emotions are integrated into all aspects of our lives. Understanding what we are feeling and gaining some distance from emotional impact are the primary goals of differentiation.

Receiving Feedback from Others. In so many ways, we all have much to gain from the feedback from others. When it comes to understanding and reflecting on our emotions, this is particularly important. As one summit pastor said, "I must listen to my spouse and others to know what is seen and perceived outside of myself."

An example of this need for feedback is seen in what we earlier wrote on nonverbal communication. Unless we are working very hard to control our nonverbal cues, we are often unaware of them. Unless we receive feedback from others, we will be unaware of what we are communicating, and we will fail to understand the emotions behind our silent messages.

Helpful feedback can come from family, peer groups and confidants. Occasionally it may come from others, like the volunteer who ran the projector and confronted her pastor about his angry expressions. However, most people, even within our circle of family and close friends, won't have the courage or concern to give us this feedback. We must seek it out.

For the pastors in the summit, the safety of their peer group provided a place to increase their emotional intelligence with lots of feedback. One pastor shared that the thing he valued most about being involved in a cohort was "the benefit of learning to deal with emotions."

QUESTIONS TO PONDER

1. How much do you value your personal prayer and worship times? Why?

2. What would your weekly schedule look like if you planned to exercise on the typically most stressful days?

3. What tasks would have to come off your plate in order to give yourself space for reflection work? What are the costs of not building in this time?

4. When are you conscious of naming your emotional state to yourself? When are you conscious of identifying the emotions of those you work with?

5. What are the emotional patterns of response to failure in your genogram?

6. When do you tend to feel intimidated by others? How do you respond to these feelings?

7. Who can provide honest feedback to you about the emotions you communicate to others?

DEVELOPING CONGREGATIONAL EQ

One of the most important outcomes of pastors working on their emotional intelligence is the impact it can have on their congregations. When the leaders of a church have low EQ, it affects the entire church. During a conversation on EQ at a summit, one pastor pondered out loud,

---

I increasingly see that I am not . . . very aware of the [emotional aspects] of my personality. . . . I see similar traits in my father. I also see my weakness in this area reflected in the church I pastor. The church is emotionally and relationally underdeveloped. I need to mature in this area.

Organizations will rarely ever rise in maturity level above that of their leaders, because systemic forces prevent the development. But when a pastor exhibits strong emotional intelligence, over time it will raise the emotional maturity of the congregation. Ordained rabbi and family therapist Edwin Friedman writes, "The capacity of members of the clergy to contain their own anxiety regarding congregational matters, both those not related to them, as well as those where they become the identifiable focus, may be the most significant capability in their arsenal. Not only can such capacity enable religious leaders to be more clear-headed about solutions, but because of the systemic effect that a leader's functioning always has on an entire organism, a non-anxious presence will modify anxiety throughout the entire congregation."[17]

In other words, one of the most important pastoral skills for helping further the maturity and growth of a church may be the pastor's ability to remain calm. It takes high EQ to remain calm in ministry leadership. Friedman's comments correspond to those of a summit pastor who said, "When pastors and their spouses work on their own emotional health, it is a real gift to the church."

Another summit pastor, Nick, shared that he had been working on his own emotional intelligence and that it had already helped his church. He confided,

> My wife has been my primary EQ consultant. God has used her more than anyone else in helping me understand how I am feeling and how it is impacting others. This, in turn, has helped me to trust God more and calm down in the midst of difficult times.

Nick went on,

> As we entered our building project, I told the congregation that the biggest challenge was not financial. Rather, it was how we would relate to one another as decisions were made and implemented. Would we demand our own way? Or would we respect and submit to one another?

Time and again, Nick found that he was called upon to be a calm presence at anxious moments.

> One particular problem stands out. We had a good-hearted man coordinating one aspect of the project who had no idea how he was impacting others. I had person after person come to me complaining about the way they had been treated. I would listen, prayerfully telling myself to calm down while they shared. Then I would pray with them and tell them to go back to the man who hurt them. That kind of differentiation is hard. I'd like to go solve the problem myself. But even though things have been messy, I see God maturing us as a congregation.

QUESTIONS TO PONDER

1. How would you describe the emotional maturity level of the people you lead? What are their emotional strengths and struggles?

2. In what ways do their EQ description and their emotional struggles correlate to your own?

3. What is your capacity to remain calm in the midst of your own and others' anxiety?

JESUS AND EQ

It is fascinating to consider how Jesus exhibited perfect emotional intelligence—being a calm presence in the midst of a highly anxious environment—and the impact it still has for us today. In a passage from Hebrews, the author explains: "For we do not have a high priest who is unable to sympathize with our weaknesses, but one who in every respect has been tempted as we are, yet without sin. Let us then with confidence draw near to the throne of grace, that we may receive mercy and find grace to help in time of need. For every high priest chosen from among men . . . can deal gently with the ignorant; and wayward, since he himself is beset with weakness" (Hebrews 4:15-16; 5:1-2).

This passage says that our high priest, Jesus, is able to empathize with us—what we would call EQ-others—because he was exposed to testing even as we are. We could say that Jesus expresses emotional intelligence toward us (that is, sympathizes with us) because he learned emotional intelligence through temptation.

At least two things come as a result of Jesus's emotional intelligence in this passage. First, we can have confidence in prayer, drawing near to the throne of grace, because we know that Jesus is sympathetic to us and to our weaknesses. He treats us with compassionate emotional intelligence.

Second, as a result, those who are appointed by God to serve his people ought to treat others with sympathy. This is illustrated by the fact that the high priest should demonstrate emotional maturity toward others ("he can deal gently with the ignorant and wayward") because he is constantly aware of his own sin. In his commentary on Hebrews, Bill Lane explains that the description of the high priest's actions "means to restrain or moderate one's feelings, and so to deal gently and considerately with another."[18] EQ-self grows and develops through a personal understanding and application of the grace and mercy of the gospel, so that EQ-others can be extended to others in Jesus' name.

QUESTIONS TO PONDER

1. When you read about the death and resurrection of Lazarus in John 11, what emotions can you observe and name?

2. How does Jesus demonstrate perfect EQ-self and EQ-others in the story? What surprises you about these observations?

CONCLUSION

We have explored the messy subject of emotions and discovered how urgently we need to grow our skills in being able to work *with* emotions. Our ministry leadership and fruitfulness depends on it. Failure to manage well our own emotions easily leads to the injury of other people and can lead to our own demise in ministry. Although our EQ has been formed while growing up, it can still be developed and matured with practice. How wonderful it is to serve our God, who knows exactly how we feel. In the next two chapters, we expand our study of intelligence into the area of understanding ourselves and others according to our differences in culture. Even if our EQ is high, we can completely misunderstand others if their cultural assumptions are not the same as our own.

RECOMMENDATIONS FOR FURTHER READING

1. Travis Bradberry and Jean Greaves. *Emotional Intelligence 2.0*. San Diego: TalentSmart, 2009.

2. Daniel Goleman, Richard Boyatzis and Annie McKee. *Primal Leadership: Realizing the Power of Emotional Intelligence*. Boston: Harvard Business School Press, 2002.

3. Peter Scazzero. *The Emotionally Healthy Church*. Grand Rapids: Zondervan, 2003.

4. Peter L. Steinke. *Congregational Leadership in Anxious Times*. Herndon, Va.: The Alban Institute, 2006.

MEDIA WORTH EXPLORING

Each of these three films explores aspects of knowing oneself and others.

1. *Wit* (2001), rated PG-13. This award-winning film with Emma Thompson is about a professor who reassesses her life and the purpose of life while fighting and dying from ovarian cancer. The professor's illness forces a reconsideration of her lifelong commitment to autonomy and the need for relationships in her hour of great need.

2. *Living Old* (2006). PBS Frontline addresses the increasing challenges of an aging U.S. society including long-term care, family dynamics and end-of-life decision making. This film, and its companion website on pbs.org, provides sobering discussion material for many who face the realities of growing old and caring for seniors.

3. *Stranger Than Fiction* (2006), rated PG-13. Will Ferrell's character hears a running commentary on his life and wonders about the meaning of life. The film prompts questions such as how the biblical storyline helps us deepen our self-awareness and our awareness of others.

4. For helpful visuals, posters and flyers for naming emotions, see Creative Therapy Associate's website. Their "Feelings Page" and "What's Behind Your Anger Wheel" are particularly helpful visuals and lists: www.ctherapy.com/web_directory.asp.

EXPLORING CULTURAL DIFFERENCES

Now the apostles and the brothers who were throughout Judea heard

that the Gentiles also had received the word of God. So when Peter went up

to Jerusalem, the circumcision party criticized him, saying, "You went to

uncircumcised men and ate with them." But Peter began and explained it to them.

Acts 11:1-4

ALONSO IS A HISPANIC PASTOR MINISTERING in the States. He shared with us his experience of being credentialed in a denomination of traditional Western European origin. After he passed his ordination examination, a respected denominational leader approached him and said, "Your worship style isn't biblical. But I'm sure after being with us for a few years, you will come to understand how true worship is to take place." Months after this incident, Alonso was still upset, alternately experiencing feelings of anger and depression. His experience is similar to that of many minorities trying to partner with Anglos.[1] All involved have much to learn about engaging well with those from other cultures.

David Livermore, executive director of the Global Learning Center, shares statistics that suggest a radical cultural transformation is occurring in the United States. He explains that 45 percent of all children in the States aged five and under are people of color. In the last ten years, the Asian population has increased 43 percent. And there are more Hispanics in the United States than there are in Spain. By 2040, Anglos will no longer be the majority population.[2]

Unless we close our eyes, we see the impact of globalization everywhere. Businesses have come to accept that they are functioning in a global workplace. This requires them to be sensitive to different cultures and to spend resources "analyzing them as they are encountered, identifying what is required of people from other cultures, and engaging in appropriate interactions with them."[3] Globalization requires that Christians, and especially pastors, recognize that, as Dave Gibbons writes, "we're living in the middle of a transition that will mark the way we do church for the next century."[4]

One result of this phenomenon has been the coinage of the term *cultural intelligence*, or CQ. It refers to the ability "to function effectively across various cultural contexts."[5] People often assume CQ means the ability to adapt to overseas environments. But as several authors point out, the ideas behind cultural intelligence are "just as likely to be relevant to someone who is moving from one region to another of his or her home country, changing business units within a large company, or moving across functional areas."[6] We don't draw on our limited CQ merely to engage our immigrant neighbors in conversation. CQ is needed for many changes in our lives.

In this chapter and the next, we will share how summit pastors recognized CQ as an important factor for resilient ministry. We will also introduce you to concepts needed for a basic understanding of CQ and point you to other helpful resources for growing your cultural intelligence. Though it would take several books to do these topics justice, the first step in increasing our CQ abilities is to raise our awareness of the many types of cultural differences and of the ways they affect our ministries. This first chapter seeks to do just that. The next focuses on how we can grow in our cultural intelligence. Then, with our eyes open to the challenges for our ministries, we will be more able to withhold judgment, observe, appreciate and work with cultural differences to the benefit of all.

WHAT IS CULTURE?

Culture has been described as "patterned ways of thinking, feeling, and reacting to various situations and actions,"[7] and as "the programming that shapes who we are and who we are becoming."[8] When teaching about culture, Tasha finds it helpful to display a city map. As a child, you didn't think about where you grew up by using a map. You unconsciously moved throughout your childhood neighborhood, learning about it by living there. Similarly, culture usually functions in the unconscious or unspoken behavior of people because it was caught, not taught. We learned our native cultures by living life.

Culture can be compared to a map that charts where and how a specific group of people lives. Culture provides the values, emotions, belief systems, ideals, ideas, customs, assumptions and practices for the group. Cultures are created by people in specific places to meet specific needs. They can change over time, and they contain both truth and error.

Maps have standard formatting and labeling characteristics. However, local maps may have different scales and keys for interpretation. Even if you and I have the same map, we may still arrive at the destination via different routes. Similarly, even if we come from the same culture, we will always view things from our own unique perspective.

Our native cultural responses are so deeply ingrained that we usually find them very difficult to change. While the impact of globalization means people look more and more alike on the outside, people will still have very different cultures, or road maps, for living on the inside. These maps include values and behaviors, as well as ways of thinking and feeling. All of these are deeply rooted in the contexts and worldviews in which individuals are raised.

WHAT CULTURAL DOMAINS AFFECT PASTORS?

Cultural domains are, according to David Livermore, "the various kind of cultures and subcultures in which we find ourselves."[9] He comments, "Most of us ministering in the twenty-first century are faced with dozens of cultural contexts even in one day of work."[10] Through discussing these matters in the Pastors Summit, we have identified seven cultural domains that affect pastors on a regular basis.

The Personal as a Cultural Domain. All people have personal backgrounds and histories that usually operate below the surface but strongly influence their behavior. The personal cultural domain is made up of many factors, including our family of origin, the broader context in which we grew up and (for many) a "home church" experience.

Personal culture from family of origin. The comment made by Pete Scazzero is worth repeating: "Almost everything I had learned about life had come from my original family." This includes deeply ingrained messages, habits and ways of behaving that create a "gravitational pull" to familiar patterns of living.[11]

Few pastors have pondered how their upbringing has shaped the way they think about culture (their "hidden map" for living life). For example, after doing a three-generation family diagram, one Anglo summit pastor shared,

---

My father and grandfather were both raised by African American nannies. And we had a black housekeeper when I was growing up. Until I did this family diagram, I never realized the impact that background has had on my relationship with people of other ethnicities.

If you take our previous suggestion to create a family diagram, one of the topics you can review is your family culture. Some questions you can ask yourself about your family cultural background include the following.

- When it came to education, career, sports, hobbies and social involvement, what were the expectations placed on you within your family? What were the responses when you attained or failed to attain in these areas?

- What events and circumstances did your family celebrate? How did they celebrate?

- What did your family believe the purpose of life is? How did your family deal with death?

- According to your family, what are the characteristics of the ideal lifestyle? The ideal father and mother? The ideal child?

- What rituals or customs or behaviors did your family perform on a daily basis? On a weekly basis? On a yearly basis?

It often requires leaving home to see that our family culture is not universal. Tasha recalls being surprised by her new college friends. Many of them did not receive big boxes of gifts on their birthdays. Neither did they expect or desire to go further for graduate degrees. Some of them called home every week. Others didn't eat dark green vegetables, and many failed to clean their plates at dinner, throwing food away without concern. Their assumptions about life were often very different from ones that Tasha unconsciously held. From the silly to the morally bound, the cultural markers that college students bring from home have many hidden differences.

Personal culture from broader contexts of childhood. Beyond our family of origin, we also have been deeply influenced by the broader cultural context of our upbringing. For some, this context was very stable throughout childhood and adolescence. Donald grew up in a small community outside of Pittsburgh, Pennsylvania. Most adult residents were employed in a variety of small family businesses, worked in the local steel plant or labored in area manufacturing plants. Many extended families either lived under one roof or within a few blocks of each another. For decades, most of the town's residents had been born there, lived there, retired there and died there. You knew your neighbors, and your neighbors knew you.

Tasha grew up in a very different environment, high in the mountains of northern New Mexico. The one known statistic about her very small hometown was that it had more doctoral degrees per square mile than anywhere in the world. High standards of educational performance were expected of the children. College and graduate schools were an assumed part of becoming an adult. Yet no one used formal titles to address each other. Children referred to adult friends by their first names. People knew their neighbors but had no extended family in the state.

In comparison, Bob grew up just outside Washington, D.C. It was typical for him to have classmates whose parents were from the diplomatic corps of another country or who worked in a government agency or on Capitol Hill. Conversations in the classroom could quickly move from sports to international affairs. One day in middle school, Bob skipped class and hitchhiked downtown to view General Douglas MacArthur's body lying in the Capitol rotunda. Then he and his friends spent the rest of the day collecting passes into the Senate and House chambers from congressional offices.

Where we grew up and who we hung out with influences our taste in food (pierogi or chili peppers?), our language (is *y'all* singular or plural?), our musical tastes (sitar or bagpipes?), our architectural perceptions (colonial or adobe?), what we wear (preppie, retro or grunge?) and our sports preferences (soccer or football—or are they the same thing?). More than these things, our childhood experiences became to us "the way the world is supposed to be" and "the way people are supposed to live in it." The strong preferences we have as adults often stem from the deep cultural assumptions of our childhood.

As we grew up, we often assumed that the rest of the world was like us until we were confronted with an alternative perspective. Bob first experienced this with his buddy Whit in the eighth grade. Whit's family had moved to the D.C. area from southern California just before the new school year. For the first few months, Whit constantly referenced "how things were in L.A." Finally, one day a classmate (not Bob) was fed up and said, "You're not in California! Get used to it or move back."

If a pastor is never exposed to different cultural expressions while growing up, or while in university or seminary, learning to live and minister in a different context could be a major adjustment. At the same time, we have seen many instances in which pastors and their families have learned to change and grow in contexts different from the environment of their upbringing. We will be looking at factors that promote such growth in the next chapter.

Personal culture from home church experience. About 40 percent of the summit pastors were raised in some type of church environment. Some grew up in a church that continues to influence them in a positive manner. Their experience was like Donald's; he will always be grateful for the grounding that his hometown church provided. Others, however, grew up in a church culture that they have no desire to replicate. One friend finds it very hard to worship if the church simply *looks* like her home church. A summit pastor shared, "My home church was spiritually dead. It was no better than a social club." The majority of summit pastors grew up with no church background at all.

The home church experience of pastors (positive, negative or no church) provides a cultural framework that continues to influence their lives. For example, one summit pastor recently went to see the movie *The Help*, which relates the story of African American women in Jackson, Mississippi, during the 1960s. He shared,

---

This movie was a reflection of the culture of my upbringing in the South. As I ponder that, I see how much I've lived in reaction to the church of my childhood. While this involves a rejection of the social customs of those days, it also includes a dismissal of some elements of that liturgical tradition which really weren't so bad.

Bob once worked with a pastor who grew up in a church with a series of male pastors who were passive and ineffectual. In his adolescence, this man came to faith in a neighboring congregation where, Bob's friend said, the pastor was "a man's man." How would you define this term "man's man"? What picture does it create in your mind? Whatever caricature it created in the imagination of this future pastor has directly influenced his view of the ministry.

QUESTIONS TO PONDER

1. What aspects of your childhood neighborhood and hometown do you most appreciate? How have these defined your expectations of how "things ought to be"?

2. What was your church or nonchurch experience from birth to adulthood? How would you describe the religious culture of your upbringing? What aspects of it can you affirm? What parts do you challenge?

3. In what ways might your childhood experiences have positively and negatively affected your current vision of the church and your perspective on leadership in it? How have these experiences from the past shaped your description of an ideal ministry?

Generation as Cultural Domain. Sociologists have outlined the various generations reflected in the Western world with category names like *builders* (born before 1946), *baby boomers* (born after World War II and before the mid-1960s), *generation Xers* (born between the mid-1960s and the 1970s) and *millennials* (also known as Generation Y).[12] Broad generalizations based on generational statistics are not always helpful, but there is no question that different cultural perspectives and commitments are reflected by each generation. And these do affect ministry.

The first example most think of in the church is the use of drums, electronic equipment and style of music for Sunday morning worship. A second example can be seen in preaching. Bob's homiletics class in seminary was taught by a well-known preacher of the builder generation. This teacher sternly emphasized that pastors should never share about their personal lives from the pulpit. Fast forward thirty-five years to the comment of one of the summit pastors:

I think you have no credibility in our cultural context if you don't honestly share your own struggles as an element of communication in your pulpit.

Another interesting illustration of generational differences has to do with leadership. The common paradigm of leadership in the builder and boomer generations is that of the hero leader. This describes authority figures who, on their own, decide where the organization should be going and how to get there. Their goal is to get people to follow them. Leadership is reduced to a combination of grand knowing and salesmanship.[13] But this perspective is changing. Authors James Kouzes and Barry Posner have captured this shift, commenting that today "truly inspirational leadership is about inspiring a *shared* vision, not about selling their own vision [that] comes from the top down."[14]

It is important for pastors to recognize that their generational framework significantly affects their perspectives. One of the best ways to become aware of these tendencies is to initiate sincere dialogue with persons of other generations, both above and below your own. Of course, this requires that we slow down long enough to ask questions and listen to these persons. If you don't have any cross-generational relationships, you should make time for them. You (and your church) will be enriched through them.

Church as Cultural Domain. The church where you currently worship or work has a distinct culture. While you might think that culture is described by the written vision and values found in official documents, those statements usually do not reflect the real ethos of the congregation. For example, we have a friend who talked to a church about becoming their pastor. He was pleased to see that the official documents listed discipleship as a church goal. So he carefully explained how he believed in discipleship. What this pastor meant by discipleship was that the majority of members should be involved in a structured small group. When he visited the church, however, he learned that their idea of discipleship was that the pastor would visit each family at least once a year in their homes.

Organizational culture can be defined as "the way we do things around here."[15] Any group with a set of shared experiences has a culture. Church organizations have distinct personalities. It is reflected in the office furniture, what members wear, what stories the organization tells itself, who the organization's heroes are and what members brag about.[16]

Every church develops and perpetuates various policies and rules, ideas and beliefs, myths and rituals, and language. As people integrate into the church, they are socialized into the ways of the community. Members' actions and attitudes mirror subtle rituals and practices reflecting expectations for proper conduct.[17] For example, a friend of ours recently moved from a church where everyone wore informal clothing (shorts or blue jeans) to a congregation in which business casual was the norm for dress. The difference in clothing reflects a major cultural transition for our friend.

Organization behaviorists Goffee and Jones share that an organization's social glue is not found in its formal structure but in the relationships of the participants.[18] They propose a model to evaluate the relational dynamics of any organization, be it a church, a community group or a business. They suggest that there are two general principles of why people interact with one another: sociability and solidarity. These can help describe the organizational culture.

On the one hand, *sociability* refers to emotional and personal relationships between people who see one another as friends or companions. Friends share certain ideas, attitudes, interests and values and are inclined to associate on equal terms with almost no expectations of deals or obligation. On the other hand, *solidarity* describes a goal-focused cooperation between people who may be very different from one another. It reflects a context in which people work together to get the job done, not necessarily because they like one another or hold to common interests and values beyond the job.

It is possible to reframe these terms into church dynamics by using *home* for sociability and *mission* for solidarity.[19] Goffee and Jones developed a typology of organizational cultures that can be applied to church systems. As you review this framework in table 9.1 below, consider your church and where it might fit within the four contexts and what direction it is moving.

A friend became the pastor of a church in Louisiana. After two weeks on the job, one of the elders, a member of an influential family, invited him to go on a fishing trip. Out in the boat the conversation focused on the church, particularly on whether or not officers ever rotated off the ruling board. Between casts the officer said, "You know, Pastor, around here, we don't rotate officers. . . . We rotate pastors." The pastor got the message. This was a tightly networked church, and he better not try to mess with this cultural rule.

Table 9.1. Ministry Organizational Culture Based on Relational Dynamics

	HIGH HOME	LOW HOME
HIGH MISSION	*Communal Organization* This is the environment most churches desire to have. It is a place where members are interpersonally attracted to one another, yet missional goals are set, accomplished and celebrated. However, communal organizations are inherently unstable. On the one hand, friendship networks tend to solidify, shifting toward a networked culture. Or programs can begin to dominate, negating relational priorities and thus moving the church toward a mercenary culture.	*Mercenary Organization* Here people cooperate together to get what each person individually desires. The prevailing attitude is, "If you help me achieve my goals and desires, I am attracted to you." Large churches often reflect this environment, where members come to have personal needs met and the staff uses people, and the resources people bring, to accomplish the agenda.
LOW MISSION	*Networked Organization* This setting has great loyalty and sincere friendships— a club-like atmosphere— where strong rituals reinforce the community. However, these strong relationships accomplish little, if anything, from a missional perspective. Many churches fit into this category.	*Fragmented Organization* In this environment, people derive benefit from the autonomy and freedom granted to members. There is a lack of coordinated efforts while people pursue their own agendas. Not many churches could remain viable as a fragmented organization.

QUESTIONS TO PONDER

1. Based on this four-part model, how would you classify your current church or ministry culture?

2. How long have you been involved in your current organization? What have you had to change or modify in order to assimilate? How has your involvement influenced the organization to change?

3. How has your involvement in this ministry changed your relationships or your sense of mission?

Denomination as Cultural Domain. If you are ministering within a denomination, you are part of a unique culture. And if you are non-denominational, you also maintain unique cultural characteristics. One dominant cultural theme is theological convictions, such as Lutheran, Wesleyan/Arminian, Roman Catholic or Reformed. Within these theological families are spectrums that range from fundamentalist viewpoints to liberal persuasions. Other cultural nuances within denominations have to do with governance structures, ethnic traditions or social concerns.[20]

Cultural subgroups within denominations, which reflect the convictions of leaders, members and churches, often exist. An example of denominational subgroups can be seen in a paper delivered by Tim Keller reflecting on his own denomination, the Presbyterian Church in America (PCA).[21] He describes three primary subgroups within this denomination, each with their own theological, sociological and programmatic agendas. One he calls the *culturalists*, because of their desire to affect the culture with the gospel. A second he calls the *pietists*, due to their emphasis on personal spirituality. And the third he calls the *doctrinalists*, based on their emphasis on theological precision. In local, regional and national meetings, the programs of these subgroups vie for attention and emphasis.

If you or your congregation is in a denomination (or your ministry is in an organization), then the culture of that broader community, as well as subgroups within it, will influence your life, ministry and assumptions.

QUESTIONS TO PONDER

1. How would you list the cultural nuances of your denomination or organization? What are the governance structures, and how are they used? What are the ethnic traditions? What are the key social concerns?

2. What issues tend to be of most concern at the organization level?

3. What things are most celebrated at the organization level?

Geography and Demographics as Cultural Domains. Sometimes people assume that they can move from one geographic region of the country to another and experience little or no difference in cultural norms. However, this naive perspective is usually shattered once people make the transition. One summit pastor from southwest Florida commented,

My church is full of "snowbirds" who decided they want to live down here. It usually takes three to four years before they figure out whether they like it or move back North.

Another pastor said,

There is a need to contextualize your approach to the people in your area, because issues over which people in different contexts are going to fight are very different.

Jim Plueddemann is the former international director of Serving In Mission (SIM) and now professor and chair of the mission and evangelism department at Trinity Evangelical Divinity School. Although he has navigated cultural contexts all of his missionary life, he shares that one of the most challenging took place in a geographical domain in the United States. He explains, "I served for three years on the board of a school in the southern part of the United States. The board asked me not to serve for a second term, and I painfully learned that there was much about Southern culture and leadership that I didn't understand. I am still reflecting on my leadership style on that board and also about the cultural leadership ethos of that school. I learned that some of the trickiest cross-cultural challenges can occur within what we think is our own culture, but in reality is a unique subculture."[22]

Even within the same geographic area, the demographic makeup of an area can change within a short period of time, and thus change the culture. Last year Bob and his wife drove through the area where they had planted a church and raised their family for seven years. They were surprised by how quickly the demographic conditions of the area had changed. One summit pastor addressed a similar transition in the community where his congregation is located. He explained,

I'd say about ten years ago we recognized that the community in which we existed as a church was undergoing massive change. Demographic change. People movement. Churches were closing their doors right and left. And so we asked, "Well, why are we here? What's our purpose?" Out of that came a sense of what we believe we are called to be in this community.

Socioeconomic Status as Cultural Domain. Pastors often confront the stark realities of social and financial differences within their congregations with no preparation for how to lead people of such diversity. Socioeconomics is the study of the complex relationship between economics and society. The main concerns of socioeconomics focus on financial resources, employment, education and ethnic diversity. Our personal cultural domains are shaped by our socioeconomic status—that is, by our social and financial experiences and realities. To the extent that these experiences are common to a location, they will help define the geographic cultural domain as well. The key socioeconomic factors that shape us are our educational level, income level, lifestyle preferences and opportunities, and profession or occupation.

When we meet someone new, we experience the weight of cultural assumptions that our society places on socioeconomic status. What is the first question a new acquaintance asks us upon being introduced? It is often, "What do you *do?*" In many other countries, one would likely be asked, "How is your family?" When we state our occupation, we know that many assumptions about us will be attached to our simple answer. For example, upon hearing of someone's profession, we probably make assumptions about their values, feelings, political preferences, lifestyle choices and daily routines. Tasha has even had people tell her what type of car she ought to be driving because of her husband's occupation. Although North Americans are technically not a class-based society, we tie many cultural values to our socioeconomic status.

Numerous participants in the Pastors Summit serve churches in communities with a wide variety of backgrounds. For example, one worked in a church whose congregants ranged from illegal immigrants to people with doctoral degrees. Others shared about neighborhoods that spanned from millionaires to Section Eight housing developments. Ministering to these diverse environments requires a willingness to learn, grow and embrace differences. Building community within such diversity requires the culture of the church itself to become one of high CQ, valuing the differences and perceiving them as opportunities for growth and maturity.

Socioethnicity as Cultural Domain. When we think of cultural intelligence, it is the socioethnic domain that usually comes to mind. While every country has an overarching culture, many subcultures exist within a single community. Today's ministries *must* account for a growing racial and ethnic diversity. As one pastor bluntly stated,

My whole ministry DNA is white, middle-class. And there's a train coming down the track that shows this will no longer be the dominant culture. My view is becoming more and more ghettoized.

The apostle Paul—a crosscultural missionary—was explicit in stating that in Christ, "there is neither Jew nor Greek, there is neither slave nor free, there is no male and female, for you are all one in Christ Jesus" (Galatians 3:28). Yet as Michael Emerson and Christian Smith explain in *Divided by Faith*, "White evangelicalism likely does more to perpetuate racialized society than to reduce it."[23]

This sad fact underlines the need for pastors and congregations to grow in the area of cultural intelligence. It is unfortunate but true that when dominant majority Christians reach out to minority culture Christians, they usually do it with an attitude of "Come—be like us." One pastor shared,

We say we want to be multicultural, but we don't want to change. We want others to adapt to us. How do I preach, how do I work with my people, how do I work on myself to develop a bigger, broader understanding?

QUESTIONS TO PONDER

1. How would you gather information in order to accurately identify the cultural realities of your geographic region?

2. How do they compare with the geographic culture of your childhood?

3. What are the demographics of your area: the education levels, occupations, employment rates and lifestyles? In what ways is discrimination of any form evident?

4. What are the ethnicities represented in your community? What are their cultural distinctives? How could your ministry welcome and celebrate some of these cultural differences?

In the next chapter we will describe cultural intelligence in more detail, discuss the most significant aspects of CQ for ministry leaders and suggest ways to develop our CQ. Then we will list a number of resources that we recommend for further study.

10

IMPROVING CULTURAL
INTELLIGENCE

Every culture, being a human construct, is a mixture of good and evil, truth and

error, beauty and ugliness. Daniel and his friends [in the OT narrative] resolved to

assimilate all that was good in Chaldean culture but were equally determined to

reject everything that was incompatible with their revealed faith.

John Stott, *Through the Bible, Through the Year*

WHY WOULD A POINT GUARD ON THE New York Knicks create a furor even among persons who cared little about his sport? For a few weeks in February 2012, the name Jeremy Lin became a household word as "Linsanity" swept the nation. Why did he create such a stir? Because this Asian American graduate of Harvard University personalized the longing of his ethnic group to be respected and understood as more than "brainy kids." Further, his words highlighted the need for all Americans to acknowledge this influential and growing minority. It has been a call for all of us to increase our cultural intelligence.

As we've noted, the term *cultural intelligence* describes the ability "to function effectively across various cultural contexts."[1] But what does it mean for ministry leaders to function effectively? It includes a number of things: communicating clearly without causing conflict from misunderstandings; behaving in a manner that accounts for cultural values and does not unnecessarily give offense; and ministering to others in love, with respect and appreciation for differences. These CQ skills are increasingly needed not only for our ministry leaders but also for the whole church.

Ultimately, we can be hopeful that we are ministering out of CQ when we see the fruit of the Spirit in our own lives and the lives of those from another culture. We are ministering out of CQ when we build trust across fences. The need to rely on CQ for ministry within one's own country is becoming as important as it is for adapting to overseas environments. For members of a dominant culture, however, learning to appreciate the differences of the Other on one's home turf can be very challenging.[2]

The multicultural transitions described in the last chapter show that ministry in the twenty-first century will involve working with people who have radically different perspectives on life and the world. It is not unlike the experience of Daniel and other Jews who were forced into the new cultural environment of Babylon. CQ involves engaging in cultural discernment and biblical wisdom in order to understand the "other" culture as well as our own.

CULTURAL DISCERNMENT WITH BIBLICAL WISDOM

Cultural intelligence includes the ability to discriminate between cultural preferences and biblical imperatives. But in order to discern between the two, one has to identify them first. It is far too easy to assume that our own cultural background represents the biblical norm and that another person's culture does not. Since our culture is usually all we've experienced, we often assume it is right. For example, the Western European framework of the Anglo majority in the States is not the only acceptable cultural pattern for Christians to follow. Although it *feels* wrong to some, others' ways of living are not necessarily unbiblical because they are different from those "back home."

Even when we can identify differences between cultures, we are still not ready to evaluate them. When it comes to discerning the difference between biblical norms and cultural preferences, we ministry leaders have much to learn. David Livermore points out that "the various studies examining cultural intelligence among American ministry leaders reveal their subjects' limited awareness of how significantly culture shapes the way one reads the Bible."[3] We read our Bibles with cultural blinders on.

CQ requires us first to examine our own culture and the preconceived ideas that we bring to the Bible. Bible study is a crosscultural endeavor. Its original hearers and writers were not from our culture. To deepen our biblical understanding, we need to use CQ to learn about the cultures in the Bible. When we grasp the intent and understanding within the original cultures, then we are able to translate the biblical principles to our own culture.

Withholding Judgment on Cultural Differences. From his wealth of global experience and expertise in anthropology, Paul Hiebert summarizes well the challenge we all face in ministering across cultures: "Two of the greatest problems faced by missionaries entering new cultures are misunderstandings and premature judgments. These are particularly damaging because we are generally unaware of them. As individuals we have strong convictions about reality. Rarely do we stop to ask whether others see it as we do, since it seems so obvious that things are as we see them."[4]

Misunderstanding and premature judgments can harm our ministries. Our lack of cultural awareness can be a primary cause of this damage. If we assume our perspective reflects the viewpoint of everyone else in our growing multicultural environment, then our interpretations of others' actions will likely be inaccurate and inappropriate.

Another root cause of misunderstanding stems from a lack of critical observations regarding our *own* cultural makeup. Everyone is culturally biased. To grow out of our bias, we need to learn to name our cultural values. Then, seeing that these values are not absolute, we can either affirm or challenge them. This will free us to appreciate other cultures. In God's common grace, all cultures will have areas worth emulating and areas needing biblical correction. However, Hiebert cautions, "We can develop such a perspective only if we avoid premature judgments and seek to understand and appreciate another culture deeply before we evaluate it."[5]

Why is it so easy to quickly make negative judgments about others before we understand them? *Negative attribution theory* helps to explain this very human and harmful pattern.[6] This theory tells us that people tend to attribute negative characteristics to things that are new and not understood. In other words, we tend to assume things in a new culture are not merely *different* but *wrong*, or at least inadequate.

Think of a young child at the dinner table. A parent sets a plate of food in front of her. One of the dishes is new, and she has never eaten it before. How does she respond? "I hate that!" To which the parent replies in frustration, "But you've never had it before." This girl's response to the new food is negative attribution at work. To fight against this tendency, we must consciously withhold judgments about others who are different from ourselves. Then we will have two further tasks to pursue: seeking knowledge about their culture and trying to communicate clearly.

One of our summit groups was made up of pastors who had been friends together in seminary. Two of these pastors had moved across the country and were working in a very different cultural environment than the others. One morning a group member told Bob that they had stayed up late into the night challenging the two ministering across the country because of a perceived attitude that their ministry was more culturally "cutting edge." The others sensed the negative attribution these two had made toward their culturally different ministries and called them out on it.

Evaluating Culture with Humility. CQ does involve making informed evaluations and judgments. The more we grow in CQ, the more our critical judgment of our *own* culture will increase, as will our ability to more wisely evaluate other cultures. You could say that CQ serves humble pie to everyone and provides learning for all. No culture has a market on the best way to be human, but each culture has uniquely valuable aspects.

The diagram below (figure 10.1) illustrates that by gaining more understanding of the culture of the other, we gain access to new ways of living that are in line with God's design. Lesslie Newbigin writes, "[We need] help in seeing our own culture through Christian minds shaped by other cultures. . . . We need the witness of the whole ecumenical family if we are to be authentic witnesses for Christ to our own culture."[7] Our final authority for cultural evaluation comes from biblical-theological principles. Scripture speaks into what is best to value, to celebrate, to contemplate and to pattern our behavior after. But no one culture has the edge on understanding Scripture over any other.

Developing CQ requires humility: humility toward other people and humility under the authority of Scripture. CQ assumes a learning process, in which we recognize that our perceptions of reality and our assumptions about "the way things ought to be" have many errors. Working on CQ requires that we abandon the assumption that everyone thinks and perceives the world the way we do.[8]

One summit cohort had a participant from Canada and another from the United Kingdom. This cohort had some lively discussions about socialized health care. When someone in the cohort made a disparaging remark about socialized medicine, these two quickly stated their satisfaction with the systems in their countries. The U.S. pastors humbly listened to their friends, reviewing and assessing their previous assumptions.

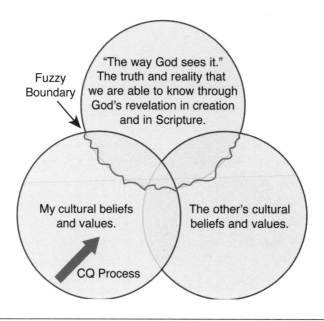

Figure 10.1. Cultural discernment and learning[9]

EQ Is Not the Same as CQ. High EQ doesn't necessarily correlate to high CQ. We can all probably think of a situation in which we offended someone of a different culture even while trying to respect or to encourage them. Years ago, Tasha invited a new immigrant family over for dinner. She was eager to be of help and encouragement to these new neighbors. Thinking it would set them at ease, she kept the evening casual. She wore jeans and was still preparing the salad when they arrived. David showed them into the kitchen and encouraged them to help themselves to one of the drinks on the counter. Tasha filled the plates in the kitchen with the main course, then placed the salad in the middle of the table. All sat at the table to eat.

Although the discussion was stilted, the evening went well—or so Tasha thought. Her one concern was that they did not seem to like the food. They did not have anything to drink and didn't touch their salad. Also, none of the guests asked for seconds. And Tasha didn't offer them any more, as their plates still had food on them. Thankfully, the friendship grew despite the many ways that Tasha's American hospitality had offended them.

Although Tasha had used emotional intelligence appropriate to her own culture, she was unable to discern and interpret the situation. Her casual dress and behavior would have been highly offensive in the Middle Eastern culture of her neighbors, so it caused them quite a bit of confusion and stress. She later learned that they actually liked the food very much and would have enjoyed a drink, salad and seconds. But according to their culture, they politely did *not* clean their plates; further, instead of serving themselves, they expected the host to serve them directly. To help themselves to seconds was unthinkable in their home culture. And to cap it off, she later learned that it was expected for her to send them home with the leftover food. Although sensitive according to her own cultural framework, Tasha's CQ was low.

How can we develop an awareness of our own cultural framework, as well as sensitivity to the cultural realities of others, all while withholding judgment and negative attributions? Developing CQ is challenging yet rewarding. Learning how to recognize and honor cultural differences advances kingdom purposes for all involved. The next two sections can help. First, we explore some basic categories for global cultures and core values. Then we look at concrete practices to adopt.

WHAT ARE CULTURAL VALUES THAT BUILD TRUST?

Every cultural domain has its own set of values, and every specific cultural context has its own unique nuances. In this section we will explore five common areas where these values are expressed. There are many other areas that could be explored. We recommend references at the end of this chapter for more detailed studies on cultural dynamics. Here we will look at the five cultural values of communication context, power, time, control and relationships. Of special importance to our pursuit of CQ is that each of them is founded on trust. Trust is the glue of relationship and societies. Whenever we examine the values of a culture, we should always consider the underlying question "What builds and breaks trust among these people?"[10]

Low vs. High Communication Context. This value category differentiates between peoples who depend on receiving accurate verbal messages (low context) and ones that rely strongly on roles and nonverbal communication (high context). A low-context culture values sending and receiving messages in a direct manner using words. People in these cultures base their understanding more on the literal meaning of what is said than on subtexts coming from facial expression, tone of voice, physical environment, cultural understandings or other nonverbal cues. Communication in a low-context culture is rarely subtle.

The seminary in which we served together is an example of a low-context culture. Our classrooms are very plain. Our faculty dress comfortably and rarely use their titles. Instead, they focus on using words (many words) to make their communication highly explicit. Their facial expressions and tone of voice may not help their communication at times. One professor is known for sounding angry when he is actually excited about discussing an idea. This can be problematic, especially for our students from high-context cultures.

A high-context culture strongly relies on nonverbal communication. As much is communicated through gestures, silence and the use of space as it is through words. Jim Plueddemann tells a fascinating story of a Canadian colleague who met with a group of Asian pastors selecting a new leader. After talking for a while, one person in the group was identified as a potential leader. The Canadian asked the others if they would support this person. Each one answered, "Yes." "Yes." "Yes." Finally, when they came to the man in question, he said, "See—they really don't want me." The Canadian was stunned, realizing that discreet cultural signals had been sent between them that he had totally missed.[11]

Our friend Susan has a highly effective ministry with abused women. These women have a difficult time expressing their pain and grief. Susan grew up in an emotionally abusive home in which any look or gesture could be interpreted negatively. She was trained to be hyperaware of the way people were feeling based on their nonverbal expressions. When first married, her husband (who came from a rather low-context family culture) was baffled when she kept asking, "What do you mean by that look?" But her capacity to understand the women she works with, especially when they cannot verbalize their pain, is almost uncanny.

QUESTIONS TO PONDER

1. Does your organization reflect low or high communication context?

2. To what extent are you accounting for your organization's low or high communication context in your own crosscultural encounters?

Low vs. High Power Distance. *Power distance* refers to how far apart leaders and followers feel from each other. Low power distance occurs when leaders and followers socialize together and address each other as peers. In these collaborative environments, followers expect to have input through a democratic decision-making process. A high power distance environment, however, is much different. Followers address their leaders formally and do not expect to socialize with them. The followers assume that leaders have more authority, respect and status symbols. And decisions are made unilaterally by leaders who assume they will be obeyed without question.

Many low power distance Americans react very strongly against the idea of high power distance in relation to their leaders. They may feel that it is unbiblical for leaders in other cultural contexts to drive high-end cars and wear expensive clothes. Rarely do they understand that these symbols are expected in a high power distance context. "Scripture seems to leave room for some flexibility regarding power distance in leadership style but not in leadership attitudes," James Plueddemann suggests. "The heart of every leader must be humble, seeking the good of others and suspicious of one's own motives."[12]

When serving as the dean of lifelong learning, Bob directed the doctor of ministry program. In this position he normally functioned in a low power distance mode. He once dealt with a very demanding applicant, however, who was a leader in a high power distance cultural context. This applicant consistently exerted his positional status in the way he signed his letters. Finally, in response to yet another demand from this person, Bob adjusted his signature, concluding with "Rev. Dr. Robert W. Burns, Ph.D., D.Min., Dean of Lifelong Learning." The applicant withdrew his demand, responding in a much more cordial fashion.

QUESTIONS TO PONDER

1. Identify your personal power distance relationships in light of your organization's broader power distance practices.

2. How would you evaluate your willingness to serve in relationships where you possess more power and those in which you possess less power?

Clock Time vs. Event Time. A *clock time* culture is one in which time is viewed as a finite commodity and people are highly aware of their own schedules as well as the commitments of others. In this environment, life involves plans, schedules and efficiency. Time is considered scarce and something to be managed. In these cultures there is usually a strong line drawn between work time and personal time.

Conversely, cultures on *event time* are more patient and spontaneous with use of time and casual about starting and ending times. A specific agenda signals a more formal relationship. And an unexpected friend popping in will usually get priority over a scheduled appointment.

Sam, one of our summit pastors, generally ran on event time. He shared how, because of his laid-back, relational style, the elders of the church decided to hire an administrative pastor to help him with the organization and administration of the church. Sam established a regular meeting at the beginning of each week with the administrator. The first few times they met, Sam was a little late. When he came in the office, the administrator had a scowl on his face. In the administrator's view, Sam was in the wrong. But from Sam's cultural perspective, it was more important to finish the conversations he was in before going to the meeting.

It is interesting, though, that Sam and his wife eventually moved as missionaries to Ireland, a country that runs much more on event time than America does. Sam discovered he was much more time-conscious than he ever believed. He shared,

---

In Ireland, they tell a joke about an Irishman asking a Mexican, "Tell me what you mean by *mañana*." "It means, 'Wait until tomorrow,'" replied the Mexican. So the Irishman responded, "Well, we don't have anything nearly that urgent in Ireland."

Sam went on,

When we arrived in Ireland, we went to purchase a car. I expected to drive it home. "Relax," I was told. "This is Ireland. You'll get your car soon enough."

QUESTIONS TO PONDER

1. What is your general attitude toward the stewardship of time?

2. To what extent are you holding on to the tension between apparent interruptions and viewing interruptions as ministry opportunities?

Precision vs. Ambiguity. Precision-oriented people are highly averse to uncertainty. They desire to maintain control over their life and circumstances, minimizing insecurity through policies and detailed planning. They value orderliness, consistency and structure. They desire precise outcomes within specific time frames. Conversely, people from high-ambiguity cultures may be offended by defined, precise goals. Life is lived "in the present," and uncertainty is accepted as a normal reality. As a result, they tend to have less respect for the details of law, and goals are framed in terms of a broad vision or general direction.

When an African American friend of ours was invited to preach in an Anglo church, he experienced this culture clash. The worship leadership of the Anglo church functioned in a precise and orderly manner. Three months prior to the service, they contacted him for the sermon text and a synopsis of his points. Two months before the service, he received an itinerary of when to report to the church, an outline of the worship flow, a comment on sermon length, and who and where to meet.

He shared his response with us. "Generally, in black churches, you are just asked to come preach. They may ask you your topic—though that is rare. They usually just say, 'Let the Spirit use you.' So, I've never been so filled with anxiety preparing to preach. I'm being stretched culturally and emotionally, and I know it. Navigating their 'waters' is very turbulent for me."

Did the leadership of this Anglo church want to create anxiety for our friend? Absolutely not! They felt that they were demonstrating care for the visiting preacher. They were totally unaware that they were creating the opposite response. Their cultural conditioning was one of planning ahead with detailed parameters. Without knowing it, their planning placed heavy constraints on our friend that he had not experienced before.

QUESTIONS TO PONDER

1. How comfortable are you with ambiguity? How much control do you require in order to function well?

2. Think of a friend who views the precision/ambiguity continuum differently than you do. How could a few intentional conversations help both of you appreciate one another's differences and build on one another's strengths?

Results vs. Relationships. Results-oriented cultures focus on individual accomplishment. Achieving goals is a higher priority than maintaining relationships. The people tend to have more fragmented interpersonal relationships, and their friendship networks are often not strong. The community exists to support individual accomplishment. As a result, moving from one location to another is the norm. The people routinely change jobs, churches, neighborhoods and even families to get what they desire.

Relationship-oriented cultures hold interpersonal harmony as a premium and believe individuals exist for the sake of the community. They usually form dense relational networks in which everyone is linked to everyone else (directly or indirectly). Cooperation is considered a higher value than competition. They place a high value on how one is viewed in the community. Therefore, maintaining one's honor within the community ("saving face") is of utmost importance.

As a church planter, Jeremy was required by his denomination to identify and work toward quarterly attendance and financial goals. But for Jeremy this was difficult. Because of his natural bent toward relationships, he felt these goals were superficial and inauthentic. So Jeremy spent most of his time networking relationally throughout the community. When it came time for denominational review, Jeremy was critiqued for not working on his goals. Then his fledgling congregation complained—first to Jeremy and then to the denomination—that he was never at work in his office. Jeremy responded by spending even more time in the community. Eventually he was replaced with a more goal-oriented person who could meet the cultural demands.

Another example can be seen in ministries in which leaders in a results-oriented culture isolate themselves from both their staff and constituents. When they do meet with staff, they may chide them for their failure to meet their goals (which the associates were not involved in setting). Further, the only time they see the people in their ministry is when they are speaking at them in large gatherings. In such contexts, there is often high staff turnover, and the people in the ministry feel alienated from the leadership.

Relationships and results are both needed in healthy ministries. It is interesting that Jesus "appointed twelve (whom he also named apostles) so that they might *be with him* and he might *send them out* to preach and have authority to cast out demons" (Mark 3:14-15, emphasis added). Here is the healthy tension of relationships (being *with* Jesus) and results (he might *send them out* to preach and cast out demons). As our friend Jerry Mabe, president of RightPath Resources, stresses, "Relationship attributes get results." Without healthy relationships, results tend to be short-lived with only a temporary impact.

The staff of Willow Creek Community Church seems to have learned that "relationship attributes get results." After spending thirty years in ministry and investing millions of dollars in sophisticated programs, they came to realize that "spiritual growth doesn't happen best by becoming dependent on elaborate church programs but through the age old spiritual practices of prayer, Bible reading, and relationships."[13] While Willow Creek continues to present quality programs, the staff and lay leadership now seek to incorporate traditional habits of spiritual formation in their ministry.

This recognition of the need for healthy, responsible relationships in order to accomplish long-lasting results is underlined by researchers Kouzes and Posner. They write: "In the thousands of [leadership] cases we've studied, we've yet to encounter a single example of extraordinary achievement that's occurred without the active involvement and support of many people."[14]

QUESTIONS TO PONDER

1. Think of a time when your organization held onto the tension between results and relationships in a healthy way. What happened? What did you learn? How has the experience influenced ongoing practice?

2. What are your opportunities to work on teams that include both results and relationships people? How could you blend your preference for the good of the group and its responsibilities?

The Correlation of Cultural Values. Denise serves on the staff of a church in the Southwest. One day, sitting in her favorite coffee shop, she struck up a conversation with JoAnn. Through the help of a support group, JoAnn had come out of a life of drug addiction and prostitution. While she remained active in her support group, JoAnn was genuinely seeking to grow in spirituality. So Denise invited her to church. After many weeks of sitting in the back rows, JoAnn took the step of attending an inquirers' class. A staff member (not Denise) heard of JoAnn's story and encouraged her to share it in a community group. Denise shared what happened.

This staff member assumed everyone would think, "How wonderful to hear about JoAnn coming to trust Christ out of her pain." However, JoAnn didn't use the "Christian language" our people have come to expect. She came from a rough background and was used to sharing with brutal honesty in her support group. After sharing with this community group, JoAnn experienced a very strong negative reaction from the people. She came to me and said, "This is not a healthy place for me." It broke my heart.

We all respond with sadness or even anger at the congregants in this story. Part of the error, however, is that Denise's staff partner didn't consider the cultural values of this church community before inviting JoAnn to share.

It is important for us to reflect on the contexts in which we minister and to understand how they reveal cultural values. Part of our discipleship agenda needs to be naming these often divergent cultures, talking about them and considering their impact on our mission as God's people.

These five areas of cultural values tend to collect into groupings. In order to see these common correlations, Jim Plueddemann uses the categories of *high-context cultures* and *low-context cultures* to group these cultural characteristics.[15] Taking a cue from Plueddemann, we would propose that cultures often reflect the following groupings:

- High-context cultures, in which nonverbal cues and space/environment are important, tend to value high power distance between leaders and followers, stress the importance of relationships (the community) over results, have a higher tolerance for ambiguity, and function on event (nonprecision) time.

- Low-context cultures, which base understanding on direct, specific verbal comments, tend to value less formal, low power distance between leaders and followers, place the accomplishment of results as paramount, seek to avoid uncertainty by plans and rules, and build expectations around precise timetables.

QUESTIONS TO PONDER

1. Overall, how would you describe your ministry using these five categories of cultural values (results vs. relationships, precision vs. ambiguity, clock vs. event time, low vs. high power distance, and low vs. high communication context)?

2. What impact do these characteristics have on members of the community?

3. How do they affect newcomers to the community? What difference does this make for the leadership?

4. In light of your overall assessment of the five categories, how would you evaluate your ministry's effectiveness in advancing its mission? What must be addressed in order to more faithfully advance the mission?

HOW DO WE DEVELOP CULTURAL INTELLIGENCE?

Years ago Bob was talking to Harvie Conn, the late missions professor at Westminster Theological Seminary. Bob had been involved in leading divorce recovery seminars. A number of African American participants said how helpful it would be to have these seminars in their community. Bob excitedly shared this idea with Harvie. With his characteristic honesty, Harvie responded, "What do you know about the culture of the black church that makes you think you could do a divorce recovery seminar for them?" Stunned, Bob thought for a moment. Then he replied, "I guess I am pretty arrogant to assume my perspective would immediately fit into another culture." Harvie responded, "Bob, don't despise your own cultural perspective. Just recognize it for what it is."

Usually we assume our cultural framework is "the way it is" for everyone else. To grow in CQ, we must recognize our cultural perspective for what it is—one particular way of viewing the world that we have inherited and developed. But as we move into ministry in a multicultural world, we must understand that our way of viewing things will often clash with the experiences and perspectives of others. How are we to learn and grow in our understanding, acceptance and appreciation of others while maintaining a respect for and appreciation of our own cultural frames?

Developing cultural intelligence is not like learning facts and figures. It is a process that integrates understanding into life through reflection and practice. In this final section, we will suggest a number of ways the summit pastors found help in developing CQ. As you have seen, the themes of our study influence each other. Many of our suggestions for developing CQ will sound familiar, since they incorporate skills and actions for ministry resilience found in previous chapters. Learning CQ requires spiritual formation, utilizing reflective practices, trying new things, exercising curiosity by asking questions and growing through hardships. Though these suggestions for practice are written for the ministry leader first, they would also be useful to consider for growing CQ in a congregation.

Learning CQ Requires Spiritual Formation. The importance of spiritual formation for resilience in ministry cannot be overstated. A primary goal of ministry is seeing people transformed into the image of Christ (Colossians 1:28-29). For this to happen in the lives of others, ministry leaders need to be examples of ongoing spiritual transformation. This is important if we are to minister to people in other cultures.

One important aspect of spiritual formation is the discovery of our own sinful patterns. We learn in John 16:8 that the Spirit of God will reveal our sin to us. As we confess our sin, we experience God's forgiveness and cleansing, which creates in us a teachable attitude of gentleness and an empathy toward others. It is this attitude that prepares us to see our own cultural preferences as *one* way of looking at the world rather than *the* way of looking at it. It also opens our eyes to the possibility that some of our ways of living are not godly or in line with biblical principles.

Another aspect of spiritual formation is walking by faith. In our fear of change and our desire for personal comfort, we naturally want to function in the security of our own cultural context. One theme in the book of Acts is how God had to push the early church out of the security of their Jewish cultural framework in order to extend the gospel to the Gentiles. Peter's visions and dramatic experience with the conversion of Cornelius in Acts 10 helped him begin to break with Jewish culture in ways Peter had thought was "unlawful." Similarly, part of our walk of faith in this century will be to move outside the ease of our traditional patterns in order to minister to and *with* others very different from ourselves. A further step will be to learn *from* and be ministered to *by* those different from ourselves.

All of this requires a willingness to pray the way Jesus prayed, "Not my will, Father, but your will be done on earth as it is in heaven." When we humble ourselves before the Lord, casting our anxieties on him (1 Peter 5:6-7), we grow into a state of mind that is prepared to learn cultural intelligence.

Learning CQ Requires Reflection. Other chapters in this book have spotlighted the importance of developing reflective capacity. Here, the goal of reflection is to make the invisible influence of culture in our lives more visible. Gaining awareness begins with reflection, "to become more conscious of the assumptions, ideas, and emotions going on within ourselves and within those we encounter."[16] In order to gain such awareness, we need to stop and consider what we're thinking, feeling and doing.

This reflection could begin by employing the discipline of journaling, which we have already discussed. As we begin to identify aspects of our cultural rules and preferences, we should write them down and consider their influence on us. Helpful reflective work can also be done through intentional discussions, or debriefs, with other people.

Crosscultural experiences can be some of the most confusing, challenging and rewarding experiences in our lives. This is because a new culture can challenge so much of who we are, how we think and what we do. The confusion that this causes throws us off balance; it causes disequilibrium. However, the bigger the disequilibrium, the bigger the potential for learning from it. But we must handle cultural disequilibrium with care, because it is possible to learn the wrong things. Without intentional reflection, crosscultural experiences can become *miseducative*; that is, we can end up decreasing in CQ if we become more fearful and judgmental of different cultures instead of more understanding and discerning.

As an example of the *miseducative* impact of a nonreflective experience, consider this story. A pastor friend of Tasha's took a group of adults from church to work with the poor in the Caribbean for a couple weeks. Upon their return, one of the travelers reported with disdain, "The people were so backward and rude." That was not a healthy learning outcome. Unfortunately, the group had not practiced journaling or debriefing on the trip. With no help toward CQ reflection during the experience, several travelers responded with defensiveness toward the disequilibrium that threatened their culture's comforts.

A few years ago, Donald and Tasha took their families to the west coast of Africa to help Ghanaians friends lead a national Christian education conference. Daily journaling and debriefing at the end of each day was a requirement, as was the keeping of daily prayer and devotionals. Even after our return, we have not stopped learning from that experience. Our children still refer to their trip journals occasionally, and new events continue to pull back the memories from that trip.

Learning CQ Requires Experimentation. A simple way to start building CQ is to deliberately place yourself into a mildly different cultural setting, such as an ethnic restaurant or a worship service in a church from a different tradition. Another way to experience cultural differences is via movies. You may want to try some of the movies we recommend at the end of this chapter. After the experience, journal or debrief with others about the differences you noticed, the feelings you experienced, and the ideas and concerns you had.

By sharing experiences and journal reflections with friends, we heighten our accountability to learn CQ. We also open up our thinking to critique and affirmation. It can be great fun and a very rich CQ experience to intentionally explore a new culture with friends. Tasha and her husband have a group of friends that take turns choosing a new ethnic restaurant to try. They arrive early, before the crowds, so that waiters might have time to answer questions about the food and their home culture. They all greatly value the shared learning experience and also use the gatherings to purposely share their travel experiences.

Another simple but profoundly moving CQ exercise is to worship at different churches with the purpose of learning. Tasha and her husband have twice taken sabbaticals from Sunday morning ministry responsibilities in order to worship at the various churches their seminary students attend. Not only were these rich worship experiences; they also proved to be tremendous CQ learning opportunities for the whole family. You can imagine the discussions over lunch about different physical spaces, music, liturgy, preaching styles and communion rituals that the children saw for the first time. "Mom," one of their teenagers exclaimed while pretending to choke, "that was real wine at communion. You didn't warn us!"

Last year Tasha and Bob traveled with their spouses to teach a class in Northern Ireland for a D.Min. cohort. Previously, these Irish pastors had traveled to St. Louis for classes. What a difference it made to be with them in their own culture: staying in their homes, eating their food, walking their streets and experiencing their ministry. We could not have understood the challenges these pastors face without having been there. In the same way, we will understand the people in our ministries far deeper if we learn about and experience their cultures: visit their homes, eat their food, walk their neighborhoods and experience their work environments.

Learning CQ Requires Asking Curious Questions. When we experience other cultures, we can pray, walk by faith and journal our reflections. But we probably will still misinterpret and misjudge the new culture according to our own cultural rules. To further our CQ, we must ask questions. This may not be easy for us, because our Western culture tends to equate intelligence and leadership with the capacity to have answers, not to ask questions.

In his book *Leading with Questions*, author Michael Marquardt debunks this "answer man" myth, asserting that people with a high IQ often fail because they don't ask questions. Further, he correlates quality leadership with the skill of asking good questions, because this ability goes hand in hand with the ability to learn.[17] In order to lead well, business literature advocates the practice of asking "why." "By repeatedly asking 'Why,' you can peel away the layers of symptoms, leading to the root cause of a problem."[18] But use this technique with care. While people in the United States may handle "why" questions well, most cultures consider direct "why" questions quite rude.

Because other cultures often function differently from our own, our first (usually unconscious) reaction is to respond in two ways. First, we conclude that we *don't like* the way the other culture behaves. Second, we often decide it is simply *wrong.* For example, an Asian partner of ours sent us an email with pictures highlighting delicacies sold by street vendors in Thailand. Our first reaction to the fried bugs and dog meat was, "We can't believe that!" The longer we considered it, the more offensive it became. But when we began asking questions about the customs in Thailand, it became obvious that our reactions were based on our own preferences rather than moral imperatives.

In our many travels, we have found most people eager to answer questions about their traditions and customs when asked graciously and with a humble eagerness to learn. It is especially helpful to have "cultural informants" to whom one can safely ask questions and seek feedback. For example, because they lived in the States for years, our Ghanaian graduates were able to keep us from committing many cultural blunders during our conference in Ghana. We asked them how to dress, what gifts to bring, how to address leaders and how to instruct our children to behave. We intentionally had them colead the workshop sessions with us in order to provide cultural interpretation as needed and to present local stories for illustrations.[19]

At the Ghana conference, Tasha led a workshop on women's ministries. She had plenty of expertise and experience to bring to the session. Still, before beginning to lecture, she decided to have participants form small groups to discuss the question "What are your main concerns about ministering to the women in your church?" Although she had read about Ghanaian culture before traveling, nothing prepared her for the list of concerns she heard. Some of the issues were the exact opposite of ones she usually heard expressed by ministry leaders in the States. As a result, she could offer few answers, but led most of the workshop by asking good questions.

Learning CQ Requires Hardships. Developing cultural intelligence will take us out of our comfort zone. More often than not, attempts to learn a new culture will be met with mixed results and setbacks. Hardships can derail us from learning if we react to our failures by saying, "Never again!" Doing so prevents us from pursuing understanding. Sadly, we have seen congregants shut down their CQ due to the challenges experienced during short-term mission trips. "I'm never going to go on a mission trip again," reported a woman to Tasha upon her return. "Leave it to the professionals!" The requirements for growing in CQ were not in place to help her process the hard experiences.

The disequilibrium that comes from crosscultural hardships can be very intense. And the Holy Spirit can use it to bring about transformation in our lives. Many years ago, Donald had the privilege of visiting fourteen churches in central Ghana on a road trip full of challenges. During the three-day adventure, he and his Ghanaian colleagues endured armed road guards, swarming cockroaches in the vehicle, scarcity of water and sleep, infrequent electricity or plumbing, nearly impassable roads, and untimely, oppositional calls to prayer by leaders of other religions. These relative hardships were accompanied by rich fellowship and celebratory worship at every stop. In fact, without fail, church members in each village along the route waited many hours for Donald and his colleagues to arrive. Disorienting hardships, especially for Donald? Yes, but momentary and relatively insignificant in light of the profound joy and mutual encouragement shared by all.

Learning CQ Requires Community. Cultural intelligence is more than an individual skill. Because culture involves people living in community, cultural intelligence is learned best as an interpersonal exercise. Anyone who has been on a short-term mission team knows that it is helpful to work through the struggles of learning CQ with the support and insights of others. But you don't need to go on a trip to experience this. We can work on our CQ simply by visiting our neighbors, ethnic restaurants and other crosscultural contexts, thus sharing the experiences and growing together.

Before Bob returned to the pastorate, he worshiped at a church in midtown St. Louis, where the founding pastor and his wife, Andrew and Lisa, were Pastors Summit participants. Their congregation has been on an adventure of learning cultural intelligence for years. The journey began even before the congregation started. This Anglo pastor and his wife adopted three African American daughters. Then when the time came for them to plant the church, they deliberately selected an ethnically diverse community for the location.

As the church grew over seven years, Andrew continued to pray that they could reflect more diversity. One day he received a call from an Asian American church in his denomination. They were also asking questions about next steps in growth and diversity. After many conversations, the two congregations joined together to form one church with two sites. Inevitably, as the congregations began to "live" together, cultural differences became more evident.

A couple years ago, a team from the congregation joined the pastor in writing an application for a pastoral renewal grant from Lilly Endowment. These grants are provided by the Endowment to help pastors and congregations take time for sabbatical and reflection. The theme of their approved grant was cultural intelligence. With two newly adopted teenage sons adding to the diversity of their family, Andrew and Lisa were convinced they needed extended time for the family to get to know one another better and to be exposed to other cultural experiences. During the summer, they visited different areas of the country and worshiped in congregations of diverse ethnic backgrounds. Andrew and his father also took a three-week trip to Asia, often visiting family and friends of people in his congregation.

Meanwhile, as the pastor's family was on sabbatical, the congregation invested their summer learning about cultural intelligence. This included picnics with menus ranging from kimchi to soul food, sermons from preachers of different cultures and a multicultural children's music camp. Each family of the congregation was urged to read the book *Cultural Intelligence* by David Livermore. And then Livermore spent a weekend with the congregation, taking them through a CQ seminar.

The results of this churchwide emphasis have been encouraging. The pastor and his family have grown in their love for one another and their understanding of different cultures. Friendships in the congregation have been deepened, and the leaders have come to appreciate the struggles involved in blending congregations. Today the church is even more deeply committed to ethnic diversity, cultural awareness and mutual understanding. While it is hard work, they happily embrace it as a taste of God's ultimate restoration of all things.

QUESTIONS TO PONDER

1. Learning CQ requires the gospel. To what degree are these six elements for learning CQ present in your life: spiritual formation, reflection, experimentation, curious questions, hardships and community?

2. What will it take for you to build on those elements most present and to address those elements least present?

3. To expand this exercise, you could rank the six elements with your elder board or executive team and then discuss how to build on those elements most present and address those elements least present.

CONCLUSION

More and more, the capacity to pursue fruitful ministry with resilience will depend upon the ability to function effectively across various cultural contexts. In these two chapters on CQ, we have highlighted the importance of understanding culture. We have also looked at common cultural domains faced by ministry leaders. The five spectrums of cultural values serve to help us start to discern our own cultural contexts. And we have considered a number of ways to grow our cultural intelligence by experiencing other contexts. By God's grace, through developing CQ, we will be able to exhibit the unity of the body of Christ to a watching world, demonstrating we are Jesus' disciples by the way we love each other regardless of, and even celebrating, our cultural differences.

RECOMMENDATIONS FOR FURTHER READING

1. James Plueddemann. *Leading Across Cultures: Effective Ministry and Mission in the Global Church.* Downers Grove, Ill.: InterVarsity Press, 2009.

2. Duane Elmer. *Cross-Cultural Connections: Stepping Out and Fitting In Around the World.* Downers Grove, Ill.: InterVarsity Press, 2002.

3. J. Nelson Jennings. *God: The Real Superpower.* Phillipsburg, N.J.: P&R Publishing, 2007.

4. Paul G. Hiebert. *Anthropological Insights for Missionaries.* Grand Rapids: Baker, 1985.

5. David A. Livermore. *Cultural Intelligence: Improving Your CQ to Engage Our Multicultural World.* Grand Rapids: Baker Academic, 2009.

6. Mary Lederleitner. *Cross-Cultural Partnerships: Navigating the Complexities of Money and Mission.* Downers Grove, Ill.: InterVarsity Press, 2010.

7. Victor H. Matthews. *Manners and Customs in the Bible: An Illustrated Guide to Daily Life in Bible Times.* 3rd ed. Peabody, Mass.: Hendrickson, 2006.

8. Everett Ferguson. *Backgrounds of Early Christianity.* 3rd ed. Grand Rapids: Eerdmans, 2003.

9. James S. Jeffers. *The Greco-Roman World of the New Testament Era: Exploring the Background of Early Christianity.* Downers Grove, Ill.: InterVarsity Press, 1999.

MEDIA WORTH EXPLORING

1. "I Am Not Supposed to Be Here" on the CD *A Fragile Stone* by Michael Card. This is a beautifully provocative song about the apostle Peter's challenge in going to Cornelius with the gospel.

2. Movie and extra features of *End of the Spear* (2005), rated PG-13. Many years after his missionary father was speared to death at the hands of Waodani tribesmen, a young man returns to the Ecuadorian jungle to meet the native who murdered his father. Film is based on a true story.

3. Movie and extra features of *The Gods Must Be Crazy* (1980), rated PG. This classic comedy explores the cultural clash and dissension caused when a soda bottle comes to an African village. The extras provide a sobering documentary about what happened to the native South African tribesman who played the lead character.

4. *An Everlasting Piece* (2000), rated R. In director Barry Levinson's comedy, set in Northern Ireland, two young entrepreneurs, one Catholic and one Protestant, take on a new toupee business. The trouble begins when competition arrives and the pair must sell thirty toupees in a race to remain on top.

5. *The Visitor* (2007), rated PG-13. A widowed college professor and two illegal immigrants learn surprising things from one another about music, friendship and suffering.

MARRIAGE AND FAMILY

STRESSED BY MINISTRY

I was at a board meeting where we were examining potential elders.

One candidate was asked, "Are you willing to make sacrifices with your family for

the sake of the church?" And it was a weird moment because I asked myself,

"What's the right answer to that question?"

A Summit pastor

DURING ONE OF OUR SUMMITS, a participant shared the following story:

A few years ago, I asked my wife what it felt like to be married to me, after twenty years of marriage and eighteen years of ministry together. I was optimistic of her positive response. She said, "I can't answer you right now. Give me some time to think about it."

A few weeks later I approached her again. "Have you thought about what it feels like to be married to me?" She replied, "Yes . . . I know that I would never divorce you. And I certainly would never kill you. However, I can't help but think the boys and I would be better off if you were not alive."

My response? I was ready to leave the ministry in order to save my marriage! I went to my elders and told them what my wife had said. I also told them I thought I should leave the ministry to save my marriage. After some quiet moments, one of the elders finally spoke. He said, "No, now is not the time for you to leave the ministry. Now is the time for you to learn what the ministry is all about." With their support, my wife and I began extended counseling together. This has resulted in some pretty dramatic changes in the way I live life and do ministry.

Another pastor responded, "The subject of ministry and marriage is one I have *never* really heard addressed in our twenty-plus years of ministry and thirty-plus years of marriage."

This story and comment demonstrate a heartbreaking theme: the effects of ministry on marriage—and marriage on ministry—are rarely discussed, yet intimately connected. Ministry is not a nine-to-five job. It is an absorbing lifestyle. The way pastors navigate this lifestyle will influence their marriage and family. Conversely, their marriage and family life will directly affect their churches.

One of the earliest and most important discoveries made in our Pastors Summit research was the critical role the spouse and family have on sustaining leaders in ministry. We responded by changing the summit format to include spouses for most of the retreats. A healthy marriage and family strengthens pastors. At the same time, marriage and family difficulties can derail ministry leaders. Therefore, the health of a pastor's marriage and family is also a priority for the well-being of a congregation.

From the summit discussions with ministry couples, we identified five primary challenges facing marriage and family for those in the ministry. (Married women pastors will want to consider how these findings might change due to gender differences. Single ministers may want to consider corollary challenges they have with close friends and extended family.) These five stressors are

- the "normal" pressures of marriage and family life

- the nature of ministry: always on the job

- the conflicting loyalties of church and home

- abandonment from always being on the job

- the unmet needs of ministry spouses for confidants

The first category simply reminds us of the usual stress that most married couples and families face in our culture. The four latter stressors are unique to ministry leaders' families and are interdependent challenges. Of course, this list is not exhaustive, but we believe it represents some of the primary issues critical for pastoral fruitfulness and resilience. In this chapter we will explore the first three stressors and describe the most helpful responses and actions identified by the summit couples. (Single pastors may find these equally important to consider in principle.)

STRESSOR ONE: THE "NORMAL" PRESSURES OF MARRIAGE AND FAMILY LIFE

Commenting on the stress of family life, a study of the University of Missouri Extension program states:

> In our society things change rapidly. With change comes stress. Today's family structure is changing drastically. The institution of marriage can be a strong, supportive force that helps family members cope with stressors as a unit. However, a large number of marriages will end in divorce and many children will spend a part of their lives with only one parent. Families go through various stages of stress even if divorce is not a factor. Families must adapt [starting from] the birth of a child [through the time] a teenager passes through adolescence to adulthood and moves away. Often the most stressful times occur when a family experiences a variety of demanding events at the same time.[1]

Pastoral families confront the common dilemmas all families face, including the demands of household chores, typical family conflicts, community involvement, childcare and activities for children as they grow. Add to these the life crises and financial struggles faced by most pastoral couples. Commenting on these challenges, a summit pastor shared,

---

One of the biggest dilemmas and stressors on marriage is not the ministry but what we're doing in all the *other* spheres of our life that everybody else is doing too: parenting and finances and all those things. These are the areas that really put tremendous amounts of stress on marriages, and they affect clergy marriages just like everyone else's.

We feel it is important to recognize these common issues that all families face in today's society. We would contend that these "normal" challenges are exacerbated by the other stressors discussed in this chapter. All of this makes the pastoral marriage and family a unique context to navigate. Therefore, ministry couples do well to regularly review their marriage and family life. Many find it helpful to do this with a counselor in order to gain insights from someone who doesn't expect to be ministered to by them.

The rest of the stressors we discuss are unique aspects of living the ministry life. Few members or regular attenders of the congregation would experience them, and even fewer would be able to understand them fully.

STRESSOR TWO: MINISTRY AS A LIFESTYLE MORE THAN A JOB

Pastors can only dream of a nine-to-five job, in which the whistle blows and the work stays behind as one heads for home. One pastor stated emphatically,

> Ministry is not a job; it's a lifestyle. Even when I'm home, I'm subject to the telephone and my inability to turn some of the church emotions off. I feel like I'm faking it with the kids much of the time.

Pastors rarely feel like they can step away from their ministry responsibilities. As we discussed in the chapter on self-care, pastors feel as though they are "on" twenty-four hours a day, seven days a week, every day of the year. It is truly difficult to disengage from the demands of ministry. One pastor explained,

> After being an active listener for a lot of other people, I really struggle being interested in my spouse and children and what's going on in *their* lives.

How do pastors respond to this strain of ministry? Many of them continue to press on, ignoring the family consequences until a crisis occurs. Unfortunately, this was a common refrain in the cohorts.

> I didn't realize the strain that ministry was putting on our marriage. I knew that it wasn't what I wanted or what it should be. Yet at the same time, I'd just keep going. Then, when we got away at the Pastors Summit, it all came crashing down. I feel like the toll on my family—the damage to me, my wife and my son—has not been worth the fruit of the ministry.

What should pastors do with these incessant pressures? How do they turn "off"? While there are no simple answers, the following are some diagnostic questions and suggested healing actions drawn from our summit conversations. These questions and stories will help you assess how well you are dealing with the ministry stress of always being "on."

How Often Do You Feel Like You Are Truly Off the Clock? Related questions include: *How many hours did you work this month? How long does it take you to unwind?* As we saw in earlier chapters, pastors need to counter the demands of ministry with responsible self-care. Our research demonstrated that exercise, days off, sabbath, vacations, sabbaticals, hobbies, firm boundaries and the pursuit of interests outside of the ministry are some of the most helpful ways to break the emotional and intellectual pressures of ministry obligations. When spouses and children are involved in these same self-care activities, the benefits multiply.

Recently a summit couple returned from a four-month sabbatical funded by a Lilly Endowment Clergy Renewal grant.[2] As they reengaged in the congregation, two of their reflections stood out. First, they were genuinely surprised at how "tightly wound up" they were *prior* to the sabbatical. They assessed that this had been their normal emotional condition of being always "on" in the ministry. Second, they were aware of how eager they were now to reengage with their congregation, with the caveat that they wouldn't wait so long to take needed breaks in the future.

Does Your Spouse Serve as a "Nuclear Dumping Ground"? *What's the emotional "radiation level" emanating from you to your spouse these days? Which friends minister to you and/or to your spouse by providing ears for venting?*

One pastor's spouse shared,

Sometimes I think it might be better if I just don't hear the criticism my spouse is facing. But then I feel like I'm abandoning the one I love.

While a pastor observed,

My spouse suffers from collateral damage. Sometimes it's a direct hit. But even when that's not happening, my spouse is collateral damage. Some bomb went off, and unfortunately, I'm the person in whose office it went off.

We have already noticed that a stressor of pastors being always "on" is their lack of intimate friendships; frequently, spouses are the only safe people with whom to share candidly the conflicts, disappointments and stress of ministry. Therefore, ministry stress easily fills the marriage. As we saw in the chapters on spiritual formation and self-care, pastors rarely have trustworthy people (confidants) in their lives with whom they can regularly process their experiences and feelings. The resulting stress on spouses became such a common topic at the summit that participants began calling spouses the "nuclear dumping ground" of the ministry.

Why nuclear dumping ground? Because pastors say things to their spouses they would *never* share with anyone else. And the effects of these conversations linger for a very long time. Ministry spouses watch their partners suffer from the criticism, crises and conflicts that come with the job. The toxicity of the emotional and relational stress can spread from the pastor to the spouse. Since the information is usually highly confidential, the receiving spouse has nowhere to share the burden and no power to settle it. Later, when ministry leaders resolve the problems, the spouse is frequently left holding the pain, unable to bring closure to the experience.

Healing actions for this ministry stress involve the pastor pursuing safe relationships, as discussed in the chapter on self-care. Pastors need to have relationships with significant allies and valued confidants (don't confuse the two) in which they can openly disclose what they are facing and how others relate to their leadership.

We are reminded of a pastor friend who was going through turmoil on his leadership board. In his rush to secure new officers, he had brought on one person with "correct" theology. As it turned out, however, this new elder did not respect the pastor's leadership or vision. This new elder became a constant problem, critically questioning every initiative coming to the board. Because the elder was well known, our friend couldn't find anyone in the church or community to talk with about it. And his wife was already burdened with the concerns of their young family, including a special-needs child.

Finally, the pastor reached out through phone calls and emails to a person over nine hundred miles away, someone who could serve as a sounding board for his frustrations. By pursuing this confidant, the pastor protected his spouse and children from the emotional burden. In the same way, developing safe, trustworthy relationships should be a priority for the health and well-being of the ministry leader's spouse. Below, we will explore this need for ministry spouses.

What Healthy Boundaries Protect Your Spouse and Children from the

Emotional Stressors of Ministry? *Do you know how your spouse and children feel about you being in the ministry? When is the last time you discussed it?*
One pastor told the group,

Our oldest daughter is five. When we're sitting at the dinner table eating, my husband [a pastor] is telling me what's happened that day. Our daughter is listening. She hears everything, to the point now where I'll say [to him], *"Names*—at least keep the names out!" But even more than the names, she feels the anxiety.

As you can tell from this story, the ministry can become an emotional burden for children. Musing on the topic, an older pastor reflected,

---

Our kids were very involved in the conflict and struggle we had in our church. They saw the good, the bad and the ugly. In some ways I'm surprised they still go to church and are believers. But they are, and I'm so thankful.

What can be done to address the emotional cost to both spouses and children? While there are wonderful people in every congregation, there can also be people who are angry and mean. Yes, the sheep can bite. Pastors and their families often bear the brunt of these negative, critical people. Therefore, pastoral couples must pursue ongoing conversations about how to manage the emotional fallout of ministry.

These conversations should include discussions about how much spouses are expected to handle. The overall objective should be for spouses to feel connected to the concerns of their partner who is pastoring but not become crippled by the emotional difficulties. Take into account that people have different capacities to manage negative issues in a healthy manner. There is a continuum between "need to know" information and knowledge that becomes too stressful to bear. Spouses need to identify where they and their children are on this continuum. It may not be easy to determine. That's why this conversation should be *ongoing*.

In addition, this conversation should include the subject of boundaries. What fences need to be established for the emotional health and safety of spouse and children? Their age, stage of life, the time of year and other contextual dynamics make a difference in how much they can or should handle at any point.

We highly recommend seeking help for discussing the management of difficult relationships, for evaluating where you are on the "need to know" continuum and for developing proper boundaries. Consider talking with other pastoral couples, particularly retired couples with years of experiences (and plenty of mistakes) to draw on. Also consider talking with a professional counselor. Not only will counselors understand the emotional dynamics of your situation; they also have had to learn how to manage similar challenges with their own families.

Do You Assure Your Children That Ministry Challenges Are Not Their Fault? How do you know? Do your children know that you believe God is good all the time? In addition to the conversations and boundaries mentioned above, what else can be done to protect the children of ministry couples from the onslaught of emotional stress?

First, we remind ourselves that kids of all ages pick up verbal and emotional signals from parents. If Mom comes home after a difficult tussle with a church member, kids will quickly pick up on the feelings of anger, frustration or confusion she feels. Unfortunately, children will often jump to the conclusion that the bad mood is a result of something *they* have done. Older children might blame the church.

We help our children by reminding them often that our emotional condition is neither their fault nor their responsibility. While they don't need to know the details of Mom or Dad's problems, they do need to know that the problems aren't about them. They also need to be comforted by the parents' confidence that the ministry challenges will not overwhelm them and that God has called the parents to this good work and is with them in it.

We know a pastor who often picks up her kids from school. One day, after a particularly bad phone call from a member, she walked out of the church office and drove directly to the school, ruminating all the way. When this pastor's daughter, who is a verbal processor, got into the car, she was full of chatter about the day. Mom's mind, however, was still on the phone call. Aware that her mother wasn't listening, the daughter stopped talking. The car became strangely silent. Being perceptive enough to realize what had happened, the pastor apologized. "Honey, I'm so sorry. Mom is feeling sad about some things that happened earlier today. But I really want to hear about your day at school. Would you please start over and share it with me?" The daughter smiled and began to recount her day.

Note how our friend was able to share her own feelings in an age-appropriate manner without disclosing inappropriate information. She communicated that the responsibility was her own. If her daughter would have asked for more details, she might gently respond that they really weren't something Mom could share. But the most important thing was for the child to know how Mom felt at that moment. Ministry children need both assurance that they are not responsible for our stressful reactions and comfort that we are not without hope in serving God with our work.

This second stressor—pastors feeling like they are always on the job—is unique to ministry and threatens the longevity of ministry leaders. In response, pastors need better self-care practices and regular time off. Their spouses do not need to be emotional dumping grounds but can have healthy boundaries and conversations about emotional ministry situations. Finally, children need to be assured that they are not to blame for ministry stress and to know that God is providing for the challenges their parents are facing.

QUESTIONS TO PONDER

1. Who helps you process the challenges of ministry stressors? Of the need for healthy boundaries for the family? Of difficult relationships at work?

2. How could an experienced pastoral couple and/or counselor assist in this work?

3. In what ways are common family life challenges being exacerbated by your ministry stressors?

4. How do the members of your family think and feel about your work life?

STRESSOR THREE: CONFLICTING LOYALTIES OF CHURCH AND HOME

Pastors generally do not have a mindset that differentiates between work and personal time. It is hard for them to distinguish between being "on" and "off" the job. One result of being on the job all the time is a conflict of loyalty between the church and their family. As one pastor mused,

---

How important should my allegiance to the church be? Does my concern
for the people of this church trump my concern for my family? How do I
reconcile these competing loyalties?

The very nature of this question signals that the ministry will take up all of
the time one allows it. As a result, pastors can be busy "doing the Lord's work"
to the neglect of their marriages. One person expressed this tension, sharing:

The reality for most of us in ministry is we're tempted to rationalize the
neglect of our marriage. I was at a board meeting where we were examining potential elders. One candidate was asked, "Are you willing to
make sacrifices with your family for the sake of the church?" And it was
a weird moment because I asked myself, "What's the right answer to that
question?" I've seen some pastors who had an explicit principle that the
church is your family, just as your spouse and kids are your family.

Another pastor shared how his wife confronted him about his loyalty: "I
was out five nights one week, and she said, 'The church is coming between
us. You can't do that.'"

When talking about this problem of conflicting loyalties with summit
pastors, we identified a number of responses to this problem. The first was
the expectation that if a pastor worked really hard during a particular season
of ministry, there would be more time for spouse and family when the
church reached a certain milestone. This milestone could reflect any number of goals, including the size of membership, the hiring of additional staff
or a level of income. The pastors challenged this "milestone mentality," however. Everyone agreed that the next goal would always be looming on the
horizon. "Do you think things will change when you reach that milestone?"
exclaimed a pastor everyone viewed as successful. "No way! Not true!"

A second unhealthy response to this problem of conflicting loyalties surfaced in a conversation between the wife of a pastor and psychologist Diane
Langberg, a guest during one of the cohort meetings. The wife shared,

---

I read about Sarah and Jonathan Edwards, and how Sarah tirelessly ran
the home and family so that Jonathan could employ his gifts in the
church by studying, writing and preparing. And I read about Susannah
and Charles Spurgeon, and how Susannah felt it was her responsibility

to sacrifice time with her husband for the sake of the gospel. So I feel guilty for complaining.

In thoughtful response to this comment, Diane said,

So many pastors' wives buy into the martyr mindset. Abandonment is not spiritual under any circumstances. Abandonment of a spouse is antithetical to the work of God. Such a person is using a woman for his own self. . . . The phrase "dying to self" has covered a lot of sin.

A third unhealthy response to the loyalty conflict swings the pendulum from neglecting the family to neglecting pastoral duties. One pastor shared,

I know about pastors who become workaholics, putting their families on the sidelines while pouring themselves into their work. That is unhealthy. But lately I've seen the opposite: pastors who neglect their pastoral responsibilities by making rigid boundaries and unreasonable expectations. It's possible to go one way or the other. We are accountable to walk carefully between responsibility to the home and to the church.

How do pastors choose wisely between family and church responsibilities? Here are some very practical and helpful suggestions that came out of the summit.

Recognize the Strategic Role of Ministry Spouses. First, it is important for pastors to identify the strategic roles spouses have in their life and ministry. While this may seem self-evident, over time many pastors may begin to take their spouses for granted. As one expressed it in a journal entry, "I realize I've undervalued her in my ministry, even while thinking that I wasn't doing that."

We found it interesting that one counselor, who was observing the interaction of participants and spouses during a summit, made the following comment about male pastors:

Churches and seminaries are issuing calls and sending men into ministry who do not have strong relational skills. But even when this is the case, they may still be successful in ministry if they are willing to accept their wife's strengths in this area and be guided and shaped by them.

When pastors—particularly male pastors—acknowledge the importance of their spouses as ministry partners and learn from them, they will find their spouses to be one of the most important resources available for their own growth. However, this will not happen if they place their loyalty to the church above their commitment to their spouses.

Ministry spouses also serve in the strategic role of chief consultant and pastor to their pastor-partners. One participant shared,

> When it comes to the point where I'm doubting my call, what is the bottom line that keeps me in the ministry? It's letting my spouse know I'm doubting my call. That takes away the loneliness of the question.

And another one shared bluntly,

> For me, when my heart is broken, when I'm angry, I don't go to the elders. I don't go to other pastors. I go to my real pastor, who is my spouse.

Because spouses play such strategic roles, their significant support work needs to be frequently acknowledged by their pastor-spouse. And they need to be honored, recognized and thanked—regularly.

Form a Ministry Partnership with Your Spouse. How do you, as a ministry couple, minister together? While this includes the shared ministry of opening the home for meals and fellowship, it expands to include all sorts of other commitments and activities. There are no formulas for determining the role of a spouse in ministry. It requires a careful, ongoing discussion around the spiritual gifts and interests of the spouse, the expectations of the congregation (and how you will address them as a couple), the needs of the family and your stage of life.

A number of pastors in the summit commented on shared ministry with their spouses. One observed,

> As I listen to the spouses in our summit, it feels like they are very interested in the Lord's work, but very confused about how they can best be involved.

Another shared this story:

> When we got married, my wife was coming from a high involvement in a ministry. While I desired to partner with her, all I had ever seen was cou-

ples where the wife was only involved tangentially. I had never seen a real ministry partnership. So I assumed my wife would develop her own activities. She was offended that I didn't involve her in ministry planning and leadership. It took a number of years to work through these hurt feelings. But even today I don't feel I have done a good job of involving her.

Other pastors and spouses described how they addressed congregational involvement. One said,

In my congregation, the spouses of previous pastors had served as unofficial, unpaid staff. I made it very clear that my spouse was like any other member of the church and wouldn't be considered unannounced head of a ministry.

The seminary students and spouses we work with are sensitive to these potential expectations, calling it a "two-for-one." During a summit, one ministry spouse shared,

When our church was just a few years old, there was an elder who thought I should have a job description. I said, "When you start paying me, you can give me one!"

One determined summit wife exclaimed,

Look. I want to be involved as a responsible member of our church. But my greatest contribution to the church is to support and encourage my spouse. No one else could or should fulfill that role I have. That is my first priority. I have led small groups, been part of starting a school, served on ministry teams and coordinated the nursery. Over the years, my other roles in the church have changed. But my commitment as the primary encourager and supporter of my spouse has remained constant.

Ministry partnership is a fluid concept that must be regularly negotiated between the pastor and spouse. Being unified in their understanding of what the spouse will do and how the spouse feels called to participate can prevent a great deal of stress.

Identify and Manage the Congregation's Expectations. Another way for pastors to address the tension between church and family is to manage the expectations of the congregation.[3] The interests of people in a congregation are many and varied. They can be held by individuals, members of a particular subgroup or the entire congregation. For example, individual members of a congregation often expect pastors to be at their special events. Another expectation often felt but not consciously recognized is that pastors will have a perfect family. As one summit pastor explained,

---

I think one of the great hindrances to our marriage is preconceived notions in the congregation of what a marriage ought to look like. . . . You get this collection of images that form this template.

This expectation of being perfect often leads ministry families to feel as though they are living a "double life," masking reality with a veneer of spirituality. A pastor sadly shared,

---

We do live double lives. We may be angry, upset, sad or hurt, yet when we're at church, we need everyone to believe that we are okay. Let's face it, the senior pastor and family are looked up to; we set the example. We are the role model for the church.

How can pastors and their families manage such expectations? First and foremost, a pastoral couple should simply name the expectations they think are stemming from their congregation. Keep a running list of the expectations you both face and make sure you have a regular conversation about them. If there are multiple people on staff, talk about congregational expectations together. Consider which ones are reasonable, which are harmless, and which are unreasonable or even dangerous to you, your family or the health of the church. Then, as a healthy part of ministry leadership, you and your staff team need to address the expectations or pressures that are unrealistic or not responsible. You might even need to plan how you will intentionally not conform to the pressure.

Disappoint Others. Often expectations found in congregations are benign, having more to do with tradition and social mores. When facing these issues, we should heed the apostle Paul's counsel to regard a weaker brother's conscience, becoming all things to all persons in order to win some to Christ.[4] At the same time, we read in the Gospels that Jesus often disappointed people by not conforming to societal expectations when it violated his understanding of God's will.[5] This work requires great discernment.

You will probably need to disappoint people when it comes to the proper care of your family or yourself. One of the summit couples shared about being criticized for not attending a church event in order to be at their son's baseball game. Their son had been struggling with self-confidence, and both were willing to disappoint others in order to support him.

It is impossible to be in ministry and not disappoint others. In order to manage the outcomes of such circumstances, pastors must help their spouses (and children) learn differentiation. In the chapter on emotional intelligence, we described differentiation as "the ability to remain connected in relationship to significant people and yet not have our reactions and behavior determined by them."[6]

In the context of others' expectations, differentiation involves resisting the pressure to form our beliefs about ourselves (or others) or to make our decisions based on the opinions of others. Such differentiation takes the support of family and friends. Sharing our perspectives and responses with safe people is a healthy way to maintain a balanced perspective. We are always in the process of learning differentiation. Murray Bowen, who developed the idea of differentiation in his work on family systems, once said that differentiation is a lifetime project, with no one ever getting more than about 70 percent there.[7]

Manage Dual Relationships. Another way for families to manage congregational expectations is to learn the dynamics of dual relationships. We mentioned the challenge of having dual relationships in our discussion on self-care in chapter six. It is an equally important concept for spouses and family members to work on. A dual relationship is one in which one person serves multiple roles in the lives of others. Pastors and their spouses (and sometimes their children) have unique dual relationships with people in the church. For example, they worship with people whom they may supervise, and they are friends with elders who are also their supervisors. At times this can be confusing and emotionally difficult. Therefore, it is important for pastors, their spouses and their children to understand this relationally challenging dynamic.

This story of dual relationships involves the entire family. At one Tuesday evening elder board meeting, the pastor had a significant conflict with an elder over a funding issue in the budget. The pastor was promoting a particular initiative that the elder publicly described as frivolous and a waste of money. During the discussion over this matter, the elder became very angry. Finally, he said that the pastor "didn't know what he was talking about." After the meeting, the elder went home and vented to his wife—within earshot of his nine-year-old son.

The next day, this elder's son confronted the pastor's son in the schoolyard, mimicking his elder-father and stating that the pastor was "an idiot." A fight ensued, which ended by both boys being suspended from school. Various relationships are at play here: both men were elders, and there were employee/employer dynamics and a pastor/member relationship. There were also the contrasting roles of elder/husband, father/son, son of elder/son of pastor and schoolmate/schoolmate. The conflict in the church meeting spread to the home and schoolyard.

Support Spouses in Spiritual Development. Another way to bridge the tension between church and family is to address the spiritual development of spouses. As we described in the chapters on spiritual formation, it is nearly impossible to manage the expectations of others unless our relationship with the Lord is vital and growing. In our relationship with God we find the strength to see clearly, to differentiate from the emotions of others and to gain the wisdom and insight to address problems. For these reasons, spouses of pastors need to be intentionally encouraged in their spiritual life.

However, it is one thing to say that ministry spouses need spiritual growth. It is another thing for pastors to consider this a priority. As one pastor's wife reflected, "How often in our marriage is our pastor-spouse representing Christ to others, but not to us?" After coming home from an emotionally and spiritually draining day, pastors want personally renewing time rather than reengagement in stressful relationships. The idea of focusing on the spiritual development of spouses feels a great deal like going back to work. As one pastor explained,

---

We all know that pastors are supposed to minister first to our family. But often we put our loved ones on hold. When the time comes to engage with them, we're just tired.

Another pastor shared,

> A couple of years ago we were driving in the car, and my spouse said, "You haven't asked about whether I'm doing my devotions for six months. You'd do that for a new Christian in our church." I just about hit a telephone pole. It was true.

Though caring for the spiritual needs of our spouses can be challenging, the apostles Paul and Peter say it is a responsibility for anyone who is married.[8] Intentionality in small ways will help ensure growth in this area.

Years ago when Bob was training some small group leaders, they all said the most difficult thing for men to do was to pray with their wives. The group viewed it as a uniquely male challenge. This also came up in a summit meeting when a pastor asked, "Why is praying together with my wife so hard?" And another said,

> I know I need to pray with my wife. But I'm tired. And unless prompted, I'm more inclined just to hit the sack. And the reason I hit the sack early is that I have so much to do the next day. So I'm thinking, *Okay, I've got to get enough rest to do A, B and C tomorrow.* And it struck me—I'm taking my spouse for granted. That's skewed thinking.

In another group, one person shared,

> Whenever we do pray together—like at 9:30 in the evening—it's exactly what we needed. But it's hard to push through the resistance to want to go unwind in other ways.

Along with the need for prayer is the importance of helping one's spouse to have time for reflection and spiritual disciplines. Listen to how the summit wives reflected on this need:

> There is no quiet in my day. Even while I'm in the shower, I hear things going on in the house.
>
> ✦ ✦ ✦
>
> My pastor-spouse can get away during the day for some quiet, but I can't.
>
> ✦ ✦ ✦

I feel part of the role of a pastor is to be contemplative. But we're so much a team that I need that too. But my life doesn't lend itself to that, and then I spiral into the whole martyr thing: *This is what I do.* I think maybe my spouse needs to give up some solitude and give it to me. I need that time to be vibrant.

Just as in the area of self-care, there may be short periods when it is not possible to focus on the spiritual growth of one's family. However, the regular investment of spiritual care for spouses and children is like daily exercise and proper diet: consistent involvement pays off over the long haul.

Ministry couples need to confront the tension between church and family by negotiating the specific challenges in the ministry environment. Taking even small steps in each of the six action areas above will reduce the strain for the whole family. These healthy steps include understanding the strategic role of our spouses, forming ministry partnerships with them, working with them to manage the congregation's expectations (even by intentionally disappointing others), managing the unique ministry dynamics of dual relationships and actively supporting the spiritual growth of our spouses.

QUESTIONS TO PONDER

1. What story do you tell yourself about the tension between work and home responsibilities?

2. How well does your spouse think you are navigating the tension?

3. To what degree do you pursue any of the above six actions? Where have you experienced help from them? Which ones need to become a new priority?

CONCLUSION

In this chapter we learned that pastors face a challenging tension between the home and family. Ministry marriages must manage similar challenges that other couples face. Some stressors, however, are unique to pastoral families. So far we have explored the impact of ministry vocation being a lifestyle more than a job, and we have looked at conflicting loyalties between church and home. In the next chapter we will explore two more unique stressors that ministry couples and their children experience.

MORE MARRIAGE AND FAMILY STRESSORS

The delicate balance between home and office is very elusive to me. . . . I want

to be a great spouse, parent and pastor. But I just wonder sometimes

if it's possible to be all three in the same year.

A Summit pastor

A RECENT GOOGLE SEARCH for "Marriage is not easy" returned over 108 million hits! Obviously, many agree. Parishioners may assume, however, that pastoral families don't face marital challenges. And they may be surprised to learn that pastoral couples face the "normal" pressures of marriage and family, as well as significant stressors that are unique to ministry life.

In the last chapter, we looked at three marriage and family stressors experienced by those in ministry leadership. Now we will look at two more particularly focused on female ministry spouses: abandonment and lack of confidants. (Male ministry spouses may find that many of these challenges and suggestions are applicable as well.) As before, while looking at these challenges, we will describe helpful responses and actions that summit participants themselves identified.

STRESSOR FOUR: ABANDONMENT BY A SPOUSE WHO IS ALWAYS ON THE JOB

This fourth stressor is often even more emotional and hidden than the conflicting loyalties of church and home. Pastors often fail to distinguish between work and personal time. A result of their being "on the job" all of the time is that the spouse and children of pastors often feel abandoned. One wife candidly shared:

> For years I thought serving in the church meant sacrificing the desires of your family. So I have overworked at home in order to let my husband serve in the church. But I've realized that I secretly hate the fact that the church seems to come first in his life, priorities and time and that I end up carrying the load of our family by myself. . . . I resent the fact that he's so exhausted (mentally, physically and emotionally) from dealing with the church's problems all day long and that he just wants "down time" when he's home. I often feel we get leftovers, if that.

Another pastor's wife said that she is pretty self-sufficient. Thus, by not insisting on connection and intimacy from her pastor-husband, she had easily become complicit in a marriage of non-intimate coexistence. She had a mindset that "this is what it will be like in the beginning of ministry, and perhaps okay for a while longer." But she assumed that "someday it'll turn around." Now she realizes that if they don't change this pattern immediately, what is "just a little snowball now is going to get bigger and bigger." And a pastor shared,

> The heart of the issue is that as a pastor you have two wives: the church and your spouse. The second wife—the church—dominates your focus and attention. My wife wishes I would give her the attention I give the church. There is resentment and jealousy.

The summit participants discussed a variety of responses to these experiences of spousal abandonment. They range from rather simple interventions to options that are more complicated. The following provides a taste of the summit discussions and solutions, organized as actions that can strengthen marriages toward secure, caring and intimate relationships.

Invest Intentional Time. A number of pastors recognized that they need to be more intentional at committing uninterrupted time to their families. This involves planning family and personal time together. It also means including one's partner in calendar decisions that may affect family commitments. A number of pastors realized that by making major time commitments (such as outside speaking engagements) without involving their spouses in the decision, they were devaluing their partner.

The main concern behind scheduled time is the need to connect—or as one spouse put it, "not to live as though we are roommates with the kids as our only reference point." Building healthy marital connection requires planning, commitment and regular calendar decision-making times together.

Provide Emotional Security. Many ministry spouses keenly feel that the church takes emotional priority over them. One summit wife said, "I often feel that our family gets leftover shepherding based more on guilt than love." Another said, "My husband is a loving man, but it hurts me that he holds his heart from me but gives it to his work."

While for some spouses emotional security stems from the intentional time we just talked about, for most it also requires a spousal willingness to make the marriage relationship a priority of the heart. One wife described this by saying,

> I just need to know . . . when it all comes down to it, I am the one he chooses. I also want the church to know that.

Her pastor-husband responded,

> I don't have the right to be wooing the bride of Christ if I'm not wooing the bride that I have. She has the right to security from me. She has the right to know that I am going to be there, come hell or high water. She has the right to know that I will turn in my resignation tomorrow if our marriage is at risk by . . . this ministry job.

Another significant area of emotional security involves protecting the sexual relationship of the marriage. An older pastoral couple, who had been invited to share from their lifetime of experiences, emphasized this theme. A primary theme of their comments focused on maintaining healthy sexual relations. They explained,

> Couples are just giving up their sex lives because they are too tired and too busy and not connecting. We would ask you to fight for this part of your relationship. It is so important. It's so central. That is the one person in the world with whom you can enjoy this part of your life. So don't let it go away. Don't let it become a non-part of your life.

Another summit guest shared how it was important for pastoral couples to talk openly about any significant attraction they might feel toward someone other than their spouse. This person counseled,

> Pastors ought to realize and expect that over the course of their ministry, there will be people they are attracted to and be prepared to deal with that. In other words, think about it before it happens. One thing to do would be to agree with your spouse that you will share if there is some chemistry between you and another person in order to bring that out into the open. Also, you need to have a sense of humor about it, and realize that if things in your life and marriage are relatively healthy, the attraction will fade away. You don't need to tell your spouse every time you think someone is attractive, but you should disclose it when there is a vibe there, or a certain vulnerability you feel.

This guest went on to talk about steps pastors should take to "affair-proof" their marriages. This included the following advice.

> Pastors have to positively project behaviors that serve as a "no vacancy" sign: i.e., don't give off any signals that could be construed as openness to romantic or sexual interactions with a person other than your spouse. One way to show a "no vacancy" sign is to constantly speak positively about your spouse; don't even joke about your spouse in a negative way. And men should never compliment women in a way that would make them feel they are being noticed sexually (i.e., their dress or appearance). You might not mean anything by it, but it can easily be misconstrued.

In summary, emotional security can be built by doing the following:

- Intentionally share heart issues.
- Protect and fully enjoy your marriage bed.
- Communicate "no vacancy" to others.
- Speak only positively about your spouse, even when joking.

Get Marriage "Checkups." A number of pastors in the summit shared how they scheduled regular marriage "checkups" with a therapist. Just like getting a yearly physical, these pastoral couples felt it was important for their marriage *and* ministry to develop an ongoing relationship with a trained professional who could serve as a confidant and speak into their lives with candor. One of the pastors has openly shared this with the congregation, urging members to consider a similar agenda for marital health.

Practice Active Listening. All of the summit couples participated in a structured exercise of active listening. One member of each couple was given the role of listener while the other was the speaker. Each listener was challenged to give their spouse-speaker full attention, without thinking about what they would say in response. The speakers answered a series of questions, giving brief "I" statements that included feelings about the topic. When the speakers finished, the listeners were asked to restate the speakers' remarks briefly, in their own words. After round one, roles were reversed to allow each partner the opportunity to practice speaking and listening.[1]

For many couples, this exercise was the first experience of intentional listening and "I" sharing they had experienced in a long time. One pair noted that it was difficult and that it felt risky at first. Several others, however, commented on how the structured exercises made the conversation safe and constructive when it might not have been otherwise.

A husband reflected in his journal,

We talked in a focused way about things that we have talked around before. The directed time has given us the opportunity to narrow in on an area in our marriage and communicate in a way that is easy to skim over in the busyness of life and ministry.

A wife summarized the experience well, sharing that the active listening exercise

---

dials the emotional temperature down dramatically while still enabling feelings to be shared and heard honestly. I was more than a little surprised by what this exercise allowed us to say to each other—to be heard.

Developing good listening skills is important for a healthy marriage. If you would like to try such an active listening exercise in your own relationship, we would encourage you to try it first with the support of a counselor. The counselor will know how the exercise functions and should be able to train you in the process, coach you through your first experience and provide you with helpful questions to get you started.

Explore Family of Origin Patterns Together. In the chapters on self-care and emotional intelligence, we reviewed the benefits of reflecting on our families of origin. In the EQ chapter we encouraged you to consider constructing and interviewing a three-generation family diagram. (Appendix D provides details for constructing and exploring a family diagram.) When couples investigate their family backgrounds *together*, it helps each partner understand the other and how their current family mirrors or is different from the ones in which they grew up.

Again, we want to stress that the purpose of exploring our families of origin is not to blame or to attack others. All families are broken. The purpose of families reviewing their backgrounds together is to grow in awareness of both sinful and healthy patterns of behavior. This work is particularly helpful for learning how to identify and respond to our own emotions and the emotions of others—especially those in our families

At one summit meeting, we asked everyone to complete a three-generation family diagram and answer a series of questions about it. One participant's journal entry stated,

---

After getting stuck again and again by a certain emotional reaction my wife has, I was powerfully impacted to hear the deeper context out of which it arises. Suddenly a tension point that typically shrinks my heart toward her has now enlarged my heart for her. I've been given a glimpse into family history and more importantly, into the logic of her heart right now, in the present.

Similarly, when Tasha and her husband, David, reviewed their family diagram, they saw two obvious patterns that explained several marital misunderstandings about how to handle conflict properly. Their families of origin dealt with conflict in very different ways. One family tended to hide problems and behave with great calmness. The other tended to become animated and verbal about disagreements. The patterns clearly extended into Tasha and David's relational tendencies. Their new understanding helped them pursue a healthier alternative.

When Bob and his wife, Janet, pondered their family history, two immediate facts jumped off the pages. First were the multiple generations of divorce and abuse in Janet's family. This realization drew their commitment to establish different patterns for their own household. It also influenced their involvement in divorce recovery ministry for many years. In looking at Bob's family, there was a generational pattern of hard work for long hours. This provided insights, conversations and impetus for change in his own workaholic patterns.

When Donald and his wife, Mary, first examined the patterns of their respective families, they discovered that Mary's family recounted family "folklore" as a way of connecting with one another. However, the Guthries engaged in wide-ranging discussions as a means to connect. In their early years of marriage, these two "normal" patterns collided to produce unintended conflict. Both Donald and Mary felt out of place at one another's in-laws' homes. Recognizing these patterns has helped them appreciate one another's communication methods and their families of origin.

Develop Healthy Connecting Habits. Much discussion took place among summit couples about healthy habits that could build stronger marital connections. Our conversations identified four habits. (Some have already come up in other chapters that focused on the ministry leader.) When practiced in the family, these habits build health and maturity for everyone.

Habit One: Take days off and keep a regular date night. In the self-care chapter, we looked at the need for regular breaks in the intense schedules of pastors. Dedicated time off, focused on family relationships, is as important for the spouse and children as it is for the pastor. Early in their marriage, Donald and Mary committed to taking several walks together every week. This simple practice, begun nearly thirty years ago, has enabled them to stay in touch with one another. When their schedules are most hectic, the walks are most necessary.

Habit Two: Pursue hobbies together. Involvement in the same activities builds bonds of shared experience that are priceless. For example, both Bob and Janet actively served as cheerleaders and carpool drivers for their sons' sporting events. Later, they supported their sons' involvement in debate and musical theatre. Tasha and David took their family hiking and camping. Despite the grumbling during the trips, afterward all were thankful for the time and adventure together. All of these experiences provided opportunities for fun as well as conversations about life that continued long after the events were over.

Habit Three: Turn off phones. A number of the summit couples commented on how often their lives are interrupted throughout the day. Smartphones have only enhanced the possibilities for interruption through calls, texts, email and other social media. Many of the couples decided they would have a dedicated time every day for the family to unplug and connect with each other. The "prime time" to unplug was during evening meals. Summit couples concluded that setting aside an unhurried dinnertime sends an important message to their congregations. They quietly communicate a boundary that the family has priority over the ministry during this time.

Habit Four: Keep short accounts of wrongs. Jesus placed great emphasis on quickly resolving conflicts and relational difficulties (see, for example, Matthew 5:21-26). When teaching his disciples to pray, Jesus included the need to address relational challenges (Matthew 6:12). And the apostle Paul counseled the Ephesians not to let the sun go down on their anger (Ephesians 4:26). So it was not a surprise when many couples shared how important it was for them to resolve conflicts quickly. Many congregations are marked by ongoing disagreements among members that boil up in meetings and other gatherings. After talking about these congregational struggles, we concluded that keeping short accounts needs to start in our own homes before we can make it a part of church life.

To summarize, the stress that ministry spouses have from feeling abandoned threatens the health of ministry families, and thus the ability of pastors to remain fruitful in ministry for a lifetime. It is important for pastors and their families to consider steps for healthy relational connection. By putting these steps into action, pastors will also help their congregations mature relationally as they model and lead out of what they are learning.

QUESTIONS TO PONDER

1. What behaviors might signal that your spouse is feeling abandoned by you?

2. How would you and your spouse rate yourselves on the six activities that encourage healthy relational connection?

3. What are a couple healthy habits you would like to build into your daily, weekly and monthly schedules?

STRESSOR FIVE: THE NEED OF MINISTRY
SPOUSES FOR CONFIDANTS

In chapter six, where we discussed social self-care, we discovered it is difficult for pastors to find confidants: people who can provide them a safe shoulder, encouragement and counsel. Because pastoral relationships take on varied roles, unguarded rapport is rarely possible with members in one's own congregation.

Pastors are not the only ones who have the special need for trustworthy relationships. Ministry spouses need confidants as well. One summit wife expressed it this way,

Who can I talk to? Not people in the congregation. We don't want to give our spouses or the church a bad name. But we really need to find someone we can connect with and not worry about being perfect.

Another explained,

A friend is someone you can call at 2 a.m. and bawl your eyes out to no matter what trouble is going on. Now tell me, can a minister's spouse ever do that?

When speaking with psychologist Diane Langberg about this issue, one pastor's wife asked, "Do you think we should be guarded in our friendships in the church?" From her wealth of experience counseling pastors, she responded:

Yes, yes, yes! Your spouse is in a position of power. Some are afraid of power; some want it, and some want to be connected to it vicariously. Many people will want to use you. You have to be prayerful and go slow. There are wonderful, trustworthy people—that's the kind of confidant you need. Be cautious. Learn what safe people look like. Write out the characteristics of a safe friend from the past. Most things you have to see demonstrated consistently over time. And remember, you're going to get hurt whether or not you let people close to you. You cannot fully protect yourself. Even safe people will hurt us.

Sometimes such friendships can be found in relationships established before entering the ministry or formed in seminary. Some have found extended family members to be safe people with whom to talk. Others find ministry spouses from other denominations a resource of insight and encouragement. And many go to professional counselors to find assurance of confidentiality.

We listened to one summit couple who shared how they desired the support of a professional therapist. Out of concern of being "discovered" that they were going to counseling, they selected a professional who respected their convictions but held different religious views. They were surprised at how much encouragement they found from someone who listened well and provided insights that were not influenced by the same religious subsystem in which they functioned.

One pastor we know entered vocational ministry after many years of working in the financial industry. After a number of years in ministry, this pastor and spouse experienced a family tragedy that deeply shook them. Yet they both were expected to publicly express a strong faith without revealing their pain and doubts. In desperation, they reached out to the pastor's former business associate in another state. Tentatively they contacted this person and discovered an open ear from one who did not expect them to "act like someone in the ministry."

It is imperative that pastoral couples talk about developing and pursuing friendships. When one assumes a role of leadership, it can be very lonely. And it can be just as lonely for the ministry spouse as it is for the pastor. As one summit wife explained,

---

I want to tell those who are following behind us that it's a lonely place. When someone told me it was going to be lonely, it gave me the freedom to be lonely, and then I knew I had to look for places to go for friendships, for support and for encouragement.

QUESTIONS TO PONDER

1. Who does your spouse turn to for support and sharing the trials of ministry life?

2. What are some other possible sources of trustworthy friendships for your spouse and for you as a couple?

3. Do you have a professional therapist to turn to in crisis and for general

counseling toward ministry resilience? If not, why not? If so, when is the last time you met with him or her?

CONCLUSION

One of the most important discoveries made in our Pastors Summit research was the critical role the spouse and family have on sustaining persons in ministry leadership and building up their resilience. In these two chapters we have looked at five stressors for ministry marriage and family identified in the Pastors Summit. We have explored the "normal" pressures and the stressors unique to those in vocational ministry leadership. These distinctive stressors stem from ministers being always on the job, having conflicting loyalties between church and family, and from spouses feeling abandoned and needing safe, supportive friendships.

Few things support and strengthen pastors for ministry more than their relationships with their spouse. However, marriage and family difficulties can disrupt and even ruin ministry. The well-being of the church and of the pastors themselves is contingent on a growing, nurturing relationship with their spouse and children. As one pastor shared:

The quality of my marriage and my parenting will probably never garner me public accolades and the esteem of my peers. I am tempted to let these things slip while I pursue public ministry opportunities, such as preaching and leadership. However, if I would do this, it won't be long before my relationship with my spouse takes a back seat to sermon preparation and time spent with my kids becomes time spent in meetings. The best way I can help my church is to be healthy myself—spiritually, emotionally and physically—and to help my spouse and children be healthy as well.

RECOMMENDATIONS FOR FURTHER READING

1. Christopher Ash. *Marriage: Sex in the Service of God*. Manchester, U.K.: Inter-Varsity Press, 2003.

2. Timothy Keller. *The Meaning of Marriage: Facing the Complexities of Commitment with the Wisdom of God*. New York: Dutton, 2011.

3. Sue Johnson. *Hold Me Tight: Seven Conversations for a Lifetime of Love.*

New York: Little, Brown and Company, 2008.

4. Gary Thomas. *Sacred Marriage: What if God Designed Marriage to Make Us Holy More Than to Make Us Happy?* Grand Rapids: Zondervan, 2000.

5. John M. Gottman and Nan Silver. *The Seven Principles for Making Marriage Work.* New York: Three Rivers Press, 1999.

6. Scott Stanley, Daniel Trathen, Savanna McCain and Milt Bryan. *A Lasting Promise: A Christian Guide to Fighting for Your Marriage.* San Francisco: Jossey-Bass, 2002.

MEDIA WORTH EXPLORING

1. For more information on Peacemaker Ministries, see www.peacemaker .net. Peacemaker Ministries is an organization that seeks to equip and assist Christians and their churches to respond to conflict in a biblical and God-honoring manner.

2. *The Story of Us* (1999), rated R. A drama-romance-comedy, directed by Rob Reiner and starring Michelle Pfeiffer and Bruce Willis, explores what happens when a couple has slowly drifted apart through the challenges of everyday life during fifteen years of marriage.

3. *Shadowlands* (1993), rated PG. This British biographical film is directed by Richard Attenborough and stars Anthony Hopkins and Debra Winger. The story of love and sorrows confronted by C. S. Lewis and his wife, Joy Davidson.

4. *When Harry Met Sally* (1989), rated R. A romantic comedy, directed by Rob Reiner and starring Meg Ryan and Billy Crystal, that originated from Reiner's return to single life after divorce. The film raises the question "Can men and women ever just be friends?"

5. *Walk the Line* (2005), rated PG-13. A biographical drama film directed by James Mangold, *Walk the Line* is based on the early life and career of country music artist Johnny Cash and his romance with June Carter.

13

LEADERSHIP POETRY

No organization works if the toilets don't work. . . .

Leadership is a mixture of poetry and plumbing.

James March, in "Too Much Efficiency Not Good for
Higher Education, March Argues"

JAMES MARCH DOESN'T HAVE A television show, and he hasn't written *New York Times* bestsellers. But when the *Harvard Business Review* awarded the "most admired management experts" title, March appeared second on the list, behind the late Peter Drucker. This emeritus professor of international management at Stanford University says that there are two essential dimensions of leadership: plumbing and poetry. "What I call 'plumbing,'" he explains, "is what most people call 'management.' And what I call 'poetry' is what most people call 'leadership.' In almost any position in life, you need the mix."[1]

Leadership requires both creative art and methodical tasks. As an art, it involves ambiguity, imagination, innovation, emotional engagement and improvisation. But the methodical tasks require technical details, repetitive chores, organization, administration, plans, orderly procedures and perhaps even restroom repair.

People don't go into pastoral ministry eager to tackle such widely varying job responsibilities. Studies show that people considering the ministry want to preach, teach, disciple, do outreach and care for God's people. When pastors enter the ministry, however, they are often shocked by how much leadership and management are involved in their work.[2] They are also surprised by how little their ministry training prepared them for these often unpleasant and misunderstood aspects of their calling.

As one pastor acknowledged,

When I got out of seminary, I was sent out as a church planter. I didn't know what I was doing. I found I was so deficient in the area of leadership. I had to self-educate—and I'm still doing that.

Another summit pastor responded, "We were trained to be pulpit-oriented. But those 'muscle groups' we were trained in aren't the muscles you need for this job."

The Pastors Summit showed us how consistently pastors chafe under the burden of leadership responsibilities. Joe Novenson, pastor of Lookout Mountain Presbyterian Church and a guest at one summit, responded to the complaints, saying,

---

I have sought to redefine "administration" as doing anything that helps people move closer to Jesus. It helps me to think of management as more than just a necessary evil but as a necessary component of discipling Christ's church.

The two-sided responsibilities of leadership are a "brutal fact" of the ministry. As one summit pastor shared, "There's a certain weight of leadership and management that's just there all the time." Therefore, it is critical for pastors and other ministry workers to embrace this area of their calling.

LEARNING THE POETRY OF PASTORAL LEADERSHIP

The poetry side of pastoral leadership is the more creative and ambiguous part of leading. Not unlike the poetry homework for a literature course, this work requires imaginative thinking, learning by trial and error, and interpreting emotions, all in the midst of pressure to produce and meet deadlines. In *The Truth About Leadership,* James Kouzes and Barry Posner boldly declare, "Learning is the master skill. The best leaders are the best learners."[3] Of course, there are many things pastors must learn. Long lists of topics could be discussed and priorities for training debated. However, when it comes to this *artistic* side of leadership, we identified four areas of learning that are critical for ministry leaders in order to develop their *practice of leadership*: reflection, hardship, systems thinking and political perception.

REFLECTION IS REAL LEADERSHIP WORK

Yes, we've already looked at reflection quite a bit in this book. Nearly every chapter has dealt with it in some way. We hope you agree that there are many facets to the idea of, and need for, reflection. So as we come to the topic of leadership poetry, a unique type of reflection comes into play. The ambiguity and complexity of leading ministry requires us to ponder intentionally.

How do leaders learn through reflection? The groundbreaking work of the late MIT professor Donald A. Schön highlights how reflection happens in practice.[4] Schön writes that professional practice takes place in situations that are puzzling, ill defined, troubling and uncertain. These situations require practitioners to make judgments and decisions while in the thick of action. Schön calls this "reflection-*in*-action." We like to think of it as *improvisation*, the kind required of a good jazz player. This type of reflection in the midst of action requires leaders to draw on a repertoire of examples and prior experiences and to connect with their emotions, often in an instant. Then they apply this wealth of material to the immediate circumstances at hand.

After the event, expert practitioners review and reconsider their decisions and the consequences of their reflection-in-action practice. Schön describes this type of reflection, which follows after the new experience, as "reflection-*on*-action." Pastors grow in leadership expertise as they practice reflection both during and after presenting situations.

One of the summit pastors shared how he routinely practices reflection-on-action.

My congregation knows that in the last week of September, I'll be away for three to five days. During that time I pull out our vision and pray and think of where we are as a church and where God is taking us.

However, reflection-on-action also takes place in less structured ways, as Ronald Cervero and Arthur Wilson write. It happens "with others in conversations on telephones, through email and faxes, and sometimes privately in offices, hallways, and restrooms or at social gatherings."[5] Reflective work cannot wait for an annual retreat.

Unlike some of the types of reflection that we discussed in earlier chapters, this kind of reflective work is not just a personal activity, focused on personal growth. Learning through leadership reflection-in-action and reflection-on-action requires conversation partners who provide insights and perspectives untapped by the individual. And it is focused on the community needs for leadership. "A person needs to take a step back to see what he did yesterday and what he did right or wrong. He needs always to reflect. But he cannot do this alone. You need good people to tell you whether you are doing right or you are doing wrong."[6]

Learning through reflection occurs through many varied methods. For example, in the Pastors Summit, individual reflection took place every Wednesday morning for at least two hours. The participants scattered—unplugged from electronic devices and unhindered by the normal pressures of ministry—to consider their lives, families and ministries in the light of God's kingdom purposes.

Another method for reflection we tried was the use of a leadership 360 evaluation tool.[7] This instrument allowed the pastors to explore their own self-perceptions as well as the experiences others have of their leadership. Participants enthusiastically responded to the opportunity of receiving and processing this kind of input. One commented, "This explains why I enjoy and succeed in some areas but struggle and fall in others." Another said, "This was the best opportunity I have ever had to address my leadership."

One other method we used to learn leadership through reflection was journaling. The summit pastors maintained a record of their insights and meditations. This was followed by a time of group sharing to discuss what they had learned. Listen to how the new insights and renewed priorities flowed.

There is an underlying presupposition that if you just master these habits or irrefutable laws, or whatever, that you can do leadership. And I know these things are important. But it can be idolatrous—I begin to think I can be successful just by mastering these methods rather than depending on the Lord.

✚ ✚ ✚

It seems to me that what attracts people to the gospel of grace is the example of grace lived out. I think that if people see that you really do struggle, then they can relate to you as a leader and can think, "If he struggles, then I guess it is okay that I still struggle."

Leaning to lead via reflection can happen in many contexts and with a variety of persons, in both formal and informal ways. Our daily reflections often go unrecognized because they take place in the normal hurry of activities. We could gain much by taking notice and slowing down to harvest them. We encouraged our participants to develop the habits of stopping to record daily reflection-in-action and of taking intentional time for reflection-on-action.

QUESTIONS TO PONDER

1. What is your capacity for reflection-in-action? What will it take for you to be willing to amplify it?

2. Where do you create regular space and time for reflection-on-action? What would have to be diminished or excluded for you to have regular time for reflection-on-action?

3. Who are good talking partners for your reflection work?

HARDSHIP PROVIDES THE CRUX OF THE CONTENT

The idea of learning through hardships has also been a regular theme of this study. Now we look at the role of hardship in the development of our leadership poetry. Earlier we referenced the seminar in which we heard from leadership guru Russ Moxley. At one point in the seminar, Moxley asked the question "What is the most effective way to train leaders?" Our responses included "continuing education," "mentors and coaching," "evaluation instruments" and "varied experiences and contexts." He explained the most effective leadership training method wasn't on our list. "As a matter of fact," he said, "the one you have missed has been found to be more effective than all the others combined."

The most effective method of leadership training, Moxley told us, is the experience of hardships. But there was a twist in his explanation. It isn't hardships themselves that provide leadership training, but hardships experienced in a supportive context with the opportunity to review the experience. This is because deep learning takes place when crisis is combined with community, a freedom to fail and the opportunity to evaluate and grow through the experience.[8] As Kouzes and Posner explain, "The only way that people can learn is by doing things they've never done before. . . . Making mistakes is part of the price people pay for innovation and for learning. . . . [But] because people know that they won't do well the first time they try something, learning new things can be a bit scary. They might embarrass themselves or look stupid. Learning is more likely to happen in a climate in which people feel safe in taking the risk of failure."[9]

Our summit pastors discussed the challenge of having support and reflection to learn from hardships. One lamented,

We're taught in ministry how to succeed and win. We're not taught how to lose and die and suffer—or how to process it when we experience it.

Another replied,

One of the biggest problems [is that] leaders see themselves as the ones who have to keep mistakes from being made. . . . There are going to be a lot of mistakes made in the church, and we're going to make a bunch of them ourselves. How do any of us learn? I would say that the things I know best I've learned from boneheaded stuff I've done. . . . Most things like that don't really kill the church or the people in the church.

In order for hardships to be a learning experience, ministry leaders need a supportive environment that allows for mistakes and difficulties and that provides a place where these experiences can be processed. Ideally this would take place with the governing board of the congregation. However, as we have seen, governing boards may not be psychologically safe places to talk about difficult experiences and failure.

More often, these conversations only happen with one's spouse. As we have already stressed, the "circle of friends" in which ministry leaders can openly talk about their mistakes and receive helpful feedback must be expanded beyond their own family. Pastors and those who work with them need to develop allies and, more specifically, confidants and peers with whom this kind of learning takes place.

Eventually, if pastors want to raise the spiritual and emotional health of their leadership boards and congregations, they will need to create conversations in which hardships can be named and discussed. Dan Allender explains, "As a therapist I know I can take no one any further than where I've chosen to go. I can never ask or expect a client to be more honest, more humble, more forgiving, or more sacrificial than I am willing to live. Consequently, if a person desires to lead others into maturity rather than mere productivity, he must go first."[10]

Congregational maturity will never adequately develop unless the leaders of the congregation embrace the difficult lessons learned by hardships and mistakes. If they don't do this, they will send a message that failure and struggle are not allowed and must be avoided. This, in turn, leads to superficiality that stunts everyone's learning and growth in the church.

QUESTIONS TO PONDER

1. What significant hardships have you experienced in the last decade?

2. To what extent did the contexts of those challenges include or exclude support?

3. To what extent were you able to reflect upon and process these experiences with others?

4. How have these hardships affected your leadership?

5. What difference has it made in your life that God was present with you during these hardships?

SYSTEMS THINKING

The third area for growth in the art of pastoral leadership involves systems thinking: understanding relational connections and their impact. Early in our research, we learned the importance of viewing the church as a living system.[11] Authors Jim Herrington, Robert Creech and Trisha Taylor describe a living system: "Whenever you engage in a relationship that is long-term, intense, and significant, you become emotionally connected to one another. Each person who is part of this interaction begins to affect, and be affected by, the anxiety and behaviors of the others."[12] The individuals in our congregations influence each other and the whole far more than we imagine.

Before looking at congregations as living systems, it is most helpful to explore the systems of our own families of origin.[13] What patterns of expectations, assumptions, behaviors and emotions did we inherit from our family systems? These patterns will have a direct impact on all those connected to us.

Systems Thinking Means Assessing Maturity and Anxiety. Systems thinking directs us to perceive the church as a gathering of people who come from very different family systems. Thus, they bring their unique family strengths and struggles into the broader system of the family of God. As one of our pastors shared,

---

It was interesting to think about the church as a family that is full of people (including the pastor) bringing their own family of origin issues together in the same place.

Another pastor related, "I'm beginning to realize that my church looks a lot like my family of origin: poor communication, conflict avoidance and a focus on high achievement."

Systems theory tells us that every system is significantly influenced by the emotional maturity and the anxiety of the people. A metaphor that Herrington, Creech and Taylor developed explains how this functions in our families and churches. They compare a system to a reservoir. The emotional maturity of the people determines the size of the reservoir. Anxiety in the system is the water level held by the reservoir. "The larger the reservoir (that is, the greater the degree of emotional maturity), the more anxiety it can contain without spilling over and producing a problem for the system. The higher the level of water (anxiety), regardless of the size of the reservoir (maturity), the closer the system is to overflowing."[14]

We think growth in maturity in general (not just emotionally) enables the family, or system, to deal with anxiety in a more healthy way. Since change of any kind produces anxiety, leading a congregation through change requires accounting for the congregation's emotional, spiritual and intellectual maturity.

As the summit pastors talked together about families and congregations, there was a natural progression from learning about systems and emotional maturity to asking how, as leaders, they could build spiritual, intellectual and emotional maturity into their family and church systems.

How can ministry leaders increase the size of their system reservoirs?

Building Spiritual Maturity in the System. When it comes to the leadership responsibilities of pastors, few things are more important than managing the system anxiety in their congregations. (Yet we have never seen that on a ministry job description!) Therefore, the ongoing development of both personal and congregational spiritual maturity is a significant pastoral leadership responsibility.

So what can pastors do to spiritually develop themselves and others? Summit pastors focused on the importance of regularly pursuing the four areas of spiritual discipline discussed in chapter four: reflection, the cultivation of personal and corporate worship, the keeping of sabbath and sabbatical, and genuine involvement in prayer and repentance.

Pastors also need to lead their elders and congregations in the development of these same disciplines. Only as pastors grow toward maturity in Christ are they able to lead their elders and congregations in similar growth. Jesus said as much in Matthew 10:24-25: "A disciple is not above his teacher, nor a servant above his master. It is enough for the disciple to be like his teacher, and the servant like his master."

Building Intellectual Maturity in the System. In Romans 12:2, the apostle Paul exhorts his friends not to be "conformed to this world." Rather, they are to be continually renewed, having their minds transformed, and they are to "take every thought captive to obey Christ" (2 Corinthians 10:5).[15]

We already noted that to see things from God's point of view often requires the crucible of hardships. But in times of intense challenge, we struggle to adopt God's way of viewing things. For example, Donald remembers when he first heard that his daughter was born with a severe hearing impairment; Bob thinks of when his second son died in childbirth; and Tasha vividly recalls the phone call at three a.m. reporting her husband's tragic accident. In hindsight, we can see how much God used those times to mature us. At these critical times, each of us faced questions of whether God is good and whether we will believe him. Building mental maturity involves trying to think after God's thoughts and contemplating what the Bible says about our circumstances, doubts and fears.

Similarly, in the life of a congregation, mental maturity develops when the people of God are encouraged to see things from God's point of view.

We're not saying leaders should present superficial proof texts and lead their people to deny anxiety or concerns. Far from it! Rather, we should teach them to name their experiences, reflect on them together, and prayerfully support each another in walking by faith and not by sight. But they need to do so with their intellect engaged and focused on the truth of Scripture.

We know a congregation in which the senior pastor, in the midst of a depressive episode, committed suicide. For many years, the members of this congregation refused to talk openly about this incident. The natural response of denial turned into the dysfunctional response of "Don't feel; don't trust; don't talk." This resulted in increased anxiety in the system. Finally, the church leadership began to name the powerful realities of this incident and talk about it together. They discussed the mysteries of God's purposes and the brokenness of our humanity. By making the implicit explicit, speaking the truth in love toward one another and seeking to understand this incident from God's point of view, people matured in their thinking, and the anxiety decreased significantly.

A few years later, the World Trade Center was destroyed by terrorists. Many members of this congregation had friends and loved ones killed in this incident. Due to the maturity developed through the previous crisis of their pastor's suicide, the congregation was better prepared to manage their own anxiety and thus care for the community after September 11.

Building Emotional Maturity in the System. In our chapters on emotional intelligence, we learned how the EQ of pastors and congregational leadership influences the EQ of the church. This is systems thinking. As one pastor shared, "Your church will take on your personality. It will reflect who you are, your background and your character."

In those earlier chapters, we reviewed ways that pastors can develop their own EQ as well as the EQ of their congregations. Here we simply want to emphasize how important conflict management is in building a congregation's emotional maturity. To use an analogy: just as children learn how to handle conflict (for good or for ill) by watching their parents work on difficulties, so congregations increase or decrease in emotional maturity by the ways their leadership manages disagreements and controversy. One summit pastor acknowledged,

I realized there was a situation that I was avoiding because of how excruciating it was. It was impacting the way I did everything else. I needed to move toward those persons, to initiate conflict with them in an appropriate way. . . . Invariably when I've gone and done that, it's been energizing instead of draining for everyone. The draining situation is the unresolved, ongoing junk.

Notice that by avoiding conflict, this pastor—and the entire system—was emotionally affected. When responsible conflict was initiated, however, the pastor and the congregation were energized. Another pastor shared,

Even when we fight as pastors, we've got to teach. We've got to teach the people how to fight fair. For example, if we have a conflict with our elders, we've got to say to them, "Look, it's okay to criticize me and my leadership and my skills, but you have to love me. And as a group, you might wind up loving me so much that you say, 'You're not right for this job.' If you love me, I could hear that. But if you withdraw your love from me, because you don't know how to confront me, and you don't know how to criticize me or face me, then that is sin." Even as we fight we've got to teach, because that is the calling God gave us.

When pastors exhibit emotional maturity, over time it will raise the emotional maturity of the congregation. Seeing things systemically means realizing that everything influences everything. The way pastors and elders lead the congregation affects far more than the immediate outcomes. The congregation takes cues for understanding how it is appropriate to think, to feel and to respond to circumstances. Therefore, pastors must consciously work to see the systemic connections in their congregations.

QUESTIONS TO PONDER

1. What stories about your ministry are told most often by its leaders and members? How do the stories told by these two groups compare? How do these stories shed light on the systemic maturity levels and anxiety in your congregation?

2. Describe (by using concrete examples) how your ministry system cele-

brates success and addresses failure. What are some of the connections between these emotional and behavioral patterns and the ones of your family of origin?

3. How did you go about resolving a recent conflict in your church? What impact do you think the process of getting through the conflict had on others?

PERCEIVING THE POLITICS OF MINISTRY

The fourth and final area of learning that is vital for leadership poetry concerns the politics of ministry. We don't often think of training our ministry leaders in politics at seminary, but we should. Ministry involves working with people. And people have differing interests; they are stakeholders who are affected by the decisions of the church leadership. The reality that they have something to gain or to lose greatly influences congregants' actions (and reactions) when confronted with decisions. Whenever people actively promote their interests, they have entered the realm of politics.

There are two forms of political activity. One focuses on gamesmanship, manipulation and getting what we want. When this takes place, politics is viewed negatively and associated with conflict and harm. During one summit discussion on politics, a pastor exploded, "What really wears us out is the junior high school stuff, all the political things . . . all the crap!"

The other form of politics involves the art of negotiating with others. We describe this political activity more positively: choosing among conflicting wants and interests, developing trust, locating support and opposition, developing sensitivity to timing, and knowing the informal and formal organizational refrains.[16] Everyone involved in ministry recognizes how much these activities describe their day-to-day experiences.

Growth in leadership of ministry politics involves the ability to perceive the differences between interests, power and authority, relationship capital, and negotiation. These themes interact with each other to make up the complex systems in which politics take place. We'll explore each of them in turn.

Interests. Ministry plans and programs reflect the various convictions found in a church: theological convictions, budget convictions, and convictions of time and resource priorities. So when ministry is being planned, participants bring their interests to the planning table. These interests develop out of the complex set of goals, values, desires, concerns and motivations that lead people in the church to act.[17] Jonathan Edwards, the esteemed philosopher and theologian of the eighteenth century, once said that the human will always chooses according to its strongest inclination at the moment.[18] This is the meaning of interests: our priority preferences at a given time.

So let's say a conflict arises on an elder board about the number of pastors the church is hiring. One group of elders strongly promotes the ministry of laypersons in the church. They believe that pastors are needed to "equip the saints for the work of ministry" (Ephesians 4:12). These elders reason, "If the pastors were equipping the saints better, we would have more mature members and less need to hire more pastors."

On the other side you have elders (often led by pastors) who say, "The expectation of this congregation is for high-quality activities. And the same passage (Ephesians 4:11) says God gives leaders to the church. You can't expect laypersons—who have full-time jobs, families and personal lives—to have the time, energy or expertise to lead. We need more staff."

Both groups have interests. Both groups identify a biblical basis for their interests. And both groups are deeply convicted that their interests are the correct priority. We now have what has been described as a "crucial conversation."[19] How should the pastor lead into these politics with conviction and love? Let's return to systems thinking to gain some help.

Power and Authority. Interests, those things people feel strongly about, are always negotiated in relationship systems, that is, in groups of people who are connected somehow. And these relationship systems are defined largely by the dynamics of power and authority. Let's explore these two concepts and how they relate to the negotiation of interests.

Discerning levels of power. Power is not an easy concept to grasp. Ministry involves working with people and always takes place in the context of relationships. Some of these relationships are fairly new; others have been preserved for generations. Regardless, the interpersonal dynamics and histories of these relationships affect the ability for anyone in the system to make decisions or to get things done. So power in ministry can be defined as the capacity to act or influence others. Contrary to how we typically account for power, the amount of power one has is largely based on the duration, strength and stability of one's relationships in the system.

Let's reflect on this concept of power in our story about conflicting interests over hiring new pastors. What are the interpersonal dynamics involved? Most of the elders who are against hiring more pastors have been in the church for over twenty years. They came to faith in Christ and membership in the church through a thriving lay renewal ministry. This ministry emphasized the importance of laypersons growing in their faith and taking responsibility in ministry. These convictions were embedded in their souls early in their walks with Christ and are viewed as foundational. Further, these elders have labored together in ministry over the years. Together they have led Bible studies, shared ministry leadership and raised children. Now many live near each other in retirement. Over the years, the congregation has venerated them as senior leaders in the faith.

On the other side of the issue, many of the elders who want to hire more pastors have grown up in the church. They came to faith under the leadership of a youth pastor who had been given permission to hire part- and full-time associates. (The older elders had agreed to hire these staff since they didn't have the time or ability to work with the youth.) Others of the pro-hiring elders are newer to the congregation. They came to faith through various parachurch ministries that had multiple-staff campus teams. They personally benefited from the quality of ministry provided by trained leaders hired to run the ministries. A few of these elders were involved together in the same college ministry. Since joining the church (or coming back after college), most of them have bonded in community groups, in which they share life together as they start their families and establish careers.

So which group has the power—the ability to act or influence—in the congregation, and where does it come from? The answer: both groups have power from their own constituencies, founded in the relational histories and commitments they have formed.

Seeing authority two ways. Now let's bring the idea of authority into the equation. All authority is derived from God. But in human systems, authority is power that "has been legitimated by the social structures within which the authority is exercised."[20]

Broadly speaking, there are two types of authority: formal and relational. Formal authority is the exercise of power that has been legitimated by recognized social structures. So, for example, both groups of elders described above have been duly trained and ordained by their congregation. Technically, the elders all have the same formal authority. However, the length of time one holds a formal position usually increases the amount of authority associated with it.

The second type of authority is based on relationships. It is derived from the relational status one has in a community and perhaps even from the place one's subgroup holds within the broader community. So while each of the elders technically has the same formal authority, each also has a level of relational authority within the congregation and its subgroups. In our story, it could be expected that the older elders have more relational authority among their peers, while the younger elders have more within their own constituency

To make things even more interesting, let's inject Mrs. Jones into our story. Mrs. Jones has been in the church for over forty years (longer than most of the "older" elders). She has taught third-grade Sunday school over all these years. This means she taught some of the elders (young and old alike) when they were in third grade. Further, she has taught all of the older elders' children, and many children of the younger elders. And she has gotten to know many of the other younger elders because she consciously chose to participate in their community group. (She says she likes the group because "they keep me young.")

Mrs. Jones is loved and respected in the congregation. Over the past forty years, people have come to her to share their burdens and seek her wisdom. It is not unusual for pastors or other elders to seek her out when faced with personal or congregational issues. So when the question of hiring more staff comes up, numerous people approach her to gain her perspective.

Who has power and authority in the church? As we saw above, both groups of elders have the formal authority of their office, and each has relational authority among their friends and peers. Then there is Mrs. Jones. She has never held a position of formal authority in the congregation beyond third-grade Sunday school teacher. But her relational authority in the congregation is enormous. An appraisal of church decisions during the past ten years would show that most significant changes aligned with the interests of Mrs. Jones. Mrs. Jones may not have any formal authority, but she has a lot of power!

While we don't disregard the importance of formal authority and the role it plays in accomplishing God's purposes, we suggest that relational authority trumps formal authority much of the time. Therefore, in order to make decisions and focus on the work of equipping God's people, leaders (including those with the most formal authority) need to recognize and develop relationship capital.

Intentionally Growing Relationship Capital. Relationship capital is a "trust savings account," of sorts. Leaders must build relationship capital with people in their system/organization, so that "money" is in the bank when withdrawals are necessary. In other words, when a leader makes a decision that others dislike, it lowers the amount of trust those people place in the leader. It is a withdrawal in their relationship to the leader. We agree with the summit pastor who said,

---

Formal authority runs out quickly. Ultimately, all power devolves down to a level of relationship. And if I haven't developed trust with people, I can only get so far.

Our research suggests that there are three elements required for building relationship capital: intentionality, time and vulnerability.

Intentionality grows relationship capital. Healthy ministry must be built on an intentional decision to develop trusting relationships. As one pastor explained,

---

I've taken a lot of time personally with elders. We've done social things together. We've done things with our spouses together. So when we come to difficult situations, there is trust. There is knowledge of each other. There is relationship. And by contrast, I'll go to denominational meetings and hear conflicts that are going on. And my first thought is, "These folks have never played golf together." There is no relationship. They don't trust each other.

Jesus interacted with many types of people, including strangers and persons who sought him out. However, a close reading of the Gospels shows that Jesus was very intentional in giving quality time to selected persons, particularly the disciples. He clearly had a focus of ministry, beginning with the twelve (some would say three or four key disciples among the twelve), then a broader group of disciples (referenced as "the seventy-two") and finally the masses of people.

Intentionality involves developing this type of ministry focus: spending time and building relationships with strategic people in the congregation. We are not talking about favoritism or building a cadre of "yes women and men." Rather, we suggest that politically perceptive ministers seek to understand the *various* interests of groups within the congregation. This involves intentionally developing more intimate and trusting relationships with current and future leaders in the congregation.

Time invested grows relationship capital. Developing relationship capital takes time. Making the effort to be present with people where they live and work communicates an interest and commitment to them. It tells people we value and respect them. Participating in recreational activities and meals together creates bonds that would never develop in formal meetings. One of the pastors explained,

> When you stay somewhere long enough, then you *do* have a voice and a certain amount of capital. The key is to very strategically spend that capital. . . . I've been at this church and in this area for eighteen years. Most pastors don't stay someplace long enough to develop the capital and actually decide to write the check and cash it in. Now I'm getting out the checkbook . . .

This comment also shows that relationship capital includes the length of time pastors stay in one place. Some denominations deliberately move pastors every two to four years. As a result, the primary relationships developed in the congregation are between lay leaders and members in the congregation, while the pastors are often (though not always) viewed as temporary residents without power. As one pastor bemoaned,

> When I came to this congregation, an older person came up to me Sunday morning and said, with a smile, "Just remember, I was here long before you showed up, and I'll be here when you're gone."

The rapid movement of pastors between churches isn't always denominational. While statistics vary, most studies show that the average duration of a pastorate is four to five years.[21] Pastors transition for many reasons, including conflict, family problems, ministry preference and burnout.[22] But studies have shown that longer pastorates create stability, which promotes church health and growth.[23] We believe a primary reason for this is that relationship capital takes time to develop. The longer a pastor stays with a congregation, the more possibility there is for informal power to develop.

Vulnerability grows relationship capital. Pastors who are appropriately vulnerable with their congregations build relationship capital. As one pastor explained, there is an analogy between sharing within one's own family and sharing in the church. He said, "You don't share all your problems with your kids, even when they're grown up; but you do share a lot."

On the one hand, pastors must identify the limits of what they will share and with whom they will share it. As one pastor said, "I meet with some men on Friday mornings; I know my limits of what I should share with them." On the other hand, pastors who only share in generalities and don't expose the realities of their own human struggles will not create authentic relationships. Rather, they project an attitude described by one participant as, "Come to Jesus and be like me, a person who doesn't need Jesus."

How transparent should pastors be about their own struggles? There are no easy answers. Honest sharing can be very powerful and very dangerous. If pastors aren't willing to take steps of vulnerability, however, it is understandable why members of the congregation follow suit. As a result, superficiality reigns and genuine relationship capital is spent rather than gained.

The three of us are friends with a pastor who, over a period of years, developed a deep dependency on alcohol. One day, after his wife discovered a hidden stash of booze, he faced the truth: he was an alcoholic. With his wife's encouragement, he began to attend Alcoholics Anonymous (AA) meetings and soon had a sponsor. While he shared with his sponsor that he was a pastor, he didn't disclose this to others in his AA meeting at first. After two years of being sober, his sponsor challenged him to share his story in more detail with his congregation. You can imagine how scared he felt. How would people react? Was this the end of his ministry?

Joined by his wife, he began by talking with some key elders in his church. Because of the trust he had developed with these leaders over the years, their surprise was followed by an interest in how they could help (rather than a move for his dismissal). After much prayer and discussion, they decided he should talk about his recovery with the entire elder board.

All agenda items were put aside for the evening, and this pastoral couple shared their story with deep sincerity and tears. The elder board responded with their own tears, saddened by their failure to understand his situation. The initial meeting was followed by months of discussion, as the elders developed a deeper understanding of addiction and learned about their pastor's recovery process. One highlight was when the pastor's sponsor came and discussed with them the twelve steps of AA.

After three years of recovery, with the support of the elder board, the pastor shared his story at a local gathering of denominational leaders. Standing in front of these leaders, surrounded by a number of his elders, this pastor spoke of the pressures of pastoral ministry, his addiction and his recovery. Instead of calls for his resignation, there was an open time of confessing how they, as fellow pastors, struggled with the difficulties of the pastorate.

After another six months, this pastor went before his congregation—with his entire elder board standing with him on the platform—and shared the same story. Then, having shared with everyone else, he had one more group to talk to. After years together at AA meetings, he finally shared with his fellow alcoholics that he was a pastor. To this day he laughs when he tells the first words spoken by one of his AA buddies. "I'll be damned!" the man exclaimed. Our friend's response? "I certainly hope not!"

The outcome of this story of thoughtful and timely vulnerability is positive. As a result, this pastor's family, congregation and denomination grew and matured. Today he continues to be held in high esteem, with significant relational capital within his congregation and community. Of course, other stories—of times that inappropriate vulnerability and immaturity broke relationship capital—could be told. Taking steps to build trust through appropriate vulnerability requires wisdom, counsel and support.

Developing relationship capital is critical in the dynamics of ministry politics. As one pastor—a former Marine—put it,

> My mentor told me relationship capital is like poker chips. When you
> make a mistake, you lose some. So you better have enough chips built
> up so when you blow it, or when you need them, you have them.

This is highlighted by the experience of another pastor, who shared,

> When I first went to my church, there was an elder there who had been
> there since 1934. I may have been the recognized leader. But he was the
> de facto leader. And when we'd sit around the table, you could tell who
> the primary influencer was when the tough questions came up. You'd
> see where their eyes would go to. That's the influencer. And I had to find
> how to work in that context. It's interesting that about twelve years into
> my ministry, he looked over at me—he was a great, godly man, who was
> good for me—he leaned over to me and he said, "Pastor, this is your
> church now." And I knew exactly what he meant by it. He acknowledged
> that the weight of influence had now shifted from him to me.

Negotiation: Political Insight in Action. Putting our political concepts
all together, we can summarize that negotiation takes place when people
use their authority and power (both formal and relational) to promote
their interests with each other. One author defines negotiation as "the
process whereby two or more parties, with a mix of aligned and conflicting interests, communicate about a decision, with a view toward reaching
an acceptable agreement."[24]

Three distinct things happen in negotiation. First, people negotiate *between* each other; second, they negotiate their interests *with* the power and
authority available to them; and third, what takes place will either maintain, strengthen or diminish the interests and power of those involved.[25]

Here's a positive story to illustrate. Say that Sally wants a significant
budgetary increase for the annual women's retreat. Being politically savvy,
she prepares a presentation for the church board. First, she gathers financial data and historical information on past retreats. She also drafts a careful program plan that includes promotional material, site descriptions and
a detailed agenda. Further, she gleans testimonies from past participants
to illustrate the significance of the retreat. Finally, she secures a three-
minute video of the proposed speaker to play for the board.

With the completion of her board presentation, Sally fulfilled the three aspects of negotiation. First, a negotiation had taken place *between* Sally and the board during the presentation and resulting discussion. Second, she negotiated *with* the power available to her (her own reputation in the congregation, excellent planning, testimonies and the speaker video clip). In response, the board unanimously approved the increase. As a result, the third aspect of negotiation occurred. Sally now has more power because her interests (the women's retreat) were highly valued by the board (and others in the congregation). And if the retreat is considered a success, this outcome will further Sally's reputation and enhance the trust the board placed in her leadership. Sally's relational power in the system increases.

QUESTIONS TO PONDER

1. Who are the powerful people in your congregation because of their informal authority and relationship capital?

2. When you consider a major upcoming ministry decision, what are the different interests at stake? Who will be the most affected by the decision? What are their interests and power (capacity to act or influence)?

3. What priority does relationship building have in your weekly schedule? Where is trust growing in your system? Where is trust breaking?

4. What are some of the negotiations you have been involved in this past week? Who was involved, and what power did they use in the process? What was the outcome? What did you and anyone else learn as a result of the negotiation?

Ethical Questions Concerning Ministry Politics. What is the difference between negotiation and manipulation? Inevitably, when summit pastors discussed negotiation, this question came up. As one pastor said,

---

I have the gift of [knowing] how to present something to get my way. So I find myself struggling with: how much of that gift do I use? Or how much should I intentionally get out of the way and let things naturally occur?

But the choice between influence and action is not as simple as the either-or presented in the quotation above. Jesus calls us to pursue leadership that is servant-oriented, grace-based and kingdom-focused.

Leaders must rely on the wisdom gained through reflection, hardship, systems thinking and political perception—all the skills, attitudes and knowledge discussed in this chapter—to lead congregations through tough changes that are full of conflict. And even then it requires creative, artistic improvisation.

How can we provide healthy leadership in the political chaos of making decisions when multiple power and interest differences collide? The answer centers on the stakeholders involved in the decision. Stakeholders include anyone who has something to gain or to lose in the decision being considered. They may be church staff, officers, members, regular attenders, children, youth, visitors and even those in the wider community.

We have found that four simple yet provocative questions help to define the issues and provide the required reflection and political perceptions ministry leaders need.

- Whose interests are at stake in this decision?

- What are the various interests?

- What do the stakeholders have to gain or to lose?

- How will the various interests be represented at the planning table?

The answers to these four questions will illuminate the direction we need to move in giving healthy leadership to the political process. As one pastor commented,

---

There are times when I think sinful interests maybe do need to be strategically worked around. But there are often valid interests that are differing from my own. And am I manipulating things so those interests can't come to the table? We pastors have to be discerning about these things.

A final ethical question must be considered for leaders wielding influence. The apostle Paul commends his apprentice Timothy to the Philippian church, "I hope in the Lord Jesus to send Timothy to you soon, so that I too may be cheered by news of you. For I have no one like him, who will be genuinely concerned for your welfare. For they all seek their own interests, not those of Jesus Christ" (Philippians 2:19-21).

As we seek to lead God's people, are we promoting our own interests over those of Jesus Christ? Are we really serving the welfare of *his* church?

This distinction is not easy to make. But by simply asking this question and considering the reasons behind our interests, we will review our options and generate strategies on how to proceed. Once we have prayerfully considered this, we can invite others at the planning table to join us in this manner of reflective thinking.

Pastors are constantly involved in politics and negotiation. Sometimes it happens in quiet consensus. At other times it occurs in uncertainty and conflict. Regardless of the context, the interests of the stakeholders will constantly be pressed forward with the power available to their constituencies. As a result, negotiation is a consistent activity in the art of ministry leadership. Negotiation is also part of our redemptive ministry that enables us to care more fully for people and to advance God's kingdom.

CONCLUSION

When people are preparing for the ministry, they don't anticipate the two-fold leadership responsibilities of poetry and plumbing that come with the job. Many ministry leaders are blindsided by the enormity of leadership challenges and demands. In order to thrive in ministry, pastors must embrace both sides of leadership as part of their calling. In this chapter we explored four themes of leadership poetry: reflection, hardship, systems thinking and political perception.

In the next chapter we will probe four essential plumbing tasks of leadership required for healthy and fulfilling ministry leadership. By looking more closely at these seeming chores, we hope to promote enthusiasm for the truly redemptive nature of the work.

RECOMMENDATIONS FOR FURTHER READING

1. Jim Herrington, Robert Creech and Trisha Taylor. *The Leader's Journey: Accepting the Call to Personal and Congregational Transformation.* San Francisco: Jossey-Bass, 2003.

2. Dan Allender. *Leading with a Limp: Turning Your Struggles into Strengths.* Colorado Springs: WaterBrook Press, 2006.

3. Ronald A. Heifetz and Marty Linsky. *Leadership on the Line: Staying Alive Through the Dangers of Leading.* Boston: Harvard Business School Press, 2002.

4. Ronald A. Heifetz, Alexander Grashow and Marty Linsky. *The Practice of Adaptive Leadership: Tools and Tactics for Changing Your Organization and the World*. Boston: Harvard Business School Press, 2009.

5. Roger Fisher and William Ury. *Getting to Yes: Negotiating Agreement Without Giving In*. New York: Penguin, 1981.

MEDIA WORTH EXPLORING

1. For more information on the "RightPath® 4 and RightPath® 6 Behavioral Profiles" and "RightPath Leadership 360" and other RightPath Resources, look at www.rightpath.com.

2. Much of the humor in the *Dilbert* comic strips by Scott Adams is based on the boss's lack of artistic leadership. For example, try searching Adams's site www.dilbert.com with the terms *manipulation, emotion at work* and *email*.

3. *Shackleton: The Greatest Survival Story of All Time* (2002, A&E Home video). This film chronicles the incredible account of how Ernest Shackleton led his stranded *Endurance* crew to safety after being locked in Antarctic ice.

4. *Invictus* (2009), rated PG-13. This film recounts the true story of the World Cup–winning South African rugby team. The film focuses on how the unlikely relationship between President Nelson Mandela and team captain François Pienaar drove the team to victory.

LEADERSHIP PLUMBING

It makes a difference how one thinks about the church. . . . When the

organizational aspect is primary—size of membership, building

and budget are decisive. When its organic nature is primary—

quality of life, attitudes, relationships are decisive.

Richard C. Halverson, in Jim Peterson's
Church Without Walls: Moving Beyond Traditional Boundaries

FOR OUR SUMMIT PASTORS, the daily nuts and bolts of leadership consisted of tasks typically grouped under the term *management*. These responsibilities differ from the artistic side of leadership, which we discussed in the previous chapter. While the poetry side of leadership deals with the ambiguous and unexpected, the plumbing side focuses on daily operational responsibilities. The five essential plumbing tasks of most concern to the pastors in our research include modeling, shepherding, managing expectations, supervising conflict and planning.

Before we explore these leadership plumbing tasks, we should consider the attitude we have toward these responsibilities and the personality characteristics needed to accomplish them. Here are two diagnostic questions to ask yourself.

- When facing a typical day at work, which tasks do I prioritize: ones that are relational or ones that accomplish results?

- Which congregational needs do I most quickly address: the *organizational* (governance structures, budgets, program planning and meetings) or the *organic* (shepherding, caregiving, discipleship and leadership development)?

Our friend and corporate consultant Jerry Mabe explains that all leaders are caught in a "leadership squeeze" between the demand to achieve results and the expectation to build relationships. Jerry believes that everyone is hardwired from birth with certain characteristics. Then, through the nurture of our families of origin and other relational contexts, these characteristics are honed and developed during youth, adolescence and adulthood. Jerry posits that our hardwiring reflects a tendency to be either relationships- or results-focused.

Both results and relationships are necessary in leadership. To pastors, the demands for results often sound like, "You need to accomplish these goals, grow the attendance and make budget." Relationship demands pressure pastors in the other direction: "You must understand my needs, listen to me and disciple me." All leaders are constantly caught in the tension between the expectations of results and relationships. Add to the leadership squeeze the fact that the church is both an organization and an organism. Leaders must give attention to both the organizational and organic needs of the church for healthy congregational life.

Congregants are not naturally concerned with both aspects of the church, however. Relationship-oriented people are naturally drawn to the church as an organism. Results-oriented people are more interested in the church as an organization. As author and educator Chuck Miller describes it, "The tension between organism and organization is very real and continual. The tension between intimacy and strategy is constant."[1]

Pastoral ministry contains a multiplicity of tasks and responsibilities, each of which incorporate expectations of organization and organism, results and relationships.[2] The diagnostic question is, "What comes out when our leadership is squeezed?"

For the rest of this chapter, we will explore the five plumbing tasks most discussed by the summit pastors. The importance of these five areas was made evident by their sheer repetition in both formal and informal conversations. As you consider each one, ponder where it might fit on the "organization–organism" spectrum. And ask yourself how your own personal wiring toward results or relationships might affect the way you approach them.

THE TASK OF MODELING

Pastors are very aware that people in the congregation and community look to them as models. And even though pastors are as frail as anyone, there is still an expectation that they provide a good example for others to follow.

First and foremost, pastors are expected to model spiritual maturity. As a summit pastor explained,

> Our primary job is to know God. All the other stuff we do is ultimately ineffective and nonsense if we aren't growing in our relationship with God. Because it is the one thing that everybody in our congregation depends on. Even though we talk about the fact that you have to have your own spirituality, the reality is that we are still considered the role model.

Being an example of spirituality involves modeling what it means to live in the grace of God. This necessarily includes sharing how one handles weakness, repentance and faith during trials. Considering this, a pastor shared,

> As I preach, as I lead, I'm honest about my own sins, failures and weaknesses. If I don't model that, well then, I'm modeling that a Christian has to have it all together. And that's not the gospel.

Walking in grace is countercultural. It can cut across the expectations of people. The summit pastors wrestled with the challenge of acknowledging weakness in a culture that wants hero leaders. One of them expressed it this way.

> The president never wants to look weak, and America would never want to see the president look weak against anybody. . . . No leader in America ever at any point wants to look weak, whether it's the high school football coach or the assistant soccer coach. And I think we take that on as well. We think, "No other leader can look weak. So I'm not going to look weak."

The pastors understood that the Scriptures openly show the weaknesses of many leaders.[3] At the same time, parishioners sometimes react poorly when pastors share their humanity. One pastor told his cohort how, after telling a story of brokenness in his family of origin, a person wrote an anonymous letter telling him he was disqualified for the ministry.

Concluding a conversation on this idea of modeling godliness, a pastor said,

I have apologized from the pulpit for things I said in a sermon the previous week. I have apologized for hurting people's feelings. I have had to humble myself before my elders, and I have found that it has turned out for the best. Overall, it has won the hearts of the people and the hearts of my elders. . . . But I have learned to take blows for Jesus' sake. . . . I learned nonviolence by choice and conscience, not by personality. And I think that is something we have to have as followers of Christ.

Therefore, while appropriate vulnerability is essential in modeling godly maturity, pastors should do so judiciously, patiently waiting for the evidence of fruit this leadership task will eventually bear. That needed patience with the sheep also connects to the next leadership task.

QUESTIONS TO PONDER

1. Who has been a model of spiritual maturity in your life? How has this modeling influenced you?

2. In what ways do you think you currently model spiritual maturity to the people in your ministry? Who could you talk to for honest feedback about your perception?

3. In what ways have you recently been an example of God's grace to others?

4. To what extent have you witnessed fruit from your leadership modeling?

THE TASK OF SHEPHERDING

We believe that pastors are not to be the sole shepherds of the congregation.[4] The scriptural pattern is for a plurality of elders to shepherd God's people.[5] In addition, the "one another" passages of the Bible emphasize the mutual shepherding responsibility all Christians have for each other.[6]

Still, pastors are responsible to be shepherds. And as our good friend and summit participant Tim Witmer says in *The Shepherd Leader*, shepherds are to *know* the sheep, *feed* the sheep, *lead* the sheep and *protect* the sheep.[7] We recognize that most pastoral tasks could be identified as shepherding. But our summit data identified four specific responsibilities as primary shepherding concerns: listening, encouraging, speaking the truth and counseling.

Listening. As you have read earlier, our participants often discussed how they needed to be *listeners*. Unfortunately, most of our discussions focused on how poorly we listen to others. Consider how the summit pastors discussed this responsibility.

When I am sitting down with someone, I find myself asking, "What do they think of me as a pastor?" Instead of listening to them and being emotionally engaged, I'm in my own little world. It's all fear of man.

✦ ✦ ✦

I realize that I don't listen well. I tend to think I know what these people ought to do. So people don't feel I listen to them as much as I should.

✦ ✦ ✦

We could say we love our people. But if we don't know how to find out about their lives, without being artificial about it, we will never connect with them in a way that causes them to feel loved. . . . We have so much more we have to fit in, so we drop the practical, relational learning about how *to be with* people.

Can you hear the leadership squeeze in these statements? One reason that pastors may be weak on the shepherding role of listening is that the skill is lost in the busyness of nonrelational activities. In addition, active listening requires a level of emotional engagement that is difficult.

These comments forced us to reconsider the importance of emotional intelligence in the pastoral calling. Without the ability to be comfortable with one's own feelings, and the ability to hear and empathize with others' strong emotions, pastors will be significantly hampered as shepherds.

In the EQ chapter we highlighted a number of suggestions on how pastors can develop these skills. Here we will simply restate that pastors need to begin working on it within the safety of their marriages and friendships and perhaps with the coaching of a professional counselor. Our research indicates that this is particularly true for male pastors. One therapist observed that summit pastors, who were all men, *talked at* one another rather than *listened to* each other.

Encouraging. A second shepherding responsibility is *encouragement.* As earlier noted, one pastor summarized, "Pastors can only encourage people over the long haul when they themselves are moved, inspired, spirited. That means self-care." As we saw in the self-care chapter, this means having people who encourage the pastors themselves. "What would have happened to Paul if Barnabas hadn't been there?" asked one of the participants. "We need encouragers in our lives and ministries." This comment led the discussion back to the topic of allies and confidants and how we can identify these people in our ministry environments.

As pastors are encouraged, they can then encourage others, as we see in the paradigm exhibited by the apostle Paul (2 Corinthians 1:3-4). They can extend encouragement in many ways, such as writing notes, developing intercessory prayer teams, recognizing people for their service and creating opportunities for people to explore their gifts and callings. One pastor said,

I think we have to be encouragers. This means praying for one another and creating an environment where the congregation is called to explore their gifts, test out different roles and skills, and freely acknowledging that if they don't do this thing well, they can try another place of service.

Our discussions on encouragement did not focus as much on the design of programs—which could be many and varied—as on the importance of simply creating an environment of encouragement. One pastor commented,

Our times of gathering ought to be times of encouragement. This is what the author of Hebrews meant when he wrote, "Let us consider how to stir up one another to love and good works, not neglecting to meet together, as is the habit of some, but encouraging one another" (Hebrews 10:24-25).

Speaking the Truth. A third aspect of shepherding—the courage and grace to *speak the truth in love*—came as a response to the discussion on encouragement (Ephesians 4:15). A pastor responded to this conversation saying,

I love to encourage people, but I don't like to confront. But you can't develop people if all you do is encourage. Then your encouragement seems disingenuous if you're not going to tell them the hard stuff.

This "truth-telling" means saying uncomfortable and challenging things even under difficult circumstances. In his study on great companies, Jim Collins identifies the ability to confront the brutal facts as one key characteristic of enduring businesses.[8] He says, "One of the single most de-motivating actions you can take is to hold out false hopes, soon to be swept away by events."[9] Similarly, if pastors do not speak the truth by addressing the brutal facts, the maturity of the church will be blunted.

Some people are naturally comfortable with confrontation. However, many pastors are naturally harmonious and find truth-telling uncomfortable, if not painful. Yet when difficult conversations are avoided out of discomfort, unintended consequences often happen. For example, when problems are not addressed directly, they usually become the topic of backroom conversations that quickly turn into gossip. Or when responses are delayed out of discomfort, the lack of reply can force people to create their own interpretation of circumstances.

One of our pastors served on a large church staff. The senior leadership team came to a consensus that a change had to be made in the community group ministry. They thought, however, that the pastor in charge of community groups would disagree with their analysis and resist any changes. And they didn't want to face the painful challenges of talking with this pastor. So instead of facing the brutal facts, these leaders developed a new community group structure, giving it a different name and pouring more resources and energy into its development than was given to the existing ministry. As a result, bitterness and a lack of trust grew among staff members. Some sided with one pastor who was "worked around." Others wondered, "Would they undermine my ministry like that?" Facing the brutal facts and having hard conversations are critical tasks in shepherding the people of God.

Counseling. A final aspect of shepherding reflected in our summit discussions was the expectation for pastors to *provide counseling*. Our participants represented many different views and philosophies of counseling. There was a consensus, however, that counseling plays an important role in shepherding. Nearly all were also concerned that the complexity and emotional burdens of counseling can quickly pull pastors away from their other responsibilities.

A significant number of our pastors felt that their counseling responsibility is bounded by pastoral issues. If needed, they refer parishioners to trusted therapists for more technical difficulties. Memorable bits of the conversation sounded like this:

Like it or not, we're general practitioners. And for a general practitioner to try and deal with your father's heart condition is irresponsible. The most responsible thing the GP could do is to refer your father to a specialist.

✤ ✤ ✤

Good counselors cost money. And I'm *free*. But I'm not very good. Knowing when to say "when" on the counseling thing, knowing when to hand them that card for the person who charges but is far more skilled and equipped, is a hard discipline.

✤ ✤ ✤

If I can't get anywhere in two counseling sessions, it's beyond my capabilities!

Identifying counselors you are comfortable referring people to is a matter of trust. It is important for pastors to identify their own convictions regarding issues of therapeutic intervention. Then they need to network with therapists in their community and at least informally interview them on Christian convictions.[10] We have found that, with appropriate guidelines, many counselors are happy to work closely with pastors and their elders as partners in the therapeutic and discipling mission of the church.[11]

QUESTIONS TO PONDER

1. Try an experiment on a typical work day of making listening well your top priority. Reflect later on what happened. What aspects of listening were most challenging for you?

2. Who are your biggest encouragers? What are five acts of encouragement you could do today at work?

3. What are some areas in which you need to practice the leadership of truth-telling? When do you plan to have those hard conversations? Pray for God to help you love well even as you confront.

4. How comfortable are you with your counseling responsibilities? Who can you go to for help and more training?

THE TASK OF MANAGING EXPECTATIONS

Our third pastoral leadership task is the business of managing expectations: our own expectations and the expectations of others. As one pastor put it,

---

This is a really interesting challenge: being who we are, and understanding who we are, over against who we want to be, or who others want us to be.

First, pastors have to manage their own expectations. While many of these expectations could be named, we found that *all* of our summit pastors struggled with the expectation for success. This particular struggle seems to be an almost universal theme in pastoral ministry. In chapter five, we looked at the "success syndrome."[12] While not all want to be TV stars, many pastors intensely desire success in ministry. One pastor shared how, in seminary, a professor predicted, "Most of you are going to pastor churches of one hundred people or less." He commented, "You could hear the air getting sucked out of everybody's wind, because there go your dreams of a large congregation."

How can pastors manage expectations for personal success? First, we need to acknowledge these expectations and how they dominate our thinking and our culture. Then, it is important to develop a responsible understanding of our limited capabilities. The J. B. Phillips paraphrase of Romans 12:3-4 is poignant in this regard: "Don't cherish exaggerated ideas of yourself or your importance, but try to have a sane estimate of your capabilities by the light of the faith that God has given to you all." One summit pastor demonstrated such a "sane estimate," saying,

---

I'm coming to the conclusion early in my ministry, just ten years down the road, that it's okay if I'm not the Donald Trump of my denomination. I've got to be okay with that.

As we come to embrace our limits in this way, we can turn to God, accept that he is in control of our calling and career, and trust him to use us for his will and purposes. One of our pastors shared how this took place in his life.

I was raised with the mindset that you can be anything and do anything. So I had these unstoppable expectations for myself. Then I had the privilege of going through seminary with a bunch of really gifted people. But the impact that it had on me was thinking that I can't be a very good pastor unless I'm like them. It took me years to realize that I was trying to be like somebody else. There came a point when I had to say, "Lord, you know what kind of a person you have made me to be. I need to live in the skin that you gave me and be effective and fruitful as that kind of person." And just to faithfully play my part of the story and let God decide how the story gets written.

Another way pastors can manage their expectations for success is to talk about it with safe, trustworthy friends. One venue by which this can happen is a peer group. If participants are carefully selected and time is taken to develop trust, pastors and their spouses can discover a place of honest transparency. One pastor expressed this well, saying,

I just realize so much more that we need each other. We are in such unique roles with the difficulty of having friendships and relationships because our lives are so consumed by the church. We so desperately need to be in relationship with other pastors and their spouses.

Pastors not only have to manage their own expectations; they have to deal with the expectations of others. This, too, is a leadership responsibility. One summit participant explained,

I think what's challenging my leadership right now are the expectations of our American culture. The demands are at an all-time high. What people expect from your church is not only a nice message but a perfect nursery, a perfect restroom and interesting programs that everybody in the family loves. All this at the same time and all under an hour long. These days we deal with some of the highest expectations and probably some of the lowest levels of commitment.

Some of the most common expectations faced by our summit pastors included the following.

- The expectation for time and energy. "There's an expectation from others that I have an endless resource of time for them, that I never will get tired of them and that they never get on my nerves."

- The expectation for friendship and availability. "People get mad quick because they feel that we, as leaders, have been unavailable to them. They say things like, 'You haven't been there for me.'" Another said that when people listen to a sermon, they develop a pseudo-relationship with the speaker and "get locked in on the idea that 'I want a relationship with the pastor.'"

- The expectation for great sermons. "A pastor is called upon to write a 'new song' every week and then go and 'perform' that 'song.' It's in front of a live audience that expects the same level of content and delivery that they have going to see The Fray in concert. And they're going to either stop buying your recordings or buy more every week. That's the pressure a pastor feels."

- The expectation to manage generational issues. "My biggest leadership challenge is trying not to alienate the older generation from the younger generation."

- The expectation that interests will be met. People think that their view of what needs to happen is accurate and must be implemented. For example, one congregation represented at the summit has both deacons and elders. The pastor explained, "Our budget was drawn up by the deacons, and it reflected cuts in almost all areas of ministry, but it gave an increase for mortgage reduction and capital expenditures. Our elders did not believe this budget reflected our ministry values. So they changed it and the deacons were ticked."

After reviewing this short sample of congregant expectations, it is understandable that a recent study shows pastors most often leave local church ministry over conflict.[13] In the Gospels, however, Jesus constantly disappointed people by not meeting their expectations. Consider Mark 3, for example, in which Jesus heals the man with a withered hand. Instead of thanking God for the healing, the religious leadership plotted how to destroy him. And when Jesus healed the Gerasene demonic in Mark 5, people asked him to leave town!

As we noted early in the book, Heifetz and Linsky write that "exercising leadership might be understood as disappointing people at a rate they can absorb."[14] As one summit pastor put it, "Sometimes the best way to love your sheep may be to disappoint them or make them angry." Regardless of how it is stated, managing the expectations of others—and being willing to disappoint them in the process—is an important leadership responsibility for all pastors.

QUESTIONS TO PONDER

- What story of success do you regularly try to live up to?

- How do you assess your limitations as a ministry leader? What aspects bother you the most? How does your cultural context speak into that? To what extent do people in your context have unique expectations on you as a leader due to the broader culture outside the church?

- What are some creative ways you can help your congregation have more realistic expectations for you and those in vocational ministry in general?

THE TASK OF SUPERVISING CONFLICT

This fourth plumbing task of pastoral leadership elicits groans from ministry leaders and spouses alike. As we have already noted, conflict is one of the primary reasons why ministers leave local church ministry. In order to address this weighty responsibility, we brought in friends from Peacemaker Ministries to meet with our summit groups. Peacemaker Ministries is an organization that seeks to equip and assist Christians and their churches to respond to conflict in a biblical and God-honoring manner. All the pastors brought a case study of a current conflict to discuss with their cohort. The conversations that took place were both difficult and enlightening.

One of the most interesting discussions focused on how we tend to view conflict as an intrusion in our ministry lives. Our Peacemaker Ministries friends reminded us that throughout the Bible, God uses conflict for personal and corporate growth. Examples of this abound, ranging from Moses' debates with God over his calling (Exodus 3–4) to the challenges of the early church integrating Gentiles into the community (Acts 15). We discovered that we need to intentionally embrace conflict supervision as a part of ministry. It provides an opportunity to teach God's people how to disagree well and love one another.

Poor Responses to Conflict. Conflict management has many facets.[15]

But the primary focus in the Pastors Summit was how we personally respond to conflictual situations. A number of poor responses were discussed. First was the tendency simply to avoid conflict. Because few enjoy disagreements, many of the pastors in the summit wanted to deny conflicts.[16] The consensus of our experience was that avoidance does not make the conflict go away. We have to face the brutal facts and address the struggle.

A second poor response to conflict is the need to "win" the disagreement. A pastor explained this inclination, saying,

> One of my personal struggles is the tendency to go toe-to-toe with people. I'm more concerned about being right than I am about really loving others and figuring out how I can pastor them.

We discovered that we are often more concerned about our own reputations than we are about helping others grow and mature. Instead of defending our own perceptions, we need to pause and repent of self-centeredness. Then we can take a stance of curiosity, asking questions to seek understanding rather than trying to show others we are correct.

A third inadequate response involves trying to control the outcome of a conflict—what one pastor described as the "God-wannabe" syndrome. Sometimes we try to control outcomes by defining the results ahead of time and then pushing everyone toward our interests. For example, in a case of marital abuse we know about, the pastor was so convinced that the abuser (a church officer) could never do such a thing that he tried to persuade the elders that the man's wife had instigated the abuse.

A second way of controlling is simply to give up working on the conflict, saying, "Because I can't control the result, I'm not going to do anything." In our conversations, we concluded that it is best to, as one pastor put it, "speak the truth in love, be obedient and trust the results to God." This is hard and few enjoy it, but it is a necessary response to the challenge of conflict management.

A final poor answer to conflict is what we called a "false resolution." This usually takes place by the pastor resigning or a member leaving the church. One of the Peacemaker Ministries staff spoke directly to this tendency.

> The worst cases I've been involved with are the ones where the pastor has said, "Let me be the one to fall on my sword and offer up my resigna-

tion. I'm just going to leave, and I'm sure everything will be better." It's not going to get better. . . . So please, don't just gratuitously offer up your resignation. . . . Take them through the process of reconciliation. After you go through the process, if leaving seems like the wise thing, then you can consider it. But I see too many pastors doing that prematurely . . . mostly because of pride and anger. It never helps.

A pastor using the threat of resignation is akin to a spouse trying to resolve an argument by using the word *divorce*. It is rarely helpful. Cutting off relationships doesn't bring health and responsible resolution except as a final reply to entrenched, sinful behavior. One pastor in the summit, realizing he had left a church in this manner, confessed that he had a "hireling mentality," because he ran when the wolves came rather than staying to protect the flock like a true shepherd.

Valid Responses to Conflict. There are no simple solutions to conflict. Each situation is unique and depends on the people involved and the circumstances surrounding the disagreement. The Bible presents a varied spectrum of responses to conflict, helpfully outlined by Ken Sande in what he calls "the slippery slope."[17] Sande outlines three basic responses to conflict: escape and attack appear on the two ends of an arch, and peacemaking appears at the middle. Within each of these three responses are a variety of options.

As we reviewed the slippery slope with the summit pastors, a number of ideas surfaced and dominated the conversation. First, conflict is a crucible for discipleship. The challenge of engaging conflict can further maturity in Christ for all involved. One pastor said,

I want to avoid conflicts. But I'm learning it is in these messes that God works out his purposes. It's all over the Bible. I just had to open my eyes to see it.

A second idea that emerged was the fact that there is a continuum of valid responses to conflict. As we discussed case after case, we learned firsthand that there isn't a "one answer fits all" solution. Within the framework of seeking God's *shalom*, there are ways of pursuing reconciliation that "turn up the heat" and other ways that reduce tensions. As an example of different but valid responses to a similar problem, summit pastors shared these two stories.

There was an elder in our congregation who was trying to get me fired. As a staff, we used this situation to move beyond his surface complaints to deeper issues of organizational struggle. By taking time to ask questions, listen and not react to his anger, we were able to probe into the real heart of the issue.

✦ ✦ ✦

People regularly want to have me fired. I generally overlook these comments as an expression of their frustration—unless they try to press on with the issue.

The importance of doing "positive church discipline" is the third idea regarding conflict. Our pastors agreed that people both inside and outside the church usually view church discipline as punitive. In the churches represented in the summit, people join by affirming membership vows. These vows state that they will submit to the discipline and spiritual oversight of the church. This discipline and oversight is usually positive and consists of gospel preaching, teaching and discipling. Church discipline can become judicial in nature when members embrace sinful attitudes, however, and when repentance doesn't occur.

These discussions also brought up the need to continue to shepherd people in the midst of conflict. One pastor's story explained it well.

If you invest in someone, they know you care. When it comes to that point of tension, it can make a difference. Once we had to excommunicate a guy. But for a full year the elders reached out to him at meals, with letters, emails and phone calls. He had left his wife and moved in with another woman. He wouldn't repent. When we finally wrote the letter of excommunication, his response was, "You couldn't have done anything better. I don't have a leg to stand on, but I'm not changing. So I'm out of here. But I respect what you've tried to do."

This story demonstrates the importance of maintaining care and concern even while confronting the brutal facts of sin.

Finally, our list of valid responses to conflict ends with the possibility of bringing in someone else to negotiate a dispute. One of our guest consultants explained it this way:

A mistake churches often make is not bringing in a third party, or not do-ing it soon enough. Unless you have a very mature congregation, people will quickly fall into a party spirit and decide who they are going to align with. And most elder boards are not equipped for conflict resolution. All things being equal, because an outside person has no established rela-tionship, they are de facto impartial.

Conflict is difficult and can end in reconciliation or rejection. Never-theless, working toward conflict resolution is an important pastoral task. As we have pointed out before, it is essential not only for the parties in-volved but also for the health of the congregation.

QUESTIONS TO PONDER

1. Do you view conflict more as a ministry distraction or as an opportu-nity to disciple?

2. To what extent are you responding to conflict with the different poor responses listed?

3. Do you feel prepared to respond positively to conflict in a current situ-ation? If not, from whom or how can you get help and encouragement? What can you learn as you reflect on healthy responses to conflict that you have observed or experienced?

THE TASK OF PLANNING

The fifth and final leadership task is *planning*. Pastors generally don't enter the ministry with the expectation of giving themselves to program plan-ning. But studies confirm what every pastor knows by experience. Tasks such as planning and administering programs, building and tracking bud-gets, developing organizational vision, values and goals, reviewing gover-nance structures, compiling statistics, and preparing worship services: these and a whole host of other things quickly find their way onto the agenda of most ministry leaders.

Looking at the details behind these activities goes beyond the scope of this book.[18] But four types of planning stood out in our summit conversa-tions as key components of pastoral leadership. These are tasks pastors often find themselves unprepared to lead: vision development, leadership selection and development, hiring and training staff, and reviewing governance structures.

Vision Development. Every pastor in the summit was keenly aware of the congregational expectation for ministry vision. As one pastor shared, "I came feeling so burdened down by the pressure to be a leader with *the* vision, vision, vision." Another added, "I know pastors who are just weighed down with this burden of vision."

But even with this pressure, all of them understood that vision development is an important leadership responsibility. A participant asked,

How do we advance what is a responsible and healthy philosophy of ministry? And how do we adjust that according to generational issues, to cultural issues and to other things, yet within the biblical and theological framework of our commitment?

Lively discussions took place around this task of developing vision. One pastor had a very positive experience getting help from a business consultant in the community known for her team-building skills. This pastor told this story.

The model I had been trained in was that vision is handed down from God to the pastor like Moses was handed the Ten Commandments from God. We had experienced a great deal of conflict when I tried to superimpose that model. So partly with hesitance, and partly with some dawning of wisdom, I slowed down the visioning process. By using the consultant, we had experience in the room guiding our attempts at collaboration. We not only developed a vision; we learned to listen to one another and respect each other in the process, even though things seemed to move at a glacial pace at times.

In this pastor's experience, one of the great frustrations was the time it takes to work together. With the "learned impatience" of our culture, leaders often feel this frustration. And when pastors decide to share the planning of vision, they often feel that they lose control of the process. What we sometimes forget in the midst of these frustrations is that broader systemic results can come from cooperative planning. Shared ownership, mutual regard, developed communication skills and heightened trust are often the unexpected outcomes of pursuing collaboration.

At the same time, as one of the pastors pointed out, a shared vision can be reached by using many methods.

> There are lots of different ways to get to that shared vision. The pastor can identify it and others confirm it. Or it can be developed by another member of the board. It can be something that comes through weeks and months of deliberation, with prayer and fasting, working together. It can come in a lot of different ways.

This pastor concluded that the most important point of any vision planning is that the staff, officers and congregation all *buy into* the vision.

> What I want to stress is that everybody agrees, "This is who we are, and this is what God has called us to. And by God's grace, we've got to do that."

Leadership Selection and Development. A second planning task necessary for pastors is the development of congregational leadership. The biblical paradigm found in Jesus' ministry, as well as the ministry of the apostles (particularly Paul's), is to identify and develop leaders who can assume responsibility for the ministry. The apostle Paul exhorts his partner Timothy to carry on this task, saying, "what you have heard from me in the presence of many witnesses entrust to faithful men who will be able to teach others also" (2 Timothy 2:2).

Some pastors have difficulty raising up new leaders and turning things over to them. It seems much easier to stay in control, not risk having others do a mediocre job and not experience the threat of others being more competent or successful. As one business leadership researcher states, however, "The acid test of a leader's success is how well his or her successor does."[19]

So when ministry leaders fail to develop others and then turn responsibility over to them, they actually harm their own effectiveness. They also curtail the growth and maturity of their system by making everything depend upon them. A summit pastor summarized a better approach, "It's important to recognize the gifts of others and enjoy seeing others exercise their gifts rather than being threatened by them." And another shared,

I remember one of my mentors saying, "If I can find someone who can do the job 75 percent as well as I can, it's wrong for me to be doing it."

The decision of *who* shall be selected to share leadership is critical. These leaders will be vested with a certain amount of formal authority. And the ways they manage that authority can have a significant impact on the church. As one pastor put it, "*Who* you put into leadership positions, humanly speaking, is just about the whole game."

A number of lively discussions took place in summit cohorts around the selection of leaders. In one group, a pastor reasoned through a common concern:

Who do we choose for leaders in the church, particularly as elders? I've noticed the tendency is to take "successful" people, check out their theology and then ordain them. But in the process, when do we check their character? We just make assumptions: if you're successful in business, check that box; if your theology is good, check that box. But the Bible focuses on a leader's character. We can't assume their character measures up because they are successful and can verbalize accurate theology.

In another cohort, a participant also spoke about the priority of character by sharing this significant story:

I added a component [to leadership selection] that had never been talked about in our church. In an officer training class, I said, "Let's look at the pastoral epistles: 1 and 2 Timothy and Titus." And from these books we laid down a series of criteria. Things like involvement in outreach, being service-minded, having a ministry, all kinds of things. It turns out we had people nominated who were super-powerful and had become committed to the church. But they weren't demonstrating spiritual leadership in any ministry.

As we talked, one guy raised his hand and said, "I don't think we're fit to be elders based on these things." I didn't deny his point, because it was true. Many of them self-selected out of the training process. So then, the next year comes and it is nomination time. And when nominations came in, I said to the elders serving as the nominating committee, "Well, let's look at the criteria." We reviewed each person, asking, "Is this

person hospitable? Involved in ministry? Quarrelsome?" And the like. All
of a sudden, the criteria began to sift them out.

Still another pastor shared this selection process:

We've got two or three stages where there is a checkpoint. They fill out
a packet of information on personal life, theology, mission and vision,
weaknesses, and all those sorts of things. We will look at each one of
those as a board."

Regardless of the methods used, the message from these pastors on
leadership development and selection was clear. First, we must make it a
priority to develop leaders. And second, demonstrable character matters
when selecting those on whom authority will be conferred.

Hiring and Training Staff. This third crucial planning task is similar to
leadership development and selection. It is the pastor's responsibility to be
careful and intentional in the selection and training of staff. When you
hire a person with a particular set of strengths, you are also hiring their
struggles as well.

One pastor asked, "Do we allow for the place of weaknesses in ourselves
and in our staff? Every great strength creates a great weakness." Another
pastor explained,

We must factor in our own strengths and struggles when hiring and consider hiring to compensate for our weaknesses. I think one of the great
issues in leadership is having people who are better than you in doing
things, who outshine you and that you can be happy they outshine you.

And another responded,

I'm a big-picture guy, and it took me years to realize that I don't know how
to get from here to there. I had to find people who could do that. I'm not
the whole package, and I really need other people.

At the same time, the issue of character loomed as important to these
pastors in hiring staff as it did for selecting leaders out of the congregation—and not just character in the areas of personal and social ethics but
also in relationship capacity. One pastor explained,

This isn't just a role we are hiring for—it's also giving them a place on the team. We're going to be in relationship. Can we get along? Can we respect and trust one another?

Hiring staff to fulfill varied responsibilities in the congregation also requires a mindset of training staff rather than expecting immediate "plug and play" competence in their role. This is particularly true in ministry, in which getting a seminary degree does not equate with skill development in ministry competencies. As one seasoned minister put it,

We were trained to be pulpit-oriented. The master of divinity is a generalist preacher's degree. When you're hiring someone with an M.Div., don't expect that they've got those other abilities developed. They've got to get training, exposure to a variety of ministries and the opportunity to live in their role for a while.

Of course, as we have seen before, hardships have been identified as an important part of leadership training. And the ministry guarantees that everyone involved will have plenty of opportunities to experience these difficulties. As one pastor said, "The newbies will make mistakes, which will raise anxiety in the system, but it's necessary for overall growth and development of leadership." And another shared, "It's not just the newbies. I'm still making mistakes and learning from them."

We have also seen that for hardships to create learning, they must be coupled with support and encouragement. If persons new to the ministry are left to themselves when experiencing hardships, the results will often be loneliness, depression and discouragement rather than personal growth and change.

One of the pastors told a story of how they developed a new staff member:

We brought a guy onto our church staff to do youth and family ministry. When interviewing him, we said, "Tell us how you develop teams for ministry." He responded, "Well, I've never done that." So we asked, "Will you let us work with you to learn to do that?" And he said, "Yeah." So for the first couple of years, even with our coaching, we watched him try to do everything by himself, until he was about to go under for the third time. But slowly he started to catch on. And now he is developing youth leaders who are developing youth to be leaders. You couldn't see that in him five years ago. But that's what is happening now. So we need to say, "This is part of our mission together. We're going to develop people."

How long a staff member can be expected to stay on the team became another item of discussion. Two pastors summarized it this way:

We've got to consider whether we are training staff to send them out or to keep them for the long haul. If we bring people in who are passionate about preaching and are excellent leaders, we have to understand that we are bringing them on to train them and to send them out. There is validity to that, but it doesn't create stability.

✤ ✤ ✤

We decided that we will not move a person from being an assistant pastor to the higher status of associate pastor unless they have clearly signed off on our philosophy of ministry, have demonstrated fruitfulness in ministry and are committed for the long haul. To us it is comparable to being made a partner in a law firm. We aren't diminishing the place of others who may leave in a few years. But we're not establishing them in a role beyond our shared expectations.

The hiring and development of staff is an important plumbing component of leadership. This includes a commitment to support and to train staff so that they might make a significant contribution to the congregation and to the broader kingdom of God.

Reviewing Governance Structures. The final planning task that emerged from our meetings is the need to regularly review and update the effectiveness of governance structures. The term *governance structures* refers to at least two things. First, it refers to the government of the congregation. This usually comes from the history and denominational background of the church. Second, within this broader polity commitment, *governance* refers to the way that decisions are made at the local, congregational level.

For example, many churches select elders as the overseers of the congregation. Their denominations often define criteria for eldership as well as the role elders have in the oversight of the congregation. But each congregation will determine the number of elders, how committees will be formed and how well the structure is working.

A second example of governance is illustrated well by asking several questions: Who develops the yearly budget of the church? Is this the task of the pastor and staff? Is this a job for the elders? Or should it be delegated to another group, such as deacons, trustees or business experts? And why is a particular way of budgeting taking place? Is it "because we've always done it that way," or because it is the best way to serve the church?

Churches grow through phases: from a church plant, to breaking through the "two hundred barrier," to reaching five hundred members and so on.[20] As churches grow, however, the leadership often does not consider how their governance structures must grow and change as well. More often than not, appropriate structures are developed late in the process. One pastor complained,

---

Nobody tells you the next phases are much harder, at least that's my experience. . . . I can handle the chaos and unsettledness of church planting, but when you have to start putting in structures and all of that, it becomes more difficult for me.

This is when it is important to network with other pastors and leadership teams that are a phase or two in front of your congregation. Learning from their experiences—and especially from their mistakes—provides insights for future planning. Of course, such planning also involves regular conversations with your own leadership team. While an extensive discussion of governance structures goes beyond the scope of this study, their importance cannot be diminished. Many leaders are hampered by outdated, traditional organizational formats that hinder their leadership and the health of the congregation.[21] Be aware, however, that changing established structures can be a daunting political challenge. Some have found bringing in a consultant to suggest changes provides a safer way to encourage review and collaboration for change.

QUESTIONS TO PONDER

1. What methods have you used in the past for developing a shared vision? What were the results of each method?

2. What is your involvement in selecting and developing other leaders? What actions and attitudes might strengthen your role and the success of others?

3. What priority has character had in your process of choosing leaders and hiring staff?

4. When is the last time you reviewed your governance structures for appropriateness in relation to your organizational mission? What ministry leaders could you network with who are a phase in front of your current ministry?

CONCLUSION

In this chapter we have explored some of the most crucial technical and administrative duties that come with pastoral leadership. We refer to this as the plumbing side of leadership. Rarely do pastors find themselves prepared to lead in these areas. It is important, however, for them to embrace these responsibilities as part of their calling. In our research, we identified five essential areas of management work for pastors to pursue for fruitful ministry: modeling, shepherding, managing expectations, supervising conflict and planning.

Our Pastors Summit participants found these studies and discussions significant to their own ministry resilience. Ultimately these explorations led to a change in perspective of their job as pastors. They came to recognize that both learning the art and attending to the details of leadership are redemptive ministry responsibilities for the care of people and the advancement God's kingdom.

RECOMMENDATIONS FOR FURTHER READING

1. Doris Kearns Goodwin. *Team of Rivals: The Political Genius of Abraham Lincoln.* New York: Simon and Schuster, 2005.

2. James M. Kouzes and Barry Z. Posner. *The Leadership Challenge.* 4th ed. San Francisco: Jossey-Bass, 2007.

3. James M. Kouzes and Barry Z. Posner. *The Truth About Leadership: The No-Fads, Heart-of-the-Matter Facts You Need to Know.* San Francisco: Jossey-Bass, 2010.

4. Patrick Lencioni. *The Five Dysfunctions of a Team: A Leadership Fable.* San Francisco: Jossey-Bass, 2002.

MEDIA WORTH EXPLORING

1. *Apollo 13* (1995), rated PG. The crisis scenes in this Tom Hanks movie provide dramatic examples of many of the leadership issues above.

2. *Twelve Angry Men* (1957), rated NR. This classic explores presumptions, prejudices and the power of persuasion in the midst of conflict.

3. *Master and Commander: The Far Side of the World* (2003), rated PG-13. There are plenty of leadership lessons to observe and discuss from this film. Pay particular attention to how Captain Aubrey's authoritative leadership is rooted in the relational capital he builds with his crew.

CONCLUDING INSIGHTS AND NEXT STEPS

Why don't the summit themes address the many and varied tasks of pastors in the ministry? It is particularly surprising that more focus isn't given to preaching.

From the reader of a booklet on the Pastors Summit

WHEN WE FIRST BEGAN WORK ON THIS PROJECT, we were hoping to discover ideas that would be helpful in strengthening the lives and families of people in vocational ministry. As the themes of the Pastors Summit emerged from the data, we were excited at how they resonated with our own life experiences. As we shared our ideas with partners in other Lilly Endowment–funded programs, we were encouraged at how their work confirmed what we were discovering.

Then we began to share these themes with the pastors who had participated in the summit. They enthusiastically endorsed our findings. So we presented our ideas in local, regional and national gatherings, seeking input, critique and confirmation. The results were overwhelmingly positive. Finally, we wrote and distributed a booklet summarizing the five themes for resilient ministry. This resulted in requests for more information from pastors, church staffs and leadership boards from around the country.

Now we find that rarely a day goes by when we are not talking with someone, somewhere, about the themes of the summit. For example, as we conclude this book, Donald is spending the weekend consulting with three churches around issues of leadership and management; Tasha is working with a leadership team fearful of growth and change; and Bob met with a pastor suffering panic attacks from not managing congregational expectations.

So while we don't believe we have found the "holy grail" of pastoral survival, we do strongly believe that an understanding of these themes, and an intentional evaluation of life and ministry through them, will greatly affect the health and resilience of pastors and other types of ministry leaders.

As we conclude, let's take a moment to quickly review the five themes presented in this book. Then we will address a number of questions we are commonly asked about our conclusions, share a retrospective look at the summit experience from some of our participants and consider how you might use this information in the future.

QUICK REVIEW OF THEMES

The five themes of the Pastors Summit are spiritual formation, self-care, emotional and cultural intelligence, marriage and family, and leadership and management. While each theme could take an entire book to develop, we have used two chapters each to introduce what we have learned about them. As we have shared these themes in multiple settings, one or more ideas have always stood out in the discussions. As a way to summarize, we will share with you a simple descriptor of each theme, together with a "big idea" or two that people often talk about with us.

Spiritual Formation. Our understanding is that spiritual formation is the ongoing process of maturing as Christians both personally and interpersonally. It is a daily response to the apostle Paul's exhortation to "train yourself for godliness" and to "keep a close watch on yourself and on the teaching" (1 Timothy 4:7, 16).

From the first days of the summit, the "big idea" we learned is that pastors can become so caught up in doing church work that they fail to do the work of the church—which begins by abiding in Christ (John 15:4). We are reminded of one pastor's comment: "People think I am closer to God than I really am." Our encouragement to everyone in ministry is simply this: long-term fruitfulness in ministry comes from the overflow of one's walk with God. Take the time necessary to cultivate your first love.

Self-Care. Taking care of oneself requires conceding that we are finite human beings with limits. Our responsibility as creatures before the Creator is to nurture and steward our capacities for the glory of God. The "big idea" of this theme is recognizing we are whole creatures with physical, emotional, mental, social and spiritual needs. One pastor shared,

> When I graduated from seminary, I acted like I was a brain on a stick—everything was about thinking and saying the right things. While this is important, I recognize I better respect myself in these other ways or my ideas won't make an impact.

Further, good self-care means helping the congregation understand that pastors are more than their role and calling. For example, they are limited human beings; they have hobbies and interests; they are siblings, children of elderly adults, marriage partners and parents; and they are followers of Jesus. Responsible boundaries are necessary.

Emotional and Cultural Intelligence. Emotional intelligence is the ability to manage one's own emotions proactively and to respond appropriately to the emotions of others. Cultural intelligence involves an awareness of regional, ethnic and generational differences and the implications of these differences personally and interpersonally.

The "big idea" we hear about this theme concerns how easy it is to assume that our perception of reality is the only way to look at things. We need to acknowledge that our understandings of reality—and our corresponding feelings—are limited. Further, we need to put ourselves in a position of learning in order to respect the experiences, views and feelings of others. When discussing these ideas in a summit, a pastor shared,

> Unless I have an ongoing experience of gospel refreshment—an embracing of brokenness and an emotional unlocking in relationships—I will not last long in ministry.

Marriage and Family. This theme focuses on maintaining spiritual and relational health with one's spouse and children. The "big idea" is that we made covenant vows to God regarding our spouse and children that will, at times, conflict with our work responsibilities and vice versa. These promises require great discernment about time and commitments. We need to balance a commitment that honors those we love and serve in our families with a commitment to those we love and serve in our churches.

Our congregations need to honor and respect these vows, and we need to expend the physical and emotional energy to fulfill them. Pastors need the people of God to support them in this challenging endeavor, even as pastors equip their flocks to wisely weave together family, work and life. A summit pastor explained, "After my relationship with Christ, the health of my marriage is the foundation of my ministry."

Leadership and Management. Leadership is the *poetry* of gathering others together to seek adaptive and constructive change, while management is the *plumbing* that provides order and consistency to organizations. In the ministry, they blend together. Pastors must handle aspects of each even if they don't feel gifted to do so.

Two "big ideas" emerge from this theme. First, pastors must embrace these responsibilities as a vital part of their calling. Second, pastors must beware of the temptation to be the "hero leader" in the congregation. Jesus is the only hero. A guest at one summit described this theme as "doing anything that helps people move closer to Jesus." Leadership and management are more than just necessary evils; they are necessary components of discipling Christ's church.

COMMONLY ASKED QUESTIONS ABOUT THE SUMMIT RESEARCH FINDINGS

As we have shared the summit themes in many locations, we have been asked thoughtful questions about their meaning and application. Here are the most common questions.

Where Do Ministry Tasks Fit In? We discovered that the summit themes speak into almost every pastoral task, including preaching. But we also learned that the resilience of pastors transcends these ministry tasks. Resilience focuses on who the pastor is and how that influences what a pastor does. Spiritual formation, self-care, emotional and cultural intelligence, and marriage and family all center on who persons are and how they function. Even the leadership and management theme tells us that relationship attributes gets results.

Pre-professional ministry training usually focuses on knowing the right content and on developing skills to accomplish ministry tasks. As important as these are, they are usually not the reasons that people leave ministry. Rather, ministry-killing issues are matters of life skills, behavior patterns and character. When we began our research, we didn't anticipate that these matters of the heart and relationships would be the areas we talked about the most. But they became the issues on which the pastors in the summit focused.

The Themes Are Simple—Isn't Ministry More Complicated? One of the greatest baseball players of all time was Ted Williams. Once he heard someone say, "Hitting a baseball is simple." His response? "Sure, hitting the ball is simple—that doesn't mean it's easy."

At first glance, the five themes don't seem exceptional or novel. The unique nature of the themes, however, is how they speak into the lives and priorities of pastors and their families, and how they emerged from pastors themselves. In the previous chapters, we have explored why these themes have stood out as important. They may seem simple to understand, but putting this knowledge into practice isn't easy. So one of the refrains you will read throughout this concluding chapter is the challenge of putting the themes into practice.

Bob and Donald have both experienced sabbaticals in the past. We had defined periods of time, a month to three months, during which we were able to break the patterns of normal work activity and focus on rest, personal renewal and special projects. Both of us approached the end of our sabbaticals with the expectation that we would not get sucked back into the hectic pace that characterized our lifestyles before the sabbaticals. But within a matter of weeks, both of us had slipped back into those patterns we sought to avoid. We know the power of systems to squeeze us into the molds of the expectations.

Because systems push members to retain behaviors, the challenge of putting these themes into practice needs to be faced by everyone in the church: the pastor, the pastor's spouse and family, the leadership board, and the congregation. In some denominational structures, the need to address these themes involves denominational hierarchy on a regional and national level.

At the same time, such change usually begins with an individual or a small group. When someone tries to implement change, the system will push back, seeking to reestablish familiar patterns. Pursuing and maintaining new patterns of personal, family and congregational life demands the maintenance of boundaries. The challenge of following new patterns requires both support (family, friends, staff and governing board) and structure (plans, time and patience). Toward the end of this chapter, we suggest some specific ideas on how to do this.

How Do the Themes Connect? At the end of our second round of summit cohorts, Bob presented these five themes to the participants. A few hours later, one of the pastors asked Bob, "Have you considered how these themes connect to each other?" He said to Bob,

---

While each theme can be looked at individually, I really think they should be considered as a whole. Each is dependent on the others. They are more like the strands of a tapestry woven into one piece.

When he went home, this pastor wove together strands of five different colors. By highlighting the unity and interdependency of the themes, he was able to approach his ministry holistically.

When considering pastoral health, all five topics should be reviewed together. We really can't reflect on self-care without considering spiritual formation. And we shouldn't review emotional and cultural intelligence unless we understand their function both in our home and leadership. To see how the themes tie together, reconsider the following comment from a summit pastor that we shared in the chapter on emotional intelligence:

I embraced this paradigm [of emotional health] five years ago. Through counseling and developing close relationships, I began experiencing emotionally healthy spirituality. However, the stress of ministry has pushed me and our marriage away from practices of emotional honesty, reflection and dialogue. I am also very prone to blame my failures on my schedule, my wife and my parishioners. I definitely can feel the difference when we take time to cultivate our marriage, when I participate at home, when I say "no" to things that are not a priority, and when I contemplate and pray.

Note how the themes function together in this quotation. The pastor spoke about embracing and working on emotional intelligence. But he didn't consider the impact that ministry stress (self-care and leadership and management issues) had on practicing EQ. As a result, his marriage took the brunt of this failure. However, taking time to work on his marriage and family, as well as spiritual formation, allows him to exercise better EQ.

We would encourage you to make time for regular checkups, looking at all of the themes and how they relate to each other in your life. One way to do this is to refer to the "Questions to Ponder" sections in each chapter. Another tool for a checkup is the list of evaluation questions in appendix B. These appendix pages can be used for personal assessment or for annual reviews with a board.

A RETROSPECTIVE LOOK AT THE SUMMIT EXPERIENCE

We surveyed the summit pastors and spouses a number of years after their participation, asking them to respond to two questions.

- What lasting impact has your participation in the summit made in your life, family and ministry?

- What hopes did you carry from the summit that have not been fulfilled?

As you can tell, these were rather broad, reflective questions that made no reference to the themes of the summit. We were not surprised, however, that the responses naturally clustered around the five summit themes.

The Lasting Impact of the Summit. In answer to the two questions, the sections below summarize this longitudinal feedback by naming the big ideas that stuck using pastors' comments and drawing on our broader summit experience.

Spiritual formation: Distinguishing self from role. Distinguishing self from role requires humility. This idea of separating one's role from one's identity is hard for anyone in ministry. So much of who we are is poured into what we do. At the same time, distinguishing our selves from our jobs is critical for our spiritual, emotional and family health. People see us in our roles more than they see us as persons. The Lord sees us for who we are. As we walk in the light by confessing our sins and experiencing forgiveness, we can embrace our limits and understand our place in God's kingdom purposes (1 John 1:9). As one pastor said,

---

I now understand the value of keeping my identity as a person and a child of God distinct from my calling/work as a pastor.

Self-care: Joining peer groups. We have a friend whose father, a retired CEO, makes his living by facilitating peer group meetings for corporate professionals. His clients pay thousands of dollars to meet together quarterly to talk about their best practices and personal challenges. In line with this practice, one primary finding of the Lilly Endowment Sustaining Pastoral Excellence program is that people in ministry benefit greatly from peer groups.

It is difficult for those in ministry, however, to find resources and to make time to participate in such groups. It would be wise for congregational leaders who are interested in the health and longevity of their clergy and staff to consider how they could provide them with peer group experiences. Later in this chapter we will explore this idea in more detail. A summit pastor commented,

> Connection with other pastors has been a lifeline. The summit has given me a band of sisters and brothers to journey with, a gift that is immeasurable.

Emotional intelligence: Managing pain and frustration. When pastors are going through the pain and frustration of ministry, they often feel like they are the only ones who experience it. We need conversation partners with whom we can process these experiences and the feelings that accompany them. For most pastors, this conversation partner is a spouse.

We affirm that the insights of spouses are vital. But we have also discovered that both pastors and spouses benefit greatly from meeting with friends from different but similar contexts. Very often during the summit, we would hear exclamations like, "You've been through that too?" and "I'm so encouraged to hear how you managed that!" One pastor said,

> The most significant impact of the summit was helping me to "normalize" the pain and frustration of ministry.

Cultural intelligence: Recognizing differences. How are we going to learn to minister together if we don't take the time to listen and learn from one another? Bob's friend Chip Sweney was commissioned by his large Atlanta church to network within the community, to learn what God was doing in other cultural contexts and to lead the church in building partnerships. Chip discovered that he had to step out of his comfort zones and begin what he described as a "painfully slow" process of relationship-building and learning from others. Over many years, this community outreach ministry developed a close network of churches committed to transforming their city together. It began by pastors taking steps to learn about one another.[1] As one pastor commented,

> The summit teased me in cultural intelligence. It was so good having pastors from different cultures in my cohort. I felt like I was on the outside of their world; they minister in contexts very different from mine. They always gave a unique perspective. It taught me that I have a lot to learn. I am a little island in a much bigger sea.

Ministry in the twenty-first century will require us to move out from our "little islands" and grow together.

Marriage and family: Prioritizing marriage. We believe pastors *and* their spouses need the support and encouragement of others in ministry. In order to touch the deep needs of our participants, summit groups brought in marriage enrichment consultants. Similarly, we would encourage ministry peer groups to involve spouses and to engage outside counselors or trained clergy to facilitate marital growth. Throughout this book, we have urged pastoral couples to seek the support and perspective of professional counselors who can serve as consultants and confidants outside of their congregational system. One pastor put it this way:

> It's easy to talk about creating and maintaining a healthy marriage and family life. It is different to actually prioritize our marriage. The summit gave us a framework for actually doing it, and our participation in the summit meetings and activities helped us practice it. The practice helped us think through real-life situations and got us moving in the right direction.

Leadership and management: Building ministry alliances. Many times in cohorts we would hear participants moan about local, regional or national denominational meetings. So we were encouraged to hear how one participant gained a new perspective on such gatherings.

> The summit has had a profound impact on me for the good in terms of my involvement in our denominational gatherings. I look at them very differently now, not seeing it so much as a theological examining committee, disciplinary court or even ministry planning team as much as a

partnership of ministers working together for a common purpose and seeking to encourage one another along the way.

Perhaps this pastor's new perspective came from discussions on how building relationship trust brings ministry results. Or maybe it came from a new realization that by getting to know others, effective coalitions can be formed. Regardless, we were encouraged that some pastors gained a new vision on how regularly scheduled meetings could be transformed into times of encouragement and partnership.

Unfulfilled Hopes After the Summit. It was important for us to learn about the disappointments people might have experienced either with the summit or in trying to put the summit themes into practice. Here we highlight a primary concern that stood out in each theme area and our reflections on them.

Spiritual formation: Neglecting spiritual health. The pressures of ministry life do not recede when we are pursuing spiritual disciplines. As one summit pastor said,

It is easy to slip into a weekly grind, getting done what must be done and neglecting my own spiritual disciplines and spiritual health. This is a never-ending struggle.

Former president Dwight Eisenhower supposedly once said, "Important things are seldom urgent; urgent things are seldom important."[2] We believe pastors must embrace this never-ending struggle, acknowledging that there will be times when we must say no to the weekly grind, and other times when crises or pressures are so high that short-term adaptations must be made. When these short-term adaptations start becoming the norm, however, our behaviors must be recalibrated to fit our commitments.

Self-care: Overlooking peer friendships. The following quotation from a pastor bemoans a lack of confidants: people who understand the challenges pastors face but are "removed enough" from the congregation.

The hole that I continue to experience is the lack of fellow laborers who share my challenges but are removed enough from my situation to support me. It is hard to take time to develop healthy and strong friendships outside of church. It just seems that congregational responsibilities always take precedence over personal social time.

The need for "personal social time" raises the idea of allies versus confidants. Allies are friends, but they have some differing interests that make certain topics of conversation off limits. Confidants are persons with whom we can share with no worries of psychological safety or of social concern or of work threats. Confidants are hard to find. It takes time and energy to identify them and to cultivate their friendship. Furthermore, the pace and activity of pastoral life makes it difficult to work on these relationships. There is no simple solution. One significant step in this direction involves investing the time to form peer groups and to employ a facilitator who can provide planning and direction for the gatherings. Appendix E describes what we learned about forming such peer groups through seven years of running the Pastors Summit.

Emotional intelligence: Busyness squeezing out reflection. Earlier in this book we presented the ideas of *reflection-in-action* and *reflection-on-action*, developed by Donald Schön. All pastors do reflection-in-action even if they don't know they are doing it. It is the unconscious musing over what is taking place at the moment. However, our experience leads us to believe that the majority of pastors do not take time for reflection-on-action, pondering what took place, how people spoke or acted and what could be learned from the experience. As one pastor said,

I still find it incredibly challenging to build reflection into my life to the degree that I want. The summit always provided glimpses of what could be, but I just find it difficult to maintain space for reflection on an ongoing basis.

To do such reflection requires an intentional commitment and a willingness to stop long enough to do it. It means saying no to the next set of demands in order to say yes to learning via disciplined reflecting. A quotation given earlier deserves to be repeated: "No one is going to ask you, 'Have you reflected today?'" Indeed, reflection is not found in the job description of most pastors. But as one of our mentors once told us, "You make time for the things you value."

Cultural intelligence: Avoiding cultural diversity. When we have inhabited one culture, it is easy to assume that our heritage and perspective are the "right" ones. This is especially true of people who have lived as part of the majority culture of a region. A first step in developing CQ is exposure to other cultural contexts. However, after this happens, we must anticipate how to learn from it. As one pastor said,

> I benefited so much being with pastors from different cultural contexts. But I don't know what to do with it. I need help bringing that into my ministry.

We need emotional and relational support, as well as structured reflection and feedback, as we identify what we are learning and how to put it into practice.

Marriage and family: Surrendering to the pressure. Do you know what often happens when newly sober alcoholics leave their treatment program? If their families have been involved in the treatment, the sobriety is usually supported. If families are uninvolved in treatment, however, they often—unconsciously or even consciously—push recovering persons back toward the old, established patterns formed prior to treatment.

Similarly, when pastors participate in peer groups, they often identify patterns and behaviors that are not healthy. When they go home and re-enter the church, however, they discover that the expectations and patterns of family and congregants remain the same. As one pastor said,

> I've experienced resistance and unhappiness in some areas where I've tried to maintain healthy boundaries on my time for the sake of marriage and family.

Now a decision must be made. Will pastors stand firm in their resolve to change? If they do, they are creating disequilibrium in their systems. In return, the systems will push back, trying to regain the previous stability and rhythms. This will happen even if these patterns are unhealthy, as the pastor's quote under the next section demonstrates.

For this reason, it is important for pastors to discuss intended changes with key participants in their systems. If these family or church members recognize the need for change and support the pastor in it, they can help others understand why change is necessary. And they can provide encouragement to the pastor, who will be "feeling the heat" from those who don't like the change.

Leadership and management: Bowing to expectations to remain the same. One summit pastor said after returning from the summit,

> What's been hard are the church's expectations that my life and ministry should continue unchanged after participation in the summit. It was fairly easy to help them see the one-time benefit of participation in the program; it's another to try to incorporate new practices into the rhythms of my work life. Helping the church see and acknowledge ways they could change in order to have a healthier pastor has been an extremely delicate—and at times, painful—process.

Similar to the comments we just made under marriage and family, incorporating "new practices into my work life," as this pastor put it, shakes up the system. It is important to involve key partners in the system—administrative staff, pastoral staff, members of the leadership board and other influencers in the congregation—in the change process. If you can identify the discomfort that has been created by your changes, and create a healthy conversation around them, you may be surprised to discover that many will be supportive.

THE STRUGGLE FOR SUMMIT COHORTS TO CONTINUE

During the Pastors Summit, eight different groups of pastors met together three times a year for two years. Even though these groups were made up of pastors from a wide geographical spectrum, it was our hope that they would find some way to continue meeting. One group has continued to meet. A participant in this cohort wrote,

> Our group is still meeting twice a year. I cannot imagine doing ministry apart from the rhythm of meeting with these folks. However you look at it, there's an unmistakable conclusion about the lasting value of our summit experiences. Our folks are still all together, continuing to do what we learned in the summit.

We also know situations in which two or three pastors come together regularly to continue their relationships. But the demands of the local congregation, together with a lack of resources, have pushed most of our participants back into the challenges of vocational ministry without the ongoing support of their summit group. Like a New Year's resolution, they recognize that the cohort should continue, but the forces of life and work erode the resolve. As a summit alumnus shared,

---

I had also hoped that our cohort would make a better effort to stay connected, but that has not happened and is probably not realistic given our lives, jobs and distance. Relationships must be given priority if they are to survive, and most of us don't have that kind of margin.

Ministry leaders deeply feel the need for peer groups like the Pastors Summit. The benefits from such cohorts have been shown to markedly increase the resilience of pastors. So what can be done to develop such groups and utilize what has been learned through our research?

HOW—AND WITH WHOM—WILL YOU USE WHAT YOU'VE READ?

If you are like most, you have picked up this book on your own and have experienced it by yourself. This is the norm. It is extremely difficult, however, to implement the ideas we've discussed by yourself. One of our summit alumni, who now leads a number of pastoral peer groups, says,

---

Reading the book will help you understand these five areas, but to implement them you have to walk with others. The genius of our summit experience was that as we were walking through it together, we were talking through it together. Each cohort became a learning community.

So, with whom will you share this book? With whom will you talk, as you consider the way these themes weave into your life? Who will help support your efforts to change areas of your life to build up resilience in ministry?

If you are married, your spouse is the first person we think you should talk with about the ideas in this book. Even though you may both read it individually before talking, we recommend you talk through each chapter. Spend time listening to the thoughts and feelings that naturally follow from reading the stories of others. And watch out for perfectionism! We are all on a journey, and we learn these lessons best as we process our experiences together over time.

We would also encourage you to share this book with a close friend. If you live near each other, consider a time of sharing over coffee once a month. If your friend is not in a paid ministry role, discuss the differences and similarities between your respective ministries (church over against business, medicine, law, education or other vocation). We are very aware that women and men in different vocations can face similar pressures as those in the pastoral vocation. Talk about these things, and consider how to encourage each other to grow in each thematic category.

How will you help your ministry system change with you as you pursue sustainable ministry practices? We suggest you teach those in your system about relevant issues raised in this book. You might start by sharing your thoughts from this book with your board, elders and other key stakeholders in your church. Many aspects of this book could supplement board and leadership training programs. The summit topics also lend themselves to small group or Sunday school discussions around healthy lifestyles and work.

Once again, we urge you to consider forming a peer group with other pastors or ministry leaders in similar positions to your own. You could meet with pastors in your community, friends from seminary or ministry training, or members of your denomination. If you want to form a peer group, there are many organizational details to consider. This book and the questions, media suggestions and bibliography we've provided in each chapter can easily form the basis for a curriculum that could provide years of ongoing reflection.

Three issues stand out as critical regarding the formation of peer groups. The first concerns the need for careful, intentional selection of participants. Consider issues like age, life stage, church size, denomination, passions, philosophy of ministry and personality (can you get along with each other?). Appendix A provides the details regarding how those in the Pastors Summit were identified and selected. The choice of cohort participants is very important.

The second involves finding funding to utilize a facilitator. This money can come from pastors' own contributions, friends or church budgets. Facilitators need to be experienced in small group dynamics. Effective facilitators can be other pastors, counselors or laypersons.

Finally, it is critical that spouses be included. Please see appendix E for more details on what we learned about how to organize and facilitate pastor cohorts. We hope the appendices will serve you well in forming your own cohort for growing resilience in the ministry.

FINAL THOUGHTS

It has been a joy and an honor for the three of us to work together on this Pastors Summit project. Imagine what it was like, when a summit group ended, to hear comments like, "This has been the best thing I've ever done in my ministry, perhaps even my life," and "I really don't think we'd be in ministry if it weren't for Pastors' Summit." We continue to receive positive feedback from pastors and spouses who participated. Just yesterday Bob was on the phone with one alumnus who shared,

---

Even though the summit seems like an eternity ago, I continue to live off the things we learned together. And I've formed a few friendships that I know will last a lifetime.

The summit has also affected our lives in many ways. For Bob, this book marks the end of a seven-year journey. This project became much more than a research interest. The pastors and spouses of the summit are now dear friends for whom he prays and hopes to remain in contact. And the themes of the summit have changed his life in profound ways. If he is going to teach and write about these issues, he must seek to live them himself. Now that Bob has reentered vocational pastoral ministry, he is even more aware of them as he works on his own resilience and the health of the staff and congregation he serves.

For Tasha, the summit research has deepened her concern for pastors, vocational ministry leaders and the health of the church. She too is challenged to pursue increased health in the areas of the summit themes. She regularly brings the themes into her classes, eager for future ministry leaders to start pursuing sustaining practices while they are in seminary.

Donald was excited by the original Lilly Endowment request for proposals (from which the Pastors Summits was funded and this research emerged). What an opportunity to care for pastors and the churches they serve! He is thankful for the many strengthening conversations, heartfelt prayers and transformed lives he has witnessed as a result of Lilly's generosity and the work of God through the summits. Like Bob and Tasha, summit themes continue to weave their way into his own personal, professional and family life.

We have been, and will be, praying for those of you who read this book. If you are a pastor or are involved in some other form of vocational ministry, our prayer is that you could patiently review these themes and continually take steps toward personal and corporate health. We also pray that the Lord would provide friends who will support you in your growth.

If you are the spouse of a pastor, we pray that you will be secure in the love of Christ and the love of your spouse, which can overflow to a love for God's people. If you are a member of a church and/or a church board member, we pray that you will help the people of your congregation understand the unique stressors and challenges faced in the ministry. By God's grace and with God's strength, healthy pastors and pastoral families are able to lead healthier, growing congregations.

RESEARCH METHODS OF THE PASTORS SUMMIT

PARTICIPANT SELECTION FOR THE SUMMIT COHORTS

Deciding who would participate was a key aspect of the program. The research involved male married pastors, thus representing the majority of U.S. pastors and providing the opportunity to include wives in the discussions. Further research would be needed to distinguish unique findings for women and single pastors. The following criteria were used in the selection of Pastors Summit participants.

1. *Existing relationships.* The three seminaries participating in the research had ongoing relationships with pastors and churches around the country, so numerous participants were selected from these existing friendships. In the social sciences, this is described as a "reputational" criterion, usually referring to recommendations made by experienced consultants.

2. *Evangelical theological commitment.* Because this initiative was directed by three evangelical seminaries, it is understandable that this would be a primary criterion for the pastors chosen to participate.

3. *Congruent pastoral experience.* In our grant request, we outlined three phases of ministry experience: novice (one to five years), seasoned (six to fourteen years), and veteran (fifteen or more years). For the first round of cohorts, we selected seasoned pastors. The criterion specified that participants display strong ministry expertise that might only be developed over time. In our initial cohorts, we did include a few unusually gifted novice pastors and wise veteran pastors. In our second round

of forming cohorts, we sought to gain greater diversity of experience by selecting participants for three groups: one of novice, one of seasoned and one of veteran pastors.

4. *Congruent positional level.* In the first round of cohorts, the participants all held similar pastoral positions. They were senior pastors, solo pastors or solo church planters. In the second round, we had a little more diversity of positions, although the significant majority still held the primary pastoral leadership role in their congregations.

5. *Variety of congregational contexts.* The original grant outlined three broad pastoral contexts: rural, suburban and urban. We sought to include a mixture of contextual experience in each cohort. However, a majority of the churches represented, particularly in the seasoned and veteran categories of pastors, were suburban.

6. *Variety of church sizes with corporate health.* Church size often seems to represent corporate maturity and strength of leadership. It is not an absolute indicator, however. Pastors in urban or rural contexts might be in a situation in which significant growth in attendance will not occur, or at least not occur quickly. At the same time, larger churches can exhibit significant dysfunction. Our participant selection focused on the areas of corporate health, leadership strength and contextually appropriate growth over and against stagnancy.

7. *Racial and ethnic minority representation.* We planned for the cohorts to serve as a unique opportunity for growth in understanding between Anglo, African American, Hispanic and Asian pastors. Our criteria called for minority participation proportional to the constituency served. As a result, there was minority representation in almost every cohort. However, for the third round of cohorts we chose to form one African American cohort and one Hispanic cohort. These cohorts provided more intimacy and psychological safety for members to address concerns of pastoral resilience within their own ethnic framework, as well as to address their experiences of interacting with dominant Anglo denominational contexts.

8. *Regional constituencies.* In the original grant proposal, we considered selecting participants within 250-300 miles of each sponsoring seminary. This criterion was considered for a number of reasons: ease of

travel to the regional locations, ease of maintaining peer relationships between meetings and lower travel expenses. A number of factors militated against these concerns, however. For example, while geographic proximity is helpful, we had documentation of significant ongoing relationships from greater distances that were maintained through regular telephone contact, email and other social media. We concluded that for our study, the quality of participant selection should not be restricted by geographical concerns. Our final sample included seventy-three pastors representing twenty-six states from across the country.

9. *Strong ministry expertise and emotional health.* In the initial grant proposal, we stated that participants should exhibit "strong ministry expertise" and "emotional health in ministry." How should these characteristics be assessed? The reputational criterion would be significant in assessing. We also used studies on ministry expertise to identify these characteristics. Four characteristics of ministry expertise stood out from this material: the length of current or former pastorate, the ability to manage time in the midst of competing demands, the ability to navigate relational demands and conflicts, and the giftedness to function within complex skill requirements. In general terms, we outlined three types of pastors: flying, floundering and driving. *Flying* pastors, sometimes described as "strong, natural leaders," are pastors of well-known, highly influential churches. *Floundering* pastors, either due to personal or corporate dysfunction, do not demonstrate strong ministry expertise or emotional health. *Driving* pastors were the focus of our initiative. They demonstrated personal maturity while also leading their congregations in corporate health and toward maturity.

Further assessment was necessary, however, in the evaluation of both ministry expertise and emotional health. We consulted a number of educational psychologists in this matter. A fruitful suggestion came from Mark McMinn, then of Wheaton College, who recommended the method of behavioral interviewing. Behavioral interviewing is a specific methodology of using structured interviews to evaluate skills and behaviors. The analysis is based on the social science theory of behavioral consistency, which states that the best predictor of future behavior is past behavior. First, desired skills and behaviors are identified. Then open-ended questions and statements are designed to elicit detailed responses. The person interviewed is asked to give specific examples of when they demonstrated particular behaviors or skills.

We developed interview questions that would elicit answers for evaluation based on a profile of behaviors that describe "strong ministry expertise and emotional health in ministry." Our interview protocol included

- personal life and time management
- conflict and personal emotions management
- ministry management and communication skills
- ability to negotiate and compromise
- personal spiritual and family life

Application Process and Confirming Documents. After initial telephone conversations with potential summit participants, the pastors were sent a brochure describing the program and the application process. Applicants were required to submit a reflection paper on their experience in pastoral ministry, as well as a letter explaining why they wanted to be involved and what they hoped to gain from participation. They were also asked to read and sign the participant covenant. Spouses were also asked to submit a letter and responses to questions concerning the commitment. Further, a reference letter was requested either from an elder or a partner in ministry. The governing board of the pastor's church was also asked to affirm participation. Finally, the pastors were given a behavior-based interview to explore their ministry expertise and emotional maturity. The interviews were done by a confidential interviewer hired by the Center for Ministry Leadership at Covenant Theological Seminary.

QUALITATIVE DATA COLLECTION AND ANALYSIS

While the summit groups began to bond by sharing their lives, our staff was actively involved in qualitative research. In distinction from quantitative research, qualitative research pursues a deep understanding and rich description of how people make meaning and sense of their experiences. The qualitative research process relies on the researcher for data collection and inductive analysis.[1] This method allowed us to gain comprehensive and descriptive data from the participants' perspectives on what is required to remain in fruitful ministry for a lifetime.

Each facilitated discussion during a summit gathering was audio-recorded. Two transcriptionists typed up transcripts of these meetings, eventually creating about twelve thousand pages of material. A team of researchers, trained in qualitative data analysis, was overseen by Bob Burns and Tasha Chapman. The team analyzed the material by focusing on the research question: "What does it take to survive and thrive in pastoral ministry?"

We used the constant comparative method to analyze the data; transcribed discussions were compared back and forth as data came in throughout the study years.[2] The transcripts were coded and categorized for themes, patterns, spectrums and insights that helped to answer the single research question.

Caroline Wilson and Bob Burns analyzed the data from the first round of summits and then involved the team on the second round. The basic five themes of resilient ministry (spiritual formation, self-care, emotional intelligence, marriage and family, leadership and management) were identified from the first round of Pastors Summit data. The cultural intelligence theme was added from analysis of data from the second round of summits. The basic five themes and other subthemes were confirmed by second-round data. Later, we went back and identified the CQ idea in the first round of data as well.

QUESTIONS FOR PERSONAL EVALUATION AND ANNUAL REVIEWS

EMOTIONAL LIFE

1. Mark and rank those that relate to you right now:

Encouraged	Energized	Focused	Affirmed
Innovative	Discouraged	Overlooked	Fulfilled
Confused	Confident	Useful	Alone
Challenged	Frustrated	Overworked	Grateful
Stressed	Optimistic	Initiator	Concerned
Integrated	Struggling	Overwhelmed	Organized
Burned out	Growing	Appreciated	Unchallenged
Goal-oriented	Task-oriented	Equipper	Team Player
Creative	Flexible	Resourceful	Current

2. Comment on any of the above.

3. How do you react when your expectations are high but the results are low?

4. How do you manage these reactions?

5. How do you deal with the loneliness of leadership?

INTELLECTUAL LIFE

1. Name three people whose biographies you would like to read.

2. Describe the professional development that you would like to experience with regard to school, work, seminars, books or new experiences.

3. What are you doing to understand the cultural trends in America and the broader cultural trends in the world?

4. With whom do you share your ideas?

5. Who shares their ideas with you?

6. What are the most significant values that reflect who you are?

PHYSICAL LIFE

1. Reflect on your current diet. What are you eating and why?

2. How do you exercise regularly and adequately? If you don't, consider what you need to do about it.

3. When was your last physical exam?

4. What are areas identified that need to be worked on?

5. What have you been doing about it?

6. What are your sleep patterns?

7. Reflect on any correlations between the way you manage your emotions and your present physical condition (including sleep, diet, exercise and overall physical condition).

SEXUALITY

1. How (and with whom) do you process your sexual issues as a pastor?

2. How do you deal with the temptation of Internet pornography?

3. How do your issues with lust hinder your ministry, leadership at home and leadership at church?

4. What role do your elders or fellow staff members play in accountability with sexual issues?

SOCIAL/RELATIONAL LIFE

1. Name two persons (or couples) you would describe as safe and trustworthy in your life.

2. Why do you feel this way about them?

3. How do you manage the tension between the competing demands of ministry and family?

4. Describe a new relationship you initiated and built with someone in the past year.

SPIRITUAL LIFE

1. How would you describe your walk with God over the past year?

2. Reflect on how you are doing in the following areas, taken from Acts 2:42-47:

   a. worship (personal and corporate)

   b. instruction (studying and learning "the apostles' doctrine")

   c. fellowship (relationships that help you to grow in faithfulness and obedience)

   d. evangelism and outreach (involvement in sharing your faith in lifestyle and word)

3. Does someone hold you spiritually accountable? (Is it "true" accountability? Are you regularly asked the hard questions?)

4. When did you last get away for a spiritual and ministry planning time?

APPENDIX C

EMOTIONS CHECKLIST

Reviewing a checklist of adjectives describing varied emotions can be very helpful in learning to accurately identify emotions.* When we better identify emotions, it deepens the understanding of ourselves and others. Try using this list at the end of the day, considering your circumstances and how you feel. Or keep the list in your journal so that you can identify feelings as you write. Or use it as a "test-retest," exploring how your feelings may have changed from one point of time to another.

Place a check next to all the adjectives that describe how you feel right now.

☐ Ambivalent	☐ Brave	☐ Depressed
☐ Amused	☐ Bright	☐ Detached
☐ Angry	☐ Calm	☐ Different
☐ Annoyed	☐ Cheated	☐ Discouraged
☐ Anxious	☐ Collected	☐ Disgusted
☐ Apathetic	☐ Confident	☐ Disinterested
☐ Ashamed	☐ Confused	☐ Empty
☐ At Peace	☐ Contented	☐ Engaged
☐ Attractive	☐ Defeated	☐ Excited
☐ Bitter	☐ Dejected	☐ Exhausted
☐ Bored	☐ Delighted	☐ Foolish

---

*Adapted from Bob Burns and Tom Whiteman, *The Fresh Start Divorce Recovery Workbook: A Step-by-Step Program for Those Who Are Divorced or Separated* (Nashville: Thomas Nelson, 1998).

☐ Fulfilled
☐ Funny
☐ Glad
☐ Glib
☐ Grateful
☐ Guilty
☐ Happy
☐ Hateful
☐ Helpful
☐ Helpless
☐ Hesitant
☐ Hopeful
☐ Hurt
☐ Impatient
☐ Independent
☐ Indifferent
☐ Inferior
☐ Insecure
☐ Inspired
☐ Interested
☐ Involved
☐ Irritated
☐ Jealous
☐ Joyful
☐ Jubilant
☐ Judged
☐ Lonely
☐ Loved
☐ Loyal
☐ Miserable

☐ Misguided
☐ Misunderstood
☐ Needy
☐ Neglected
☐ Nervous
☐ Neutral
☐ Optimistic
☐ Overjoyed
☐ Overwhelmed
☐ Pessimistic
☐ Phony
☐ Pleased
☐ Powerful
☐ Preoccupied
☐ Puzzled
☐ Questioning
☐ Quiet
☐ Rejected
☐ Relieved
☐ Reluctant
☐ Resentful
☐ Resilient
☐ Respectful
☐ Restless
☐ Romantic
☐ Sad
☐ Satisfied
☐ Secure
☐ Selfish
☐ Sexual

☐ Sexy
☐ Shy
☐ Silly
☐ Smart
☐ Sorry
☐ Strong
☐ Stupid
☐ Suicidal
☐ Supported
☐ Surprised
☐ Tense
☐ Terrible
☐ Thankful
☐ Touched
☐ Tough
☐ Trusting
☐ Ugly
☐ Unappreciated
☐ Unhappy
☐ Unsure
☐ Upset
☐ Useful
☐ Violent
☐ Weary
☐ Welcome
☐ Well
☐ Whole
☐ Willing
☐ Wise
☐ Worried

CONSTRUCTING AND INTERVIEWING A FAMILY DIAGRAM

A GENOGRAM IS A VISUAL DESCRIPTION of behavioral systems in a family over the course of three or more generations. It serves as a helpful tool for leaders to "see" the family system to which they belong and how their family of origin has influenced their leadership, both positively and negatively. Families don't ultimately determine us. God's grace, gifting and sovereign purposes can shape and even override the influences of our family. At the same time, God ordained our family of origin as one means of his divine design for our lives. Therefore, one way for us to "number our days that we may get a heart of wisdom" is to review how we were shaped by our family of origin (Psalm 90:12).

STEPS TO CREATING AND EXPLORING YOUR GENOGRAM

1. Draw a family tree with three generations: you and your family, your family of origin (parents and siblings), and your parents' families of origin (your grandparents, aunts and uncles). Use a circle to represent females and a square to represent males. To the best of your ability, place the year of birth and, if applicable, the year of death, for each person.

2. Use the symbols guide (below) to illustrate the types of relationships that existed between key persons in the genogram.

3. To provide insights for reflection on a particular theme, mark each person with a symbol to represent her or his typical behavior on a par-

ticular issue. For example, for each person, note how they responded to success or to failure.

4. Make observations on any patterns, contrasts or spectrums that you discover in behaviors across the genogram. Note patterns of gospel health or of sinfulness.

5. Reflect on your observations in light of your own behavior. How have you superimposed unhealthy patterns of behavior on God? How have you continued the family patterns in your home? How have you continued the family patterns in your ministry leadership? How do your strengths and struggles correlate to family patterns? What can you do to strengthen the healthy patterns? How can you leverage your strengths to correct the sinful patterns?

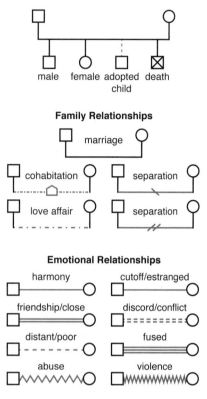

Figure D.1. Genogram symbols guide

ADDITIONAL GENOGRAM QUESTIONS

Foundational Genogram Questions

1. Who was the dominant person in your family?[1] How did you learn to relate to that person? Who taught you to relate to that dominant person in that manner? Who was the dominant person in your parents' family of origin? If you have heard, how did your parents (and their siblings) relate to that person?

2. What were the major life-altering events and crises in your family of origin? In previous and subsequent generations? How did individuals and families respond and react to these events? What were some of the long-term effects of these events on individuals and families as a whole?

3. The following presents a spectrum of emotions one might feel: sad, glad, mad, strong, afraid, weak, confused, anxious, calm. Using these descriptors, identify the dominant feelings for each member of your family system. What was the predominant feeling describing your entire family of origin? What impact has this emotional environment had on your ministry leadership?

Leadership Models and Methods

1. Ken Blanchard has identified four "natural" leadership patterns.[2] The patterns form around two types of specific leader behaviors with individuals. To what degree is a leader acting to support the other and to provide direction?

   - high supportive, low directive
   - high supportive, high directive
   - low supportive, low directive
   - low supportive, high directive

2. To the best of your ability, label the leadership pattern exhibited most often by your parents and grandparents. How would you describe your natural pattern?

3. Who were your models growing up? What impact did these models have on your expectations for yourself as a leader?

4. Using words or short phrases, describe your father as a leader. Describe your mother as a leader. Describe your grandparents as leaders.

5. Identify who you believe are the three key leaders in your congregation (elders or otherwise) or your business.

   - What criteria do you use to identify these three leaders?
   - What do you know about the family of origin of these three leaders?
   - How do you think your family of origin has shaped who you consider these three leaders to be?

Emotional Experience and Expression

1. Describe any hobbies or sports family members participated in, as well as the level of their involvement.

2. How did your parents respond to you when you were in a highly reactive emotional state? How do you respond to your children when they are highly emotional? Comment on any similarities between these family patterns and the way that you respond to the emotions of your elders or others in the congregation or to your employees in your business.

3. *The Leader's Journey* defines acute anxiety as "our reaction to a threat that is real and time-limited. We react to the threat, respond to it, and then eventually return to a normal state of mind and body. . . . With chronic anxiety, however, the threat is imagined or distorted, rather than real. Consequently, it is not time-limited; it does not simply go away."[3] Every emotional system sustains some level of chronic anxiety.

   a. How would you describe the family system in which you grew up with regard to the level of chronic anxiety? Were you led to think of the world as basically secure or basically threatening? What did people in your family fret over? What difference has growing up in this environment had on the way you lead? Consider an anxious time in your current family. How has your "training" in your family of origin affected the way you handled that situation?

   b. How would you describe the ministry system you are engaged in with regard to the level of chronic anxiety? Do leaders in the system see the world about them as threatening? How does this manifest itself? Are there frequent emergencies and crises? When a crisis occurs, does the leadership take it in stride and solve the problem, or are they likely to develop symptoms? Review a difficult or crisis situation you have faced as a ministry in the light of these questions.

   c. How do you think your three key leaders would describe the chronic anxiety of the congregation? How do they respond when a crisis occurs?

Relational Connectivity

1. What is your place in the constellation of your family of origin: oldest, youngest, middle? Were you a brother with younger sisters? Younger brothers? Older sisters? Older brothers?

   a. How did the unique spot in the family that you occupied shape you in learning to relate to others?

   b. How did it shape you in the way you lead and the way you respond to others' leadership?

2. Describe the kind of community and social involvement reflected in the members of your family system. What roles did your family members play in this involvement?

3. In *The Leader's Journey*, the authors identify four symptoms of chronic anxiety that are indicative of an anxious system: *conflict* (often identified with "all or nothing" thinking); *distance* (keeping the peace by maintaining superficial or no contact); *overfunctioning* and *underfunctioning* (compensation of an individual or group within a system to take on too much responsibility for another person or group); and *projection* (projecting anxiety onto an individual or a part of the system).

   a. Which of these four symptoms do you most typically see in your congregation? How about in your own family?

   b. How do you, as a leader in the system, participate in this? How do your elders or staff participate in this?

   c. How do key leaders in the congregation participate in these four symptoms of an anxious system?

4. *Individuality*: God has created us as unique individuals. The complexity of the human DNA makes every one of us distinguishable from others (Psalm 139:1-14). *Togetherness*: God calls us to community (Ephesians 4:1-3). In this context, we are called to be sensitive to the needs of others, serve others and "fit in" with each other.

   a. How would you describe your family of origin with regard to individuality and togetherness?

   b. How would you describe your nuclear family with regard to individuality and togetherness?

   c. How would you describe your three key leaders with regard to individuality and togetherness?

   d. How would you describe your church with regard to individuality and togetherness?

Metrics and Means of Success

1. Describe the level that each family member completed in school.

2. Identify the job experience of those in your genogram. Describe the employment and career patterns that you see (including homemaking). What types of leadership responsibilities are evident in those job roles?

3. When it came to education, career, sports, hobbies and social involvement, what were the expectations placed on you within your family system? What was the response when you attained or failed to attain in these areas?

4. Describe how your family of origin planned and accomplished goals. Were plans and goals ever made? If so, where did these goals fall on a spectrum between individual goals versus family goals? Did the family plan these together, were they imposed "from on high" or did everyone make up their own goals when they wanted? How were goals accomplished (individually, in partnerships or as a group)?

5. Who were the heroes and heroines in your family? Why or for what were they honored?

6. What was "applauded" in your family? How and for what were you applauded in your family?

Failure, Loss and Pain

1. Who were the unrecognized or disregarded members of your family? Why were they treated this way?

2. How was failure viewed in the family? How have you superimposed these standards on God? How have you reflected these in your leadership of others?

3. What was criticized in your family? How and for what were you criticized in your family?

4. What "secrets" are in your family tree? What are you not allowed or supposed to talk about?

Spiritual Influences and Experiences

1. What were the views of God in your family of origin? What did it mean to be religious? What did it mean to be a Christian?

2. What events formed your view of God and humanity?

3. What events informed your understanding of Jesus?

4. What spiritual understandings were formed in your childhood that you now consider very helpful and significant?

5. What spiritual understandings or beliefs were formed in your childhood that you now consider dangerous or destructive?

Application Questions

1. How would you relate your sense of call into ministry to your family of origin? To your extended family?

2. Dissociating from the emotional anxiety of your system while staying connected to the people is hard work.

   a. Identify three methods you use to manage your feelings during times of anxiety. Where, how or from whom did you learn these methods? Do you consider these methods healthy or an avoidance method? Why?

   b. How well do your three key leaders dissociate from anxiety yet stay relationally connected to people?

3. Who in your congregation do you struggle to connect with—in other words, when you leave their presence you think, *This man or woman just doesn't get me?*

   a. What characteristics of these trigger such an emotionally allergic reaction?

   b. Can you think of anyone in your history to whom you had a similar response?

BEST PRACTICES FOR FORMING PEER COHORTS

This is the only place people want me to be me.

I miss who I am outside this. It's impossible to miss who I am here.

At a Pastors Summit cohort gathering

Appendix E provides you with our counsel for forming peer cohorts for building resilience for pastors or other ministry leaders. These pages contain summaries of the details that we found to be most important and helpful. We arrived at these practices out of seven years of designing and facilitating Pastors Summit groups. The participants gave thorough input and feedback on the gatherings as the program progressed, so this is really a summary of practices that pastors think meets their needs best. Many alumni from the program hoped to continue with their current group or start their own regional summit cohort, so we initially gathered this information for them.

KEY PARTICIPANT MOTIVATIONS FOR COMMITTING TO A COHORT

We use Summit participants' own phrases to list them.

- To be with others who "get it" and "understand my world and know my job as a pastor."

- To have a support group where there are "no faces or fronts, where I can simply be myself, in all my glorious ruin."

- To meet a deep need "for an environment where I don't have to prove anything."

KEY REASONS TO INCLUDE SPOUSES IN COHORTS

- To increase the motivation and commitment of both spouses to attend.

- To hold more meaningful conversations about the life impact of vocational ministry, which occurs more easily when spouses are present.

- To pull male married pastors out of "shop mode" to deal with heart issues, which occurs more easily when their wives are present.

- To increase the emotional work, the empathy and listening focus of the group.

- To avoid the risk of one spouse having a powerful experience that could bring more division to couples if both are not present.

LOGISTICS AND STRUCTURE

Cohort Group Size: Six to eight pastors + spouses + facilitators
Small-group research correlates with our experiences of these key factors:

- At twelve, the group crosses out of small-group dynamics, so try to limit numbers to a dozen participants.

- Most small groups function like support groups.

- Include spouses as much as possible, requiring spouse participation at least once per year.

- For all to have the opportunity to tell their stories and to feel heard, group meetings require fifteen minutes per person minimum for discussion on a single topic.

Timing and Schedules for Cohort Gatherings

1. Gatherings of forty-eight hours (Tuesday lunch through Thursday lunch) worked best for the pastors.

2. Pastors found three gathering times per year, with at least one time with spouses, to be just right.

3. The gathering schedule and learning process must be designed intentionally.

4. The first gathering requires a planned experience for all to share in order to break down barriers. (See notes on first gathering below.)

5. The first gathering is best held with only the pastors so that they can feel enough ownership and value to convince the spouses to commit with them.

6. Initial sessions will need more structure and detailed planning than later ones.

7. Reflection time should use guides and must be enforced in the schedule.

8. Ground rules should be discussed and reviewed each session. For example, facilitators should remind the group of their commitment to completely unplug and shut off phones, to keep all discussions confidential ("What comes here, stays here"), to drop the "shop talk" and to keep the gathering an "advice-free zone" so that no one tries to fix another's challenges.

Sample Pastors Summit Schedule

Tuesday	
12:00 p.m.	Lunch and settle into rooms
1:30 p.m.	Worship and announcements
2:00 p.m.	Reconnect: How can we pray for you? For your marriage and family? For your ministry?
5:30 p.m.	Dinner
7:00 p.m.	Book and case studies
Wednesday	
6:00 a.m.	Personal devotions
7:30 a.m.	Breakfast
8:30 a.m.	Worship and devotion
9:00 a.m.	Personal reflection time
11:00 a.m.	Gather with partner to share/pray
12:00 p.m.	Lunch and free time
1:30 p.m.	Afternoon discussion/activity
5:30 p.m.	Dinner
7:00 p.m.	Evening team-building activity (movie with reflection questions, sports venue, bowling, etc.)
9:00 p.m.	Break for evening

Thursday	
6:30 a.m.	Personal devotions
7:30 a.m.	Breakfast and check out of rooms
8:30 a.m.	Worship and announcements
9:00 a.m.	Debrief of this summit experience: What did you see, hear, learn?
10:30 a.m.	Break
10:45 a.m.	Plans for next summit experience: What topics would you like to discuss? What books would you like to read? What expert would you like to invite?
12:00 p.m.	Lunch and leave

Room and Board

- Offsite locations, where participants have no connections and no responsibilities, are a must.

- Cook meals together, if needed, as part of a facilitated group project.

- Consider asking congregants to donate the use of vacation homes for use.

Administration

- Facilitator must provide regular communication with all participants.

- Assignments and materials for participants should be provided in advance.

- Reservations for lodging and meals need to be made in advance.

- Meal organization and preparation requires careful advance planning. It is worth the time and expense to have nice meals. Ask caterers from congregations to help.

Topics for Books and Resources to Provide for Advance Reading and Discussions

The Summit participants found it very helpful to have assigned reading to do before meeting together. The readings launched the discussions. See bibliography lists at the end of most chapters for specific suggestions.

- spiritual formation

- vocational calling

- self-care

- emotional intelligence

- cultural intelligence

- marriage and family

- leadership and management

- ongoing ministry training

- personality or leadership profiles and 360s, like MBTI® and RightPath®

- movie reflection questions

- outlines and summaries of books

PRIORITIES FOR THE FIRST COHORT GATHERING

- The participants should be away from home and work during the entire meeting, including overnight.

- Participants must unplug for meeting times by turning off all cell phones and computers and leaving them in the bedrooms.

- Spend Tuesday afternoon on introductions, including information such as name, ministry context and timing, where you grew up, family background, college and major, how you met your spouse, kids' names and ages, a favorite movie and why, a favorite activity and why.

- Spend Tuesday evening after dinner discussing a topic, with a book summary, for focusing on "shop" or addressing a current ministry need. The first meeting should focus on immediate felt needs in the work of ministry, but the group will need to get beyond this during later meetings. For example, select a "big picture" ministry book such as *Culture Making: Recovering Our Creative Calling* by Andy Crouch or *Deep Church: A Third Way Beyond Emerging and Traditional* by Jim Belcher.

- Spend Wednesday afternoon all together, sharing thoughts and concerns that came up during the personal reflection time and then doing a creative team-building activity (like a high ropes course).

SAMPLE OF PERSONAL REFLECTION QUESTIONS
FOR WEDNESDAY MORNING

- What issues/topics have you focused on today?

- What questions have emerged?

- What conclusions have you drawn?

- Have you identified any action items for personal development? If so, please list them here.

- What resources will you need to pursue these action items?

PARTICIPANT YEARLY EXPENSES

The following two lists show the expenses we expected a summit group to incur in 2010 if they followed the model described above. These figures are calculated for ministry leaders to attend three times a year, for forty-eight hours over two nights, with spouses coming twice a year. The facilitator cost is equally divided by the eight pastor participants.

Category	Low Cost	High Cost
Lodging (double occupancy)	$0	$600
Print/literature	$0	$150
Meals	$250	$555
Outside "expert"	$0	$2,500
Percentage of facilitator cost[1]	$581	$1,203
Yearly cost total	$831	$5,008

Goal = Church expense no more than $5,000/year

YEARLY COST FOR OUTSIDE FACILITATOR

This includes a roughly $750 honorarium plus expenses for facilitator. The facilitator should be paid based on a fixed fee per participant or on an agreed-upon hourly rate, based on their vocation and needs.

Category	#Mtgs	Low/High Cost per Mtg[2]	Low/High Cost per Yr
Facilitator stipend	3	$855/$1,555	$2,565/$4,665
Spouse facilitator stipend[3]	2	$855/$1,205	$1,710/$2,410
Facilitator travel	3	$25/$400[4]	$75/$1,200
Spouse facilitator travel	2	$25/$400	$50/$800
Facilitator expenses[5]	3	$50/$110	$150/$330
Spouse facilitator expenses	2	$50/$110	$100/$220
Yearly cost total		$1,860/$3,780	$4,650/$9,625

ANOTHER SUMMIT MODEL TO MINIMIZE EXPENSES

We are currently running several new Pastors Summit groups using a different model in order to minimize the funding needed. After six months, this model seems to be providing the benefits of the other cohort model toward sustaining pastors in ministry.

The biggest costs for a summit include travel, lodging and meals. Therefore, this new model involves choosing participants from within a hundred-mile radius. This minimizes travel expenses, and no lodging or meals are involved. These groups commit to meeting ten times per year for three-hour meetings. The spouses join the pastors for four out of the ten gatherings. We have found that although the pastors' abilities to get completely "out of role" are limited by this schedule, they are able to unplug with the aid of a skilled facilitator. Later, the groups plan to raise funds from their churches for a couples' gathering over two to three nights. The main expense with this model is the facilitator fee.

RECOMMENDED SOURCES OF FUNDING

- A line item in the church budget for continuing education of the pastor.

- A grant from a church-planting network or other ministry network for continuing education for the ministry leader based on network requirements.

- A scholarship fund established by anonymous donors for the continuing education of the pastor or ministry leadership.

- A part of the pastor's tithe given for the summit ministry. Some believe this follows well the Old Testament example of the Levites tithing to provide for the priests.

PEER PARTICIPANT RECRUITING CRITERIA TO CONSIDER

The ideal cohort size is six to eight couples, recruited according to the following criteria. Initially the lead initiator and organizer, in conversation with the facilitator, selects participants.

- Established relationship: Often initial recruits will suggest friends who might participate.

- Pastoral experience and position: Solo pastor, senior pastor, church planter or associate/assistant pastor. We recommend the peers share the same position.

- Geographic proximity: A radius of 250-300 miles works well unless financial resources are significant enough for airfare. Diversity of locale can add safety but also adds cost. The closer together pastors are geographically, the more territorial concerns and competition may be felt. Different denominational affiliations can mitigate this challenge in creating intimacy.

- Theological conviction: We recommend the peers share similar theological commitments that can be openly stated in the group.

- Denominational commitment: This obligation is not the same as a philosophical agreement. Successful cohorts can form with peers from different denominations if they share similar philosophies of ministry.

- Ministry philosophy: Participants should have a similar philosophy of ministry or openness to other ministry styles.

- Openness and eagerness to learn: This is often demonstrated by the desire of the pastor and spouse to participate.

- Ministry expertise and health: It is worth considering the pastor's emotional health, and the pastor's church's reputation of corporate health, leadership strength and a contextually appropriate growth over and against stagnancy. Emotional health can be observed in how people acknowledge their need for repentance and humility and tell stories in response to questions about their actions. Ministry expertise may be represented in (1) length of current (or former) pastorate, (2) the ability to manage time in the midst of conflicting demands, (3) the ability to navigate relational demands and conflicts, (4) the giftedness to function within complex skill requirements. Similar expertise level enables a peer group to bond more easily.

- Congregational contexts: Urban, suburban or rural. We found it helpful to have a variety represented as much as possible.

- Age/stage: Breakdown of years in ministry, such as one to five years, six to fourteen years, and fifteen or more. This often reflects experience in ministry as well as pastors' marriage and family situation. Groups representing the same age/stage often share similar interests and challenges.

However, such similarity reduces the opportunity to gain from varied life and ministry experiences. Selection should recognize the strengths and weaknesses found in the way this criterion is used.

- Racial and ethnic minority representation: Cohorts could serve as a unique opportunity for growth and understanding between Anglos, African American, Hispanic and Asian pastors within our churches.

- Ministry board and spousal support: We found it important for pastors to have the support of both.

- Agreement to a common commitment: Commitments must be discussed from the beginning. The first session should be "open" for a trial experience, but all should understand that a commitment will be requested after the first meeting. Commitments should include attendance, length of time (we recommend starting with three meetings a year for two years), spouses attending at least annually, completion of reading and reflection before each gathering, and transparency, including the willingness to share weaknesses and failures as the group grows together.

How to find participants

1. Build a list of potential participants. Build up potential names through your own relationships, through "consultants" and through reputation.

2. Pass the names through a criteria list.

3. Approach each person with the concept and commitments. Approach individually and relationally, in a context in which a conversation can take place—if possible, at a meal or coffee time.

SAMPLE PARTICIPANT COMMITMENT PLEDGE

Depending on God's grace, as a participant in the Pastors Summit I, _____, make a pledge of intention to do the following:

1. Attend all meetings, unless providentially hindered. I will call my summit facilitator if I am unable to attend and will take the responsibility to find out what was missed in my absence.

2. Thoughtfully and honestly write a personal development plan that I will revise and develop over the course of my two-year involvement.

3. Visit my cohort's website online discussion forum (password protected) at least once a week, and post at least two comments a month.

4. Arrange for my (and my spouse's, when applicable) absence from regular duties during cohort meetings, including those related to family, church, work and friends.

5. Participate fully in cohort discussions and activities. I will give an accurate account of my experience, reflections and spiritual progress during cohort meetings and online discussions. I will seek to be appropriately transparent, willing to share weakness, struggle and failure as the cohort grows together.

6. Unplug from electronic devices and work responsibilities. I will turn my cell phone off and will not email or surf the Internet during meetings. I will do my best to bring no work with me and will refrain from working during breaks at the gatherings.

7. Care for the members of my cohort (and their spouses) as individuals, family members and church leaders.

8. Protect the confidentiality of my cohort by keeping whatever is shared with my summit cohort confidential so as to encourage openness and honesty.

9. Complete all assignments before and after cohort meetings to the best of my ability.

I understand that the Pastors Summit will last for two years (*provide dates*).

Pastor's Signature:_____ Date: _____

Spouse's Signature:_____ Date: _____

Please sign both copies. Keep one and return the other to the cohort facilitator. Thank you.

WHAT DOES IT TAKE TO BE A FACILITATOR?

The pastors' peer cohort facilitator needs to be able to fill the role of pastor to the pastors. A co-facilitator will need to offer similar support to the spouses when they are present. Our findings indicate that the presence of a facilitator for the spouses was of significant importance to the effectiveness of the cohort for the pastoral couple. Where a facilitator's spouse is not able to serve as a co-facilitator, it will be necessary to secure the services of an outside facilitator for the benefit of the spouses.

Facilitator Responsibilities

- Direction of the meeting agenda from arrival, meals, combined and breakout sessions through departure (twenty to twenty-two hours).

- Possible coordination of the schedule and meetings with local host and facility/property prior to meeting (depending on whether a participant is arranging location).

- Providing recommendations or planning for food and beverages prior to meeting.

- Planning and facilitating combined and breakout sessions (co-facilitator plans and facilitates for spouses).

- Preparation for each of three two-day meetings, reading and study, review and preparation of materials and agenda (from eight to twenty-four hours).

- Availability to cohort members for occasional personal consultation.

Facilitator Criteria to Consider

1. Pastoral experience preferred. Other caregiving professionals (counselors) or skilled facilitators could be considered.

2. Experience in facilitating small groups and/or support groups.

3. A "safe" person: one who can keep confidences and who will not influence the pastors' careers in the denomination.

4. Recognition that this work of facilitating is a ministry. The peer group is not the facilitator's support group. She/he needs to have a different support system. The facilitator must recognize that facilitators are not participants—that is, they will be *in* the groups but not *of* the groups.

5. High EQ: Strong self-awareness and self-management, as well as social awareness and relationship management.

6. Ability to ask good questions and live with the tension (ambiguity) of not providing answers. The facilitator is not an "answer person" or "speaker."

7. Affirmation of the facilitator's own church board (if this person is a pastor). This commitment to be a facilitator should be seen as a part of this person's ministry and built into her/his job description.

FACILITATING: *IN* BUT NOT *OF* THE COHORT

The main job of the facilitator is to create space for growth and change by providing structure, support, and challenge in healthy tension. (See figure E.1.) Leading others through difficult but necessary growth is complex work, especially because it requires people to act *together* in order to make progress. In other words, it requires collaborative learning. This transformative process can also be anxious or fearful work, because it necessitates that people give up comfortable habits of thinking and behaving for an unknown but promising future.

For learning to take place in any system, three factors must be held in healthy tension: structure, support and challenge. If any one area of the three is weak in the environment, learning will not take place and healthy progress will not be made. Likewise, if any one area is emphasized too much, the learning space will collapse. For example, when there is an overemphasis on structure, the learning environment can become inflexible and rigid, which limits creativity to address new challenges. If support is overly stressed, the climate can become smothering and enmeshed. And if challenge dominates, the learner can become performance-driven or discouraged.

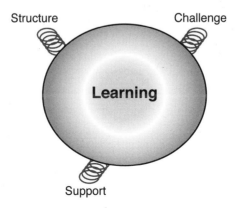

Figure E.1. Creating space for learning

Structure: Providing a Framework

- Have a flexible agenda, with open spaces and firm work times.

- Require reading and preparation before each session.

- Invite guest experts to heighten session focus.

- Give no leadership responsibilities to participants.

- Discern the needs and concerns of the group before choosing content focus and resources. Have the group speak into the decision, and listen to current discussions for next gathering topic ideas.

The Pastors Summit provides, in the words of consultant Roy Oswald, a chance "to go somewhere and have someone else be in charge for a while." Facilitators must "take charge of the event and offer groups content, structure, and rituals by which they [pastors] can feel taken care of. Clergy can become quite infantile in a retreat setting . . . [which] should come as no surprise."[6] Thus, there is the need for planned structure and clear facilitation by leadership for the time together. We found that herding cats, in the form of pastors, is especially hard work for the facilitator during the first couple of sessions.

Support: Creating a Safe Community

- Be prepared to counsel participants one-on-one.

- Consider having a guest counselor come to a gathering to meet with pastors or ministry couples.

- Offer obvious authority and gracious facilitation, which are required to help the group establish trust.

- Leave lots of time for sharing and praying together and in smaller groups.

- Help the participants set up some accountability structures and plans for communicating between gatherings for support in areas of growth they are focusing on.

These excerpts from Roy Oswald's book describe this need for support well:

A pastor once described his job this way: "I feel like a chunk of cheese from which everyone wants just a nibble."[7] When we lose control of our lives in this way, we need strong support in order to get our lives back. It will mean saying "no" to people, which will upset both them and us. Few of us can do this without a group of people behind us to support us. For clergy, the most helpful support systems are those that allow them to be "out of role" for a time.[8] Periodically we need to move into a state where we do not have to be in charge and can allow ourselves to be cared for.[9]

In the absence of strong leadership at the center of most groups, the trust level usually doesn't develop and meetings get reduced to "bitch and brag" sessions. . . . But having a support group where the trust is high and where we can share our pain and vulnerability is worth its weight in gold. The reason I believe in having a paid facilitator . . . [is that pastors must] perceive strength and caring at the center of the experience. In short, we need to hire someone to be a pastor to us when we gather as peers to review our lives.[10]

Challenge: Turning Up the Heat to Learn

- Provide weighty and relevant content, which opens the door to relational work and quality conversations.

- Be prepared for small-group dynamics, which are adaptive challenges themselves.

- Be aware that over time, a facilitator gains the right to push on the participants' life issues.

- Provide accountability, create dissonance around key issues and challenge assumptions toward learning.

NOTES

Chapter 1: Life in Pastoral Ministry

[1]If you Google the phrase *pastors leaving ministry,* multiple websites declare that 1,500 pastors are leaving the ministry every month. This statistic is often attributed to Focus on the Family, Cru (Campus Crusade for Christ) and other ministries. From what we can identify, these "statistics" have been taken from magazines and articles, not studies developed from reliable research methods.

[2]Dean R. Hoge and Jacqueline E. Wenger, *Pastors in Transition: Why Clergy Leave Local Church Ministry* (Grand Rapids: Eerdmans, 2005), p. xi.

[3]We thankfully acknowledge our friend Stafford Carson, formerly of Westminster Theological Seminary (East) and now pastor of First Presbyterian Church, Portadown, Northern Ireland, who shared his extended study on fruitfulness with us.

[4]Jackson W. Carroll, *God's Potters: Pastoral Leadership and the Shaping of Congregations* (Grand Rapids: Eerdmans, 2006), pp. 98, 106.

[5]Gary W. Kuhne and Joe F. Donaldson, "Balancing Ministry and Management: An Exploratory Study of Pastoral Work Activities," *Review of Religious Research* 37, no. 2 (1995): 160.

[6]Carroll, *God's Potters*, p. 103.

[7]Peter Brain, *Going the Distance: How to Stay Fit for a Lifetime of Ministry* (Kingsford, NSW: Matthias Media, 2004), p. 17.

[8]Carroll, *God's Potters*, p. 2.

[9]See, for example, Paul's statement to Timothy that one should not look to bodily training while failing to emphasize godliness (1 Timothy 4:7-8).

[10]The apostle Paul emphasized that elders must manage their households well. See 1 Timothy 3:4.

Chapter 2: The Five Themes of Resilient Ministry

[1]See the many references to "one another" in Scripture, such as John 13:34-35, Ephesians 5:21 and Hebrews 10:24-25.

[2]Two examples include: references on Scripture reflection, including Deuteronomy 6:6-9, Joshua 1:8 and 2 Timothy 3:16; and references on prayer, including Matthew 6:9-13 and Luke 11:1-13.

[3]John Stott, *Through the Bible, Through the Year* (Oxford: Candle Books, 2006), p. 210.

[4]Peter Brain, *Going the Distance: How to Stay Fit for a Lifetime of Ministry* (Kingsford, NSW: Matthias Media, 2004), p. 24.

[5]Daniel Goleman, Richard Boyatzis and Annie McKee, *Primal Leadership: Realizing the Power of Emotional Intelligence* (Boston: Harvard Business School Press, 2002), p. 30.

[6]United States Census Bureau, "An Older and More Diverse Nation by Midcentury," August 14, 2008. See www.census.gov/newsroom/releases/archives/population/cb08-123.html.

[7]Jackson W. Carroll, *God's Potters: Pastoral Leadership and the Shaping of Congregations* (Grand Rapids: Eerdmans, 2006), pp. 98, 106.

[8]D. S. Schuller, M. P. Strommen and M. L. Brekke, ed., *Ministry in America: A Report and Analysis, Based on an In-Depth Survey of 47 Denominations in the United States and Canada, with Interpretation by 18 Experts* (San Francisco: Harper & Row, 1980), p. 34.

[9]Gary W. Kuhne and Joe F. Donaldson, "Balancing Ministry and Management: An Exploratory Study of Pastoral Work Activities," *Review of Religious Research*, 37, no. 2 (1995): 160.

[10]Robert Banks and Bernice Ledbetter, *Reviewing Leadership: A Christian Evaluation of Current Approaches* (Grand Rapids: Baker Academic, 2004), pp. 17-19.

[11]Jim Collins, *Good to Great: Why Some Companies Make the Leap . . . and Others Don't* (New York: Harper Business, 2001), pp. 65-89.

[12]Ronald A. Heifetz and Marty Linsky, *Leadership on the Line: Staying Alive Through the Dangers of Leading* (Boston: Harvard Business School Press, 2002), p. 142.

[13]Donald C. Guthrie and Ronald C. Cervero, "The Politics of Moving Continuing Education to the Center of the Institutional Mission," in *A Lifelong Call to Learn: Approaches to Continuing Education for Church Leaders,* ed. Robert E. Reber and D. Bruce Roberts (Nashville: Abingdon, 2000), p. 182.

[14]John Forester, *Planning in the Face of Power* (Berkeley: University of California Press, 1989).

Chapter 3: Evaluating Spiritual Formation

[1]The apostle Paul uses these phrases in Philippians 2:12 and 3:14, Romans 12:2 and Ephesians 4:15.

[2]An example of this can be seen in 1 John 2:12-14, where the author references "little children," "young men," and "fathers."

[3]See Paul's rebuke for lack of growth toward spiritual maturity in 1 Corinthians 3:1-3.

[4]Kevin Harney, *Leadership from the Inside Out: Examining the Inner Life of a Healthy Church Leader* (Grand Rapids: Zondervan, 2007), p. 47.

[5]Eugene Peterson, *Working the Angles: The Shape of Pastoral Integrity* (Grand Rapids: Eerdmans, 1987), p. 3.

[6]C. S. Lewis, *The Last Battle*, The Chronicles of Narnia (New York: Scholastic, 1956), chap. 16.

[7]Perhaps a more ideal description of a healthy identity would involve not a separation of identity from role but an increasingly fuller integration of faith and spiritual growth with our life tasks and concerns.

[8]Jim Herrington, R. Robert Creech and Trisha Taylor, *The Leader's Journey: Accepting the Call to Personal and Congregational Transformation* (San Francisco: Jossey-Bass, 2003), p. 131.

[9]Ibid., p. 150.

[10]Charles Stone, *Five Ministry Killers and How to Defeat Them* (Minneapolis: Bethany House, 2010), pp. 166-67.

[11]Peter Scazzero, *Emotionally Healthy Spirituality: Unleash a Revolution in Your Life in Christ* (Nashville: Thomas Nelson, 2006), p. 32.

Chapter 4: Pursuing Spiritual Formation

[1]Jim Loehr and Tony Schwartz, *The Power of Full Engagement* (New York: Free Press, 2003), p. 166.

[2]The means of grace is a theological concept used since the Reformation. It indicates the ordinary ways that Christ blesses us with the benefits of redemption in order to sustain and to grow our Christian faith and life by his grace, power and presence through the Holy Spirit. Included are especially the Word (2 Timothy 3:16-17; 1 Peter 1:23–2:3), prayer (Matthew 6:5-15), and the sacraments of baptism (Acts 2:37-41; Colossians 2:11-12) and communion (1 Corinthians 11:23-34).

[3]Jim Herrington, R. Robert Creech and Tasha Taylor, *The Leader's Journey: Accepting the Call to Personal and Congregational Transformation* (San Francisco: Jossey-Bass, 2003), p. 145.

[4]Ronald Heifetz and Marty Linsky, *Leadership on the Line: Staying Alive Through the Dangers of Leading* (Boston: Harvard Business School Press, 2002), p. 199.

[5]Ibid.

[6]Ibid.

[7]"Building Resilience: What Hardships Teach About Leading," *Leading Effectively* e-newsletter, December 2003, www.ccl.org/leadership/enewsletter/2003/DECresil ience.aspx?pageId=432; based on Russ Moxley and Mary Lynn Pulley, "Hardships," in *The Center for Creative Leadership Handbook of Leadership Development,* 2nd ed. (San Francisco: Jossey-Bass/CCL, 2003).

[8]John Stott, *Romans: God's Good News for the World* (Downers Grove, Ill.: InterVarsity Press, 1994), p. 242.

[9]As shared in James Plueddemann, *Leading Across Cultures: Effective Ministry and Mission in the Global Church* (Downers Grove, Ill.: InterVarsity Press, 2009), p. 31.

[10]Mary Lynn Pulley and Joan P. Gurvis, "The Ultimate Learning Experience," *Across the Board* (July/August 2004): 45.

[11]Popular evangelical resources include Dallas Willard, *The Spirit of the Disciplines: Understanding How God Changes Lives* (San Francisco: HarperSanFrancisco, 1999); Richard Foster, *Celebration of Discipline: The Path to Spiritual Growth* (San Francisco: HarperSanFrancisco, 1998); R. Kent Hughes, *Disciplines of a Godly Man* (Wheaton, Ill.: Crossway Books, 2001); and Donald S. Whitney, *Spiritual Disciplines Within the Church: Participating Fully in the Body of Christ* (Chicago: Moody Press, 1996).

[12]The most exhaustive list of sixty-two is presented in Adele Ahlberg Calhoun, *Spiritual Disciplines Handbook: Practices That Transform Us* (Downers Grove, Ill.: InterVarsity Press, 2005).

[13]Boud, Keogh and Walker's (1985, 1996) original adult learning model consisted of three stages: "(1) returning to and replaying the experience, (2) attending to the feelings that the experience provoked, and (3) reevaluating the experience." Sharan B. Merriam and Rosemary S. Caffarella, *Learning in Adulthood: A Comprehensive Guide*, 2nd ed. (San Francisco: Jossey-Bass, 1999), p. 226.

[14]See, for example, Calhoun's description of meditation in *Spiritual Disciplines*, pp. 172-75.

[15]David A. Livermore, *Cultural Intelligence: Improving Your CQ to Engage Our Multicultural World* (Grand Rapids: Baker Academic, 2009), p. 193.

[16]Ibid., p. 50.

[17]Peter Scazzero, *Emotionally Healthy Spirituality: Unleash a Revolution in Your Life in Christ* (Nashville: Thomas Nelson, 2006), pp. 48-50.

[18]Foster, *Celebration of Discipline*, p. 30.

[19]Richard F. Lovelace, *Dynamics of Spiritual Life* (Downers Grove, Ill.: InterVarsity Press, 1979), p. 155.

[20]Eugene Peterson, *Working the Angles: The Shape of Pastoral Integrity* (Grand Rapids: Eerdmans, 1987), p. 45.

[21]Richard C. Halverson (1916–1995) was the pastor of Fourth Presbyterian Church in Bethesda, Maryland, chaplain of the United States Senate for fourteen years, and chair of the board for World Vision.

[22]Peterson, *Working the Angles*, p. 19.

[23]Ibid., p. 28.

[24]Ibid., p. 47.

[25]Scazzero, *Emotionally Healthy Spirituality*, p. 171.

[26]Peterson, *Working the Angles*, p. 47.

[27]Ibid., pp. 50-51.

[28]Scazzero, *Emotionally Healthy Spirituality*, pp. 157, 160, 165.

[29]Eugene H. Peterson, *Working the Angles: The Shape of Pastoral Integrity*, reset ed. (Grand Rapids: Eerdmans, 1993), p. 82.

[30]Willard, *Spirit of the Disciplines*, p. 187.

[31]Calhoun, *Spiritual Disciplines*, p. 93.

[32]C. John Miller, *Repentance and 20th Century Man* (Fort Washington: Christian Literature Crusade, 1980), p. 108.

[33]1 John 1:7; 2 Corinthians 12:9-10; 13:3-4.

[34]A number of summit pastors began to use *The Divine Hours*, a series of Daily Office prayers developed by Phyllis Tickle (New York: Doubleday, 2000). Another example is the daily worship guides developed by Mike Farley (http://crossroadspresworship .net/daily-worship-guides). Farley's resource contains simplified versions of the models of morning and evening prayer found in liturgical books like the Anglican *Book of Common Prayer* and the Presbyterian *Book of Common Worship*. For more information, contact Mike Farley at mifarley@sbcglobal.net.

[35]Willard, *Spirit of the Disciplines*, p. 252.

Chapter 5: Burning On, Not Burning Out

[1]Peter Brain, *Going the Distance: How to Stay Fit for a Lifetime of Ministry* (Kingsford, NSW: Matthias Media, 2004), p. 24.

[2]Ibid., p. 23.

[3]Ibid., p. 10.

[4]Dave Gibbons, *The Monkey and the Fish: Liquid Leadership for a Third-Culture Church* (Grand Rapids: Zondervan, 2009), p. 160.

[5]Thanks to our friend Alan Taha, who identified much of this research in "Physical Self-Care Practices for Sustainable Pastoral Leadership in Local Church Ministry" (DMin diss., Covenant Theological Seminary, 2010).

[6]Fred Lehr, *Clergy Burnout: Recovering from the 70-Hour Work Week and Other Self-Defeating Practices* (Minneapolis: Fortress, 2006), p. 5.

[7]Ibid. A pastor quoted by the authors explained, "But the pay isn't the biggest thing. The low pay combined with high stress and long hours, I think that's the triple combination that's really lethal" (p. 59).

[8]Gary L. Harbaugh, *Pastor as Person: Maintaining Personal Integrity in the Choices and Challenges of Ministry* (Minneapolis: Augsburg, 1984), p. 47.

[9]David N. Mosser, "Managing the Public Life, Freeing the Personal Life," *The Christian Ministry* 23, no. 2 (1992): 10-13.

[10]G. Lloyd Rediger, *Beyond the Scandals: A Guide to Healthy Sexuality for Clergy* (Minneapolis: Fortress, 2003), p. 22.

[11]Jeffrey E. and Natalie Cooper Barnett, "Creating a Culture of Self-Care," *Clinical Psychology Science and Practice* 16, no. 1 (2009): 18.

[12]Charles R. Figley, "Compassion Fatigue: Psychotherapists' Chronic Lack of Self-Care," *Psychotherapy in Practice* 58, no. 11 (2002): 1434-35.

[13]See also Harbaugh, *Pastor as Person,* p. 72; and Gwen Wagstrom Halaas, *The Right Road: Life Choices for Clergy* (Minneapolis: Fortress, 2004), p. 44.

[14]Brain, *Going the Distance,* pp. 20-21.

[15]Garry Gunderson and Larry Pray, *Leading Causes of Life* (Memphis: The Center of Excellence in Faith and Health, 2004), p. 164.

[16]See Lois E. LeBar, *Focus on People in Church Education* (Westwood, N.J.: Revell, 1968). These frames are used more recently by Jim Loehr and Tony Schwartz in *The Power of Full Engagement* (New York: Free Press, 2003) and by Chuck Miller in *The Spiritual Formation of Leaders* (Maitland, Fla.: Xulon Press, 2007).

[17]John Calvin, *The Institutes of the Christian Religion*, vol. 1, ed. John T. McNeill, trans. Ford Lewis Battles (Philadelphia: Westminster Press, 1960), p. 35.

[18]The use of the Leadership 360 will be discussed in chapter eight. For more information on RightPath Resources, see www.rightpath.com.

[19]The pastors who took both instruments (MBTI and RightPath) benefited from each of them. However, the general impression was that the RightPath profiles provided more detailed and accurate information.

[20]Peter Scazzero, *Emotionally Healthy Spirituality: Unleash a Revolution in Your Life in Christ* (Nashville: Thomas Nelson, 2006), pp. 95-96.

[21]See Exodus 20:4-6; 34:6-7 and 2 Samuel 12:10. Scazzero, *Emotionally Healthy Spirituality,* p. 96.

[22]Ibid., pp. 109, 114.

[23]See Isaiah 53:6 and Romans 3:23. The reality of sin means that all people and families struggle with dysfunction.

[24]See Jeremiah 31:29-30; Psalm 51 and 2 Corinthians 5:16-19. One resource to explore how family brokenness can be addressed is Bob Burns and Michael J. Brissett Jr., *The Adult Child of Divorce* (Nashville: Thomas Nelson, 1991).

[25]To learn how to develop a family diagram, see Jim Herrington, R. Robert Creech and Trisha Taylor, *The Leader's Journey: Accepting the Call to Personal and Congregational Transformation* (San Francisco: Jossey-Bass, 2003), pp. 87-102; Scazzero, *Emotionally Healthy Spirituality,* pp. 93-115; and Monica McGoldrick, Randy Gerson and Sueli Petry, *Genograms: Assessment and Intervention*, 3rd ed. (New York: W. W. Norton, 2008).

[26]These three reasons are adapted from Herrington, Creech and Taylor, *The Leader's Journey,* pp. 92-93.

[27]Ronald Heifetz and Marty Linsky, *Leadership on the Line: Staying Alive Through the Dangers of Leading* (Boston: Harvard Business School Press, 2002), pp. 187-88.

[28]Donald R. Hand and Wayne L. Fehr, *Spiritual Wholeness for Clergy: A New Psychology of Intimacy with God, Self and Others* (Herndon, Va.: Alban Institute, 1993), p. 61.

[29]Scazzero, *Emotionally Healthy Spirituality,* p. 26.

[30]H. Norman Wright, *The Christian Use of Emotional Power* (Old Tappan, N.J.: Fleming H. Revell, 1974), p. 30.

[31]Daniel Goleman, *Working with Emotional Intelligence* (New York: Bantam Books, 2000), p. 56.

[32]See, for example, H. Norman Wright, *Winning Over Your Emotions: Helpful Answers That Will Change Your Life* (Eugene, Ore.: Harvest House, 1998); Dan B. Allender and Tremper Longman, *The Cry of the Soul: How Our Emotions Reveal Our Deepest Questions About God* (Colorado Springs: NavPress, 1994); and Larry Crabb, Inside Out (Colorado Springs: NavPress, 2007).

[33]A couple of books that can be helpful in identifying and managing depression are Les Carter and Frank Minirth, *The Freedom from Depression Workbook* (Nashville: Thomas Nelson, 1995) and Richard Winter, *The Roots of Sorrow: Reflections on Depression and Hope* (Eugene, Ore.: Wipf and Stock, 2000).

[34]Herrington, Creech and Taylor, *Leader's Journey*, p. 18. Peter Scazzero explains, "Developed by Murray Bowen, the founder of modern family systems theory, differentiation refers to a person's capacity to 'define his or her own life's goals and values apart from the pressures of those around them.' . . . Differentiation involves the degree to which you are able to affirm your distinct values and goals apart from the pressures around you (separateness) while remaining close to people important to you (togetherness). People with a high level of differentiation have their own beliefs, convictions, directions, goals, and values apart from the pressures around them. They can choose, before God, how they want to be without being controlled by the approval or disapproval of others. . . . Bowen emphasizes that in families there is a powerful opposition when one member of that system matures and increases in their level of differentiation" (Scazzero, *Emotionally Healthy Spirituality*, pp. 82, 90). The Bowen reference comes from Michael Kerr and Murray Bowen, *Family Evaluation: The Role of the Family as an Emotional Unit That Governs Individual Behavior and Development* (New York: Norton Press, 1988), pp. 97-109.

[35]Edwin H. Friedman, *A Failure of Nerve* (Bethesda, Md.: The Edwin Friedman Estate/Trust, 1999), p. 236. Also discussed in Edwin H. Friedman, *Generation to Generation: Family Process in Church and Synagogue* (New York: Guilford, 1985).

[36]Brain, *Going the Distance*, p. 21.

[37]Bryan E. Robinson, *Chained to the Desk: A Guidebook for Workaholics, Their Partners and Children, and the Clinicians Who Treat Them*, 2nd ed. (New York: New York University Press, 2007), p. 7.

[38]Jim Loehr and Tony Schwartz, *The Power of Full Engagement: Managing Energy, Not Time, Is the Key to High Performance and Personal Renewal* (New York: Free Press, 2003), p. 40.

[39]C. A. Rayburn et al., "Men, Women, and Religion: Stress Within Leadership Roles," *Journal of Clinical Psychology* 42, no. 3 (1986): 540-46.

[40]D. Martyn Lloyd-Jones, *Spiritual Depression: Its Causes and Cure* (Grand Rapids: Eerdmans, 1965), p. 21.

Chapter 6: Pacing Our Lifestyles

[1]Ronald Heifetz and Marty Linsky, *Leadership on the Line: Staying Alive Through the Dangers of Leading* (Boston: Harvard Business School Press, 2002), p. 199.

[2]Ibid.

[3]Jerry White and Mary White, *Friends and Friendship: The Secrets of Drawing Closer* (Colorado Springs: NavPress, 1982).

[4]Ibid., p. 37.

[5]Charles Stone, *Five Ministry Killers and How to Defeat Them* (Minneapolis: Bethany House, 2010), p. 189.

[6]Henry Cloud and John Townsend, *Safe People: How to Find Relationships That Are Good for You and Avoid Those That Aren't* (Grand Rapids: Zondervan, 1995).

[7]Janet Maykus and Penny Long Marier, "A Study of the Effects of Participation in SPE Pastoral Leader Peer Groups, Survey Report and Analysis," April 2010, www.austin seminary.edu/uploaded/continuing_education/pdf/SPE_Survey_Report_and_Analysis_April_2010.pdf.

[8]Holly G. Miller, *Sustaining Pastoral Excellence: A Progress Report on a Lilly Endowment Initiative* (Indianapolis: Lilly Endowment, May 2011).

[9]Roy M. Oswald, *Clergy Self-Care: Finding a Balance for Effective Ministry* (Herndon, Va.: The Alban Institute, 1991), p. 137.

[10]Gary W. Kuhne, "Needs Assessment in Continuing Professional Education: Applying the Work Content Triad Approach with Evangelical Protestant Clergy" (PhD diss., Pennsylvania State University, 1991), pp. 103, 138.

[11]John Broadus, *On the Preparation and Delivery of Sermons*, 4th ed., ed. Vernon L. Standfield (1870; reprint, New York: Harper and Row, 1979).

[12]Ibid., p. 16.

[13]Oswald, *Clergy Self-Care*, p. 121.

[14]This pattern was also identified by Oswald in ibid., p. 125.

[15]Jim Loehr and Tony Schwartz, *The Power of Full Engagement: Managing Energy, Not Time, Is the Key to High Performance and Personal Renewal* (New York: Free Press, 2003), p. 37.

[16]Ibid., p. 12.

[17]For various views and ideas on how pastors can celebrate sabbath, see Gordon MacDonald, *Ordering Your Private World* (Nashville: Thomas Nelson, 2003); Oswald, *Clergy Self-Care*; Eugene H. Peterson, *Working the Angles* (Grand Rapids: Eerdmans, 1987); Peter Scazzero, *Emotionally Healthy Spirituality* (Nashville: Thomas Nelson, 2006).

[18]Bob Wells, "Which Way to Clergy Health?" *Pulpit & Pew: Research on Pastoral Leadership,* www.pulpitandpew.org/which-way-clergy-health, reprinted from *Divinity,* Fall 2002.

[19]Alan Taha, "Physical Self-Care Practices for Sustainable Pastoral Leadership in Local Church Ministry" (DMin diss., Covenant Theological Seminary, 2010), p. 9.

[20]First Timothy 4:8 states, "for while bodily training is of some value, godliness is of value in every way, as it holds promise for the present life and also for the life to come."

[21]Taha, "Physical Self-Care," p. 20.

[22]Kathleen J. Greider, *Reckoning with Agression: Theology, Violence, and Vitality* (Louisville: Westminster John Knox, 1997), p. 115.

[23]David F. Wells, *The Courage to Be Protestant: Truth-Lovers, Marketers, and Emergents in the Postmodern World* (Grand Rapids: Eerdmans, 2008), p. 164.

[24]Taha, "Physical Self-Care," p. 94.

[25]Ibid., p. 95.

[26]Ibid., p. 98.

[27]Ibid., p. 99.

[28]Ibid., p. 103.

[29]C. Welton Gaddy, *A Soul Under Siege: Surviving Clergy Depression* (Louisville: Westminster John Knox, 1991), p. 157.

Chapter 7: Understanding Emotional Intelligence

[1]As defined in Marcy Levy Shankman and Scott J. Allen, *Emotionally Intelligent Leadership* (San Francisco: Jossey-Bass, 2008).

[2]See Daniel Goleman, *Working with Emotional Intelligence* (New York: Bantam Books, 1998), p. 4; and Daniel Goleman, Richard Boyatzis and Annie McKee, *Primal Leadership: Realizing the Power of Emotional Intelligence* (Boston: Harvard Business School Press, 2002), p. 12.

[3]David R. Caruso and Peter Salovey, *The Emotionally Intelligent Manager* (San Francisco: Jossey-Bass, 2004), p. xxi.

[4]Goleman, *Working with Emotional Intelligence*, pp. 44-45; and Goleman, Boyatzis and McKee, *Primal Leadership*, p. 30.

[5]D. A. Carson posits that the negative attitude among Christians toward emotions comes from the influence of certain strands of Greek metaphysical thought. These views "insist that emotion is dangerous, treacherous, and often evil. Reason must be set against emotion, and vulnerability is a sign of weakness." D. A. Carson, *Divine Sovereignty and Human Responsibility* (Atlanta: John Knox Press, 1981), p. 215. Wayne Grudem implies that a negative view of emotions may stem from a tripartite view of anthropology. See Wayne Grudem, *Systematic Theology: An Introduction to Biblical Doctrine* (Grand Rapids: Zondervan, 1994), p. 482.

[6]Wayne Grudem states, "In the area of emotions, our likeness to God is seen in a large difference in degree and complexity of emotions" (*Systematic Theology*, p. 447). And John Frame explains, "Theologians have sometimes thought that emotions are unworthy of God. . . . Scripture ascribes many attitudes to God that are generally regarded as emotions . . . [such as] God's compassion, tender mercy, patience, rejoicing, delight, pleasure, pity, love, wrath, and jealousy. . . . God, speaking in Scripture, regularly expresses emotion and appeals to the emotions of his hearers" (Frame, *The Doctrine of God* [Phillipsburg, N.J.: P & R, 2002], pp. 609, 611). And B. B. Warfield expressed similar sentiments in his article "On the Emotional Life of Our Lord," in *The Person and Work of Christ*, ed. Samuel G. Craig (Phillipsburg, N.J.: P & R Publishing, 1950).

[7]Peter Scazzero, *Emotionally Healthy Spirituality: Unleash a Revolution in Your Life in Christ* (Nashville: Thomas Nelson, 2006), p. 12.

[8]Goleman, Boyatzis and McKee, *Primal Leadership*, p. 30. Daniel Goleman also describes EQ as "the capacity for recognizing our own feelings and those of others, for motivating ourselves, and for managing emotions well in ourselves and in our relationships." Goleman, *Working with Emotional Intelligence*, p. 317.

[9]Goleman, Boyatzis and McKee, *Primal Leadership*, pp. 30, 40.

[10]Caruso and Salovey, *Emotionally Intelligent Manager*, p. 11.

[11]Jim Herrington, R. Robert Creech and Trisha Taylor, *The Leader's Journey: Accepting the Call to Personal and Congregational Transformation* (San Francisco: Jossey-Bass, 2003), p. 34.

[12]Scazzero, *Emotionally Healthy Spirituality*, pp. 100-101, 103.

[13]Goleman, *Working with Emotional Intelligence*, p. 7.

[14]Ibid., p. 22.

[15]Scazzero, *Emotionally Healthy Spirituality*, p. 44.

[16]Adapted from John Forester, *Planning in the Face of Power* (Berkeley: University of California Press, 1988), p. 75.

[17]Refer to appendix A on how the pastors in the Pastors Summit were identified and selected.

[18]Goleman, Boyatzis and McKee, *Primal Leadership*, pp. 40, 45.

[19]Gary W. Kuhne, "Needs Assessment in Continuing Professional Education: Applying the Work Content Triad Approach with Evangelical Protestant Clergy" (PhD diss., Pennsylvania State University, 1991), pp. 103, 138.

[20]Alfred Poirier, *The Peacemaking Pastor: A Biblical Guide to Resolving Church Conflict* (Grand Rapids: Baker Books, 2006).

[21]Donald T. Miller, *Martin Luther King, Jr., On Leadership* (New York: Warner Business Books, 1998), p. 43.

[22]This idea of hearing the "song beneath the words" is suggested by Ron Heifetz and Marty Linsky in *Leadership on the Line: Staying Alive Through the Dangers of Leading* (Boston: Harvard Business School Press, 2002), p. 55.

Chapter 8: Developing Emotional Intelligence

[1]Jim Loehr and Tony Schwartz, *The Power of Full Engagement: Managing Energy, Not Time, Is the Key to High Performance and Personal Renewal* (New York: Free Press, 2003), p. 8.

[2]R. W. Thayer, *Calm Energy: How People Regulate Mood with Food and Exercise* (New York: Oxford University Press, 2001).

[3]Loehr and Schwartz, *Power of Full Engagement*, p. 90.

[4]Charles R. Figley, "Compassion Fatigue: Psychotherapists' Chronic Lack of Self-Care," *Psychotherapy in Practice* 58, no. 11 (2002): 1,434.

[5]In Loehr and Schwartz, *Power of Full Engagement*, see especially chapter three, "The Pulse of High Performance: Balancing Stress and Recovery" (though this is a theme throughout their book). In Alan Taha, "Physical Self-Care Practices for Sustainable Pastoral Leadership in Local Church Ministry" (DMin diss., Covenant Theological Seminary, 2010), see especially pp. 93-96.

[6]Daniel Goleman, Richard Boyatzis and Annie McKee, *Primal Leadership: Realizing the Power of Emotional Intelligence* (Boston: Harvard Business School Press, 2002), p. 219.

[7]A helpful study on journaling as a spiritual discipline is found in Donald S. Whitney, *Spiritual Disciplines for the Christian Life* (Colorado Springs: NavPress, 1991), pp. 195-211.

[8]Adele Ahlberg Calhoun, *Spiritual Disciplines Handbook* (Downers Grove, Ill.: InterVarsity Press, 2005), p. 57.

[9]David R. Caruso and Peter Salovey, *The Emotionally Intelligent Manager* (San Francisco: Jossey-Bass, 2004), p. 136.

[10]These elements have been modified from a list given by Caruso and Salovey in ibid., pp. 136-37.

[11]Ibid., pp. 69, 73.

[12]Ibid., p. 90.

[13]Ibid., p. 95.

[14]For more on developing a family diagram, see the chapter on self-care and appendix D for diagram interview questions. You may also want to consult the descriptions given on pp. 87-102 of Jim Herrington, R. Robert Creech and Trisha Taylor, *The Leader's Journey: Accepting the Call to Personal and Congregational Transformation* (San Francisco: Jossey-Bass, 2003); pp. 93-115 of Peter Scazzero, *Emotionally Healthy Spirituality: Unleash a Revolution in Your Life in Christ* (Nashville: Thomas Nelson, 2006); or in Monica McGoldrick, Randy Gerson and Sueli Petry, *Genograms: Assessment and Intervention*, 3rd ed. (New York: W. W. Norton, 2008).

[15]This is a modified version of a comment made by Peter Scazzero in *Emotionally Healthy Spirituality*, p. 114.

[16]Herrington, Creech and Taylor. *Leader's Journey*, p. 18. See note 34, chapter 5.

[17]Edwin H. Friedman, *Generation to Generation: Family Process in Church and Synagogue* (New York: Guilford Press, 1985), p. 208.

[18]William Lane, *Hebrews 1-8*, Word Biblical Commentary 47, ed. David A. Hubbard and Glenn W. Barker (Nashville: Thomas Nelson, 1991), p. 116.

Chapter 9: Exploring Cultural Differences

[1]For simplicity, we use the term *Anglo* to refer to white people in the United States, primarily of European descent, who have been in the country for a couple generations. We employ this term, and all other terms used to designate various races or ethnicities, without any derogatory connotations attached. We hope to give no reason for offense to any reader.

[2]David Livermore, "Serving with Cultural Intelligence" (seminar, Crossroads Presbyterian Fellowship, Maplewood, Mo., June 11, 2011).

[3]P. Christopher Earley, Soon Ang and Joo-Seng Tan, *CQ: Developing Cultural Intelligence at Work* (Stanford, Calif.: Stanford Business Books, 2006), p. 1.

[4]Dave Gibbons, *The Monkey and the Fish: Liquid Leadership for a Third-Culture Church* (Grand Rapids: Zondervan, 2009), p. 111.

[5]Soon Ang and Linn Van Dyne, "Conceptualization of Cultural Intelligence," in *Handbook of Cultural Intelligence: Theory, Measurement, and Applications*, ed. Soon Ang and Van Dyne (Armonk, N.Y.: M. E. Sharpe, 2008), p. 10.

[6]Earley, Ang and Tan, *CQ*, p. vii.

[7]Ibid., p. 21.

[8]Soong-Chan Rah, *Many Colors: Cultural Intelligence for a Changing Church* (Chicago: Moody Press, 2010), p. 38.

[9]David Livermore, *Cultural Intelligence: Improving Your CQ to Engage Our Multicultural World* (Grand Rapids: Baker Academic, 2009), p. 93.

[10]Ibid., p. 45.

[11]Peter Scazzero, *Emotionally Healthy Spirituality: Unleash a Revolution in Your Life in Christ* (Nashville: Thomas Nelson, 2006), pp. 100-101, 103.

[12]Livermore, *Cultural Intelligence*, pp. 102-8, provides a helpful review of these generational breakdowns, with characteristics reflected in each one.

[13]Adapted from Ronald Heifetz and Donald Laurie, "The Work of Leadership," *Harvard Business Review*, December 2001. Reprint R0111K.

[14]James Kouzes and Barry Posner, *The Truth About Leadership* (San Francisco: Jossey-Bass, 2010), p. 68.

[15]Robert Goffee and Gareth Jones, *The Character of a Corporation* (New York: Harper Business, 1998), p. 9.

[16]Livermore, *Cultural Intelligence*, p. 94.

[17]Earley, Ang and Tan, *CQ*, pp. 166-67.

[18]This discussion of Goffee and Jones is based on the presentation of their organizational framework found in Earley, Ang and Tan, *CQ*, pp. 160-67.

[19]This spectrum between *home* and *mission* was developed by Randy Pope, lead teacher at Perimeter Church in Atlanta, Georgia.

[20]Denominations tend to fall into one of three governance frameworks: hierarchical, congregational or representative.

[21]In 2007, Tim Keller presented a paper describing these subgroups based on an analysis developed by George Marsden in his essay "Reformed and American," in *Reformed Theology in America* (Grand Rapids: Baker, 1997), pp. 1-14. To the best of our knowledge, Keller's paper remains unpublished.

[22]James Plueddemann, *Leading Across Cultures* (Downers Grove, Ill.: InterVarsity Press, 2009), p. 43.

[23]Michael Emerson and Christian Smith, *Divided by Faith: Evangelical Religion and the Problem of Race in America* (New York: Oxford University Press, 2000), p. 170.

Chapter 10: Improving Cultural Intelligence

[1]Soon Ang and Linn Van Dyne, "Conceptualization of Cultural Intelligence," in *Handbook of Cultural Intelligence: Theory, Measurement, and Applications*, ed. Soon Ang and Van Dyne (Armonk, N.Y.: M. E. Sharpe, 2008), p. 10.

[2]By "dominant culture," we mean when a person's cultural context "aligns closely with those who hold the greatest degree of [formal] authority, control, and resources within the broader cultural context" (David Livermore, *Cultural Intelligence: Improving Your CQ to Engage Our Multicultural World* [Grand Rapids: Baker Academic, 2009], p. 221).

[3]Ibid., p. 17.

[4]Paul G. Hiebert, *Anthropological Insights for Missionaries* (Grand Rapids: Baker, 1985), p. 111.

[5]Ibid., p. 103.

[6]Duane Elmer, *Cross-Cultural Connections: Stepping Out and Fitting In Around the World* (Downers Grove, Ill.: IVP Academic, 2002), p. 58.

[7]Lesslie Newbigin, *Foolishness to the Greeks* (Grand Rapids: Eerdmans, 1986), p. 146.

[8]L. Robert Kohl, *Survival Kit for Overseas Living* (Yarmouth, Me.: Intercultural Press, 2001), p. 56.

[9]Adapted from Duane Elmer's epistemology drawing, Trinity Evangelical Divinity School, Deerfield, IL, DES921 Social Science Research, September 16, 2003.

[10]Elmer, *Cross-Cultural Connections*, p. 99.

[11]James Plueddemann, *Leading Across Cultures* (Downers Grove, Ill.: InterVarsity Press, 2009), p. 77.

[12]Ibid., p. 103.

[13]"Willow Creek Repents?" *Out of Ur* (blog), October 18, 2007, www.outofur.com/archives/2007/10/willow_creek_re.html.

[14]James Kouzes and Barry Posner, *The Leadership Challenge*, 4th ed. (San Francisco: John Wiley & Sons, 2007), p. 223.

[15]Plueddemann, *Leading Across Cultures*, p. 87.

[16]Livermore, *Cultural Intelligence*, p. 152.

[17]Michael Marquardt, *Leading with Questions: How Leaders Find the Right Solutions by Knowing What Questions to Ask* (San Francisco: Jossey-Bass, 2005), pp. 12-13, 18.

[18]Six Sigma Financial Services, "Determine the Root Cause: 5 Whys," accessed May 8, 2012, http://finance.isixsigma.com/library/content/c020610a.asp.

[19]We recommend Mary Lederleitner, *Cross-Cultural Partnerships* (Downers Grove, Ill.: InterVarsity Press, 2010) as a helpful resource to explore organization partnerships and collaboration in crosscultural ministry.

Chapter 11: Marriage and Family

[1]Bryan Adcock, Lucy Schrader and Brenda Procter, "Managing Stress," Building Strong Families, University of Missouri Extension, last modified July 26, 2010, http://extension.missouri.edu/bsf/stress/index.htm.

[2]For more information on the Lilly Endowment Clergy Renewal program, see www.lillyendowment.org/religion_ncr.html.

[3]See chapter eight on the leadership challenge of managing the expectations of others.

[4]See Romans 14:1–15:7 and 1 Corinthians 9:19-23.

[5]Note, for example, how Jesus broke societal expectations of the sabbath many times because it did not conform to God's original sabbath purposes; see Mark 2:23-28 and 3:1-6.

[6]Jim Herrington, R. Robert Creech and Trisha Taylor, *The Leader's Journey: Accepting the Call to Personal and Congregational Transformation* (San Francisco: Jossey-Bass, 2003), p. 18.

[7]Edwin H. Friedman, *A Failure of Nerve: Leadership in the Age of the Quick Fix* (Bethesda, Md.: The Edwin H. Friedman Estate/Trust, 1999), p. 236.

[8]See Ephesians 5:25-33 and 1 Peter 3:7.

Chapter 12: More Marriage and Family Stressors

[1]For a discussion of how to do the speaker/listener technique, see chapter twenty-two of Lori Gordon, *Passage to Intimacy*, rev. ed. (self-published, 2000).

Chapter 13: Leadership Poetry

[1]March, quoted in Lan Liu, *Conversations on Leadership: Wisdom from Global Management Gurus* (San Francisco: Jossey-Bass, 2010), p. 159.

[2]Studies by Blizzard, as well as those of both Kuhne and Kuhne and Donaldson, were cited in previous chapters. Other studies emphasize the same finding. See H. Richard Niebuhr, *The Purpose of the Church and Its Ministry* (New York: Harper and Brothers, 1956); Peter Jarvis, "The Parish Ministry as a Semi-Profession," *The Sociological Review* 23, no. 4 (November 1975): 911-33; and Roy Oswald, *Crossing the Boundary Between Seminary and Parish* (Herndon, Va.: The Alban Institute, 1980).

[3]James M. Kouzes and Barry Z. Posner, *The Truth About Leadership: The No-Fads, Heart-of-the-Matter Facts You Need to Know* (San Francisco: Jossey-Bass, 2010), pp. 120-21.

[4]Donald A. Schön, *The Reflective Practitioner: How Professionals Think in Action* (New York: Basic Books, 1983). Others who have worked in this area of identifying professional learning include Ronald Cervero, Peter Jarvis and Chris Argyus.

[5]Ronald M. Cervero and Arthur L. Wilson, *Working the Planning Table: Negotiating*

Democratically for Adult, Continuing and Workplace Education (San Francisco: Jossey-Bass, 2005), p. 81.

[6]Cho-yun Hsu, "Cho-yun Hsu: Leading the Confucian Way," in Liu, *Conversations on Leadership*, p. 225. Cho-yun Hsu is the university professor emeritus of history and sociology at the University of Pittsburgh, teaching leadership and management from a historical perspective.

[7]We used the Leadership 360 of RightPath Resources. For more information see www.rightpath.com.

[8]Russ Moxley is the former director of nonprofit initiatives and senior program associate at the Center for Creative Leadership. See Moxley, "Hardships," in *The Center for Creative Leadership Handbook of Leadership Development*, ed. Cynthia D. Mc-Cauley, Russ S. Moxley and Ellen Van Velsor (San Francisco: Jossey-Bass, 1998), pp. 194-213.

[9]James M. Kouzes and Barry Z. Posner, *The Leadership Challenge*, 4th ed. (San Francisco: Jossey-Bass, 2007), pp. 202, 204-5.

[10]Dan Allender, *Leading with a Limp: Turning Your Struggles into Strengths* (Colorado Springs: WaterBrook Press, 2006), pp. 151-52.

[11]We first discovered this term in Jim Herrington, Robert Creech and Trisha Taylor, *The Leader's Journey* (San Francisco: Jossey-Bass, 2003). These authors use the family systems framework of Murray Bowen to understand the relational dynamics of pastors and their congregations. Numerous other authors employ family systems analysis in studying the church. See, for example, Edwin Friedman, *Generation to Generation: Family Process in Church and Synagogue* (New York: Guilford, 1985); Douglas Hall, *The Cat and the Toaster: Living System Ministry in a Technological Age* (Eugene, Ore.: Wipf & Stock, 2010); Ronald Richardson, *Creating a Healthier Church* (Minneapolis: Fortress Press, 1996) and *Becoming a Healthier Pastor: Family Systems Theory, Leadership, and Congregational Life* (Minneapolis: Fortress, 2005); and Peter Steinke, *How Your Church Family Works: Understanding Congregations as Emotional Systems* (Herndon, Va.: The Alban Institute, 1993) and *Congregational Leadership in Anxious Times: Being Calm and Courageous No Matter What* (Herndon, Va.: The Alban Institute, 2006).

[12]Herrington, Creech and Taylor, *Leader's Journey*, p. 29.

[13]See chapters seven and eight for more on understanding our families of origin.

[14]Herrington, Creech and Taylor, *Leader's Journey*, p. 33.

[15]See also Philippians 4:8-9 and 2 Peter 3:1-3.

[16]John Forester, *Planning in the Face of Power* (Berkeley: University of California Press, 1989), p. 75.

[17]Ronald M. Cervero and Arthur L. Wilson, *Planning Responsibly for Adult Education: A Guide to Negotiating Power and Interests* (San Francisco: Jossey-Bass, 1994); Roger Fisher and William Ury, *Getting to Yes: Negotiating Agreement Without Giving In* (New York: Penguin, 1981); Gareth Morgan, *Images of Organization* (Thousand Oaks, Calif.: Sage, 1998).

[18]Quoted in R. C. Sproul, *Chosen by God* (Wheaton: Tyndale House, 1986).

[19]Authors Kerry Patterson, Joseph Greeny, Ron McMillan and Al Switzler describe a crucial conversation as a discussion that occurs when "(1) stakes are high, (2) opinions vary, and (3) emotions run strong." See their book *Crucial Conversations: Tools for Talking When Stakes Are High* (New York: McGraw-Hill, 2002), p. 3.

[20]J. N. Bartholomew, "A Sociological View of Authority in Religious Organizations," *Review of Religious Research* 23, no. 2 (1981): 118-32. See also Max Weber, *From Max Weber: Essays in Sociology*, trans. H. H. Gerth and C. Wright Mills (New York: Oxford University Press, 1958), p. 248.

[21]We have found no clearly verifiable and reliable statistics on the duration of pastorates. However, there is a great deal of commentary on this topic on the Internet. We identified this number after reviewing multiple websites and reviewing current studies.

[22]See Dean R. Hoge and Jacqueline E. Wenger, *Pastors in Transition: Why Clergy Leave Local Church Ministry* (Grand Rapids: Eerdmans, 2005).

[23]Dale Weldon, *The Impact of a Long-Term Pastorate* (DMin diss., Covenant Theological Seminary, 2001); Paul Borthwick, "How to Keep a Youth Minister," *Leadership* 4, no. 1 (1983): 75-81.

[24]Adapted from Michael Newman, *Defining the Enemy: Adult Education in Social Action* (Sydney: Stewart Victor Publishing, 1994), p. 153.

[25]A helpful introduction to negotiation, the first book that came out of the Harvard Negotiation Project, is Fisher and Ury, *Getting to Yes*.

Chapter 14: Leadership Plumbing

[1]Chuck Miller, *The Spiritual Formation of Leaders: Integrating Spiritual Formation and Leadership Development* (Maitland, Fla.: Xulon Press, 2007), p. 190.

[2]The most extensive research conducted that evaluated ministry roles and responsibilities is the Profiles of Ministry project sponsored by the Association of Theological Schools. This 1974 study, readministered in 1987, included well over twelve thousand participants and identified sixty-four criterion characteristics.

[3]Consider stories of the patriarchs, kings, prophets, apostles and early church leaders such as Abraham, Jacob, David, Isaiah, Peter and Paul.

[4]Helpful studies on eldership include Donald J. MacNair with Esther L. Meek, *The Practices of a Healthy Church: Biblical Strategies for Vibrant Church Life and Ministry* (Phillipsburg, N.J.: P & R, 1999), chapter seven; and Cornelius Van Dam, *The Elder: Today's Ministry Rooted in All of Scripture* (Phillipsburg, N.J.: P & R, 2009). See also Sean Michael Lucas, *On Being Presbyterian: Our Beliefs, Practices and Stories* (Phillipsburg, N.J.: P & R, 2006).

[5]See, for example, Acts 14:23; 20:17; Titus 1:5; Hebrews 13:17; 1 Peter 5:1-5.

[6]Passages to consider include Romans 12:3-13; Ephesians 4:11-16; 1 Thessalonians 5:11, 14-22; 1 Peter 4:10-11.

[7]Timothy Z. Witmer, *The Shepherd Leader: Achieving Effective Shepherding in Your Church* (Phillipsburg, N.J.: P & R, 2010).

[8]Jim Collins, *Good to Great: Why Some Companies Make the Leap . . . and Others Don't* (New York: HarperCollins, 2001), pp. 65-89.

[9]Ibid., p. 74.

[10]We suggest informally interviewing therapists on theological topics such as the authority of Scripture, the importance of personal regeneration and the role of the church in discipleship. Other ethical concerns such as separation, divorce and remarriage, sexual standards, abortion, homosexuality and gender dynamics would also be appropriate. Some pastors will also want to explore a counselor's philosophical framework of counseling. A helpful book on pastoral counseling and referral is

David Benner, *Strategic Pastoral Counseling: A Short-Term Structured Model* (Grand Rapids: Baker Academic, 2003).

[11]Pastors should talk with counselors about release forms that will allow the counselor to share appropriate information with them.

[12]Kent and Barbara Hughes first touched a nerve in pastors twenty-five years ago with *Liberating Ministry from the Success Syndrome*. The fact that this book is still in print in an updated version (Wheaton: Crossway Books, 2008) shows the enduring nature of this issue.

[13]See Dean R. Hoge and Jacqueline E. Wenger, *Pastors in Transition: Why Clergy Leave Local Church Ministry* (Grand Rapids: Eerdmans, 2005), p. 39.

[14]Ronald A. Heifetz and Marty Linsky, *Leadership on the Line: Staying Alive Through the Dangers of Leading* (Boston: Harvard Business School Press, 2002), p. 142.

[15]Suggested books on conflict supervision include Ken Sande, *The Peacemaker: A Biblical Guide to Resolving Personal Conflict* (Grand Rapids: Baker Books, 2004); and Alfred Poerier, *The Peacemaking Pastor: A Biblical Guide to Resolving Church Conflict* (Grand Rapids: Baker Books, 2006).

[16]We recognized during the summit that some personality types are not anxious about conflict and are willing to take it "head on." An informal review of the summit constituency, however, determined that most would be happy to avoid conflict altogether.

[17]Sande, *Peacemaker*, p. 22.

[18]A helpful book on program development that can be adapted well for ministry is Rosemary S. Caffarella, *Planning Programs for Adult Learners: A Practical Guide for Educators, Trainers, and Staff Developers*, 2nd ed. (San Francisco: Jossey-Bass, 2002).

[19]Manfred Kets de Vries, "Leadership on the Couch," in Lan Liu, *Conversations on Leadership: Wisdom from Global Management Gurus* (San Francisco: Jossey-Bass, 2010), p. 202.

[20]To consider the developmental stages of a church, see Alice Mann, *The In-Between Church: Navigating Size Transitions in Congregations* (Herndon, Va.: The Alban Institute, 1998).

[21]Books that may be helpful in reviewing governance structures are John Carver, *Boards That Make a Difference: A New Design for Leadership in Nonprofit and Public Organizations*, 3rd ed. (San Francisco: Jossey-Bass, 2006); John Edmund Kaiser, *Winning on Purpose: How to Organize Congregations to Succeed in Their Mission* (Nashville: Abingdon Press, 2006); Fredric L. Laughlin and Robert C. Andringa, *Good Governance for Nonprofits: Developing Principles and Policies for an Effective Board* (New York: AMACOM, 2007); and Larry W. Osborne, *The Unity Factor: Developing a Healthy Church Leadership Team* (Vista, Calif.: Owl's Nest, 1989).

Chapter 15: Concluding Insights and Next Steps

[1]To learn more about Chip Sweney's experience, see Sweney, *A New Kind of Big: How Churches of Any Size Can Partner to Transform Communities* (Grand Rapids: Baker Books, 2011).

[2]The exact source of this quotation is not available, though it has been used by a number of authors and in training materials. Charles E. Hummel, author of *Tyranny of the Urgent* (Downers Grove, Ill.: InterVarsity Press, 1994), p. 5, says that an experienced factory manager once told him "important things are seldom urgent."

Appendix A: Research Methods of the Pastors Summit

[1]Sharan B. Merriam, *Qualitative Research: A Guide to Design and Implementation* (San Francisco: Jossey-Bass, 2009), pp. 13-14.
[2]Ibid., p. 30.

Appendix D: Constructing and Interviewing a Family Diagram

[1]The following books and tools were used to develop these questions: Jim Herrington, R. Robert Creech and Trisha Taylor, *The Leader's Journey: Accepting the Call to Personal and Congregational Transformation* (San Francisco: Jossey-Bass, 2003); Rita DeMaria, Gerald Weeks and Larry Hof, *Focused Genograms: Intergenerational Assessment of Individuals, Couples, and Families* (Philadelphia: Brunner/Mazel, 1999); Peter Scazzero, *The Emotionally Healthy Church: A Strategy for Discipleship That Actually Changes Lives* (Grand Rapids: Zondervan, 2003); Peter Scazzero, *Emotionally Healthy Spirituality: Unleash a Revolution in Your Life* (Nashville: Thomas Nelson, 2006); and *RightPath Leadership 360 Manual* by RightPath Resources®.
[2]Ken Blanchard uses this model in his leadership profile assessments. See his website at www.kenblanchard.com/Issues_Organizational_Development/Effective_Leadership _Solutions/Blanchard_Leadership_Assessments/individuals/.
[3]Herrington, Creech and Taylor, *Leader's Journey*, p. 35.

Appendix E: Best Practices for Forming Peer Cohorts

[1]Assumed at 1/8 of listed yearly cost for facilitators.
[2]Expenses are calculated using a $750 honorarium plus a $35/hr benchmark for outside work. Each summit would include one to eight hours of travel, two to five hours of prep work (reading, planning), and zero to ten hours of logistical work (depending on needs/desire of cohort).
[3]Cost for spouse facilitator does not include any pregathering logistical work.
[4]Travel costs could be as minimal as fifty miles (roundtrip) at $.50/mile to airline tickets and meals in transit.
[5]Expenses include food, lodging and materials based on cost for participants.
[6]Roy M. Oswald, *Clergy Self-Care: Finding a Balance for Effective Ministry* (Washington, D.C.: The Alban Institute, 1991), p. 134.
[7]Ibid., p. 129.
[8]Ibid., p. 130.
[9]Ibid., p. 132.
[10]Ibid., p. 137.

For more information about this book
and the work of the authors visit:

www.resilientministry.com